GLOBAL PEACE

AND THE RISE OF ANTICHRIST

Dave Hunt

The Berean Call

BEND • OREGON

· DAVE HUNT CLASSIC ·

The DAVE HUNT CLASSIC series features formerly out-of-print, bestselling titles presented in their original typeset form (some bluriness or artifacts are normal). Each book features a special collector's edition cover design that preserves the original artwork in an attractive and affordable library-look binding. This series provides readers with a valuable snapshot of the author's insight regarding prophetic world events as viewed from a historic perspective. In reflecting on what was understood of past events at the time they occurred, it is possible for contemporary generations to gain an even clearer understanding of biblical prophecy as the future unfolds in the current signs (and headlines) of our time.

Contents

1 | *The Counterfeit Christ*

S OMEWHERE, AT THIS VERY MOMENT, on planet Earth, the Antichrist is almost certainly alive—biding his time, awaiting his cue. Banal sensationalism? Far from it! That likelihood is based upon a sober evaluation of current events in relation to Bible prophecy. Already a mature man, he is probably active in politics, perhaps even an admired world leader whose name is almost daily on everyone's lips. Or he could be the head of a multinational corporation, a little-known international banker of great wealth and behind-the-scenes influence, or a sports hero—or he may arise suddenly from total anonymity. Somewhere he is being meticulously groomed, though as yet he probably has no more inkling than do those who encounter him daily of the ultimate role for which Satan is preparing him and will, one momentous day, utterly possess him.

Whoever and wherever he is, one passion rules this remarkable man—a lust for power. Even so, benevolence, prudence, integrity, and principle mark his circumspect public behavior. Certainly he seems to be no more evil than the accepted norm in today's amoral society. It may be that to this point in his life he is still convinced that his motives are altogether pure and unselfish.

The obsession that drives this extraordinary man to excel in whatever he does has tempered the brilliant qualities and inflamed the explosive charisma that makes him Satan's chosen Messiah to rule the world. Just as Judas's lust for money made him vulnerable to Satan, so this man's passion for power has made him similarly vulnerable. Satan has found in him the one through whom he can effect an even more fiendish betrayal of Christ. The Antichrist is so driven by his dream to rule— yes, perhaps in his own eyes, to *save*—the world, that he will pay any price, even satanic possession, to make his mark in history. So it has been predestined and so it will be.

Antichrist! The media has so conditioned our minds that the very word instantly conjures up the image of a sinister man who exudes evil from every pore. But Hollywood caricatures play into the hands of the real Antichrist, since no suspicion will rest upon this one whose admirable qualities so well conceal his dark designs. When the time has come for his ascension to power—it will be in the midst of an unprecedented global crisis—he will be hailed as the world's savior, and so he will appear to be.

The apostle Paul dispels popular misconceptions and gives us the awesome facts: "Satan himself is transformed into an angel of light. Therefore it is no great thing if his ministers also be transformed as the ministers of righteousness . . ." (2 Corinthians 11:14,15). Nor is the Antichrist an ordinary "minister" of Satan. We may therefore be certain that he will appear as the purest "angel of light" that Satan can produce. Indeed, his very title implies as much.

While the Greek prefix "anti" generally means "against" or "opposed to," it can also mean "in the place of" or "a substitute for." The Antichrist will embody both meanings. He will oppose Christ while pretending to *be* Christ. That masquerade is made all the easier in today's society, where the distinction between good and evil has in many cases become obscured past recognition and where our most prestigious universities and seminaries have all but eliminated the concept of moral absolutes from their thinking.

Society has been undergoing a step-by-step preparation for the advent of Satan's Messiah, and in our moment in history it has at last produced a generation so perverted that it will mistake the Antichrist for Christ. In the name of freedom and right of choice, this most blest of nations has condemned its unborn to the cruelest of deaths, it has made a mockery of the sanctity of marriage, it entertains itself with films and music centered on themes of sadism, Satanism, and sexual perversions, it has all but destroyed millions of its youth with drugs, and it has created an urban war zone and a poisoned planet. Evil will soon be ripe for harvest.

Even if one should expect such moral and ecological devastation in a fallen world, what of the church? Those who call themselves Christians, and even born-again evangelicals, listen to the same music, attend the same movies, watch the same television programs, worship the same jaded and lost heroes, and live much the same lifestyle. Compared with the generation of 50 years ago, they are biblically illiterate. This is especially true when it comes to the subject of prophecy. Their consciences may be pricked and they may even repent of their sins at periodic revivals or emotional Sunday evening services, but it would scarcely occur to any of them that more is involved—that their generation is ripening for the Antichrist to make his appearance.

Antichrist? Most people take him about as seriously as Santa Claus or the Tooth Fairy. All they know about him are the trashy distortions bred of horror films. Yet the awful truth is far more terrifying, even though at first the world will seem to have entered a golden age of peace and prosperity under the most brilliant and benevolent leader in history.

Jesus warned that *many* would come claiming to be the Christ. These numerous lesser antichrists who were already in the world, as the apostle John explained in 1 John 2:18, would prepare the way for the real Antichrist who would appear in the "last days." Behold the ultimate deception: Satan posing as God, the Antichrist masquerading as the true Christ, and not just the world, but an apostate church as well, totally taken in by the charade. Instead of a frontal assault against Christianity, the evil one will pervert the church from within by posing as its founder. He will cunningly misrepresent Christ while pretending to *be* Christ. And by that process of substitution he will undermine and pervert all that Christ truly is. Anything less than such a diabolically malevolent strategy would be unworthy of Satan's genius.

This is an altogether different scenario from that envisioned by most people. If they believe in a literal Antichrist at all, they presume he will be an obviously evil ogre whom any child would immediately recognize. In fact, he will be the closest counterfeit of Christ that Satan can produce. Completely deceived by this brazen masquerade, the world will hail him as its deliverer.

And right there is where the plot thickens. If the Antichrist will indeed pretend to be the Christ, then his followers must be "Christians"! The church of that day will, without a dissenting voice, hail him as its leader.

Such a perverse and total deception is beyond the ability of the imagination to conceive. It is certainly not what the average person has been led to believe, much less what the media has implanted in the minds of the public at large. Yet this is the picture which the Bible presents and to which current events ever more clearly seem to point. Such is the thesis which we will pursue in the following pages.

It is immediately apparent that such an unthinkable scenario requires certain preconditions to make it credible. First of all, the apostate church in the last days must become so corrupted that it actually opposes what Christ taught while at the same time insisting that it is faithful to Him. Satan's lie must be honored as God's truth without the church leaders who deceive and those who are deceived even knowing that such a metamorphosis has occurred. Moreover, that perversion must have taken place from within the "last days" church itself even before the Antichrist appears.

Could Paul have meant anything less when he warned, "Let no man deceive you by any means; for that day shall not come except there come a falling away [apostasy, turning from the faith] first, and [then] that man of sin [the Antichrist] be revealed, the son of perdition" (2 Thessalonians 2:3)? While the apostasy no doubt is related to a simultaneous general moral decay in society affecting every arena of life from the family to education, business, and politics, the primary meaning is a *departure from the truth of God's Word.* Sound doctrine will be despised (2 Timothy 4:1-4). For many people objective truth will have been replaced by feelings and experience. For others, intellectualism and skepticism will have justified what seems to be a very reasonable new faith.

Jesus Himself, who raised the question as to whether there would be any faith whatsoever on the earth when He returned (Luke 18:8), used language similar to Paul's. When His disciples asked Him what would characterize the last days just prior to His return, He explained that it would be a time of the greatest religious deception the world had seen to that point, or would ever see again. He prefaced His remarks with this solemn warning: "Take heed that no man *deceive you*" (Matthew 24:4; cf. 24:5,11,24).

Those who heed such warnings will not succumb to the spirit of the last days. Like God, who weeps over a rebellious world and delays His judgment to give men time to repent, they will have a passion to bring His truth to the world. Everyone who loves God more than this world and to whom His evaluation of one's life means more than the fickle opinions of men will be kept from the delusion that will sweep the world. Those who fear God and keep His Word have no fear of what others may think or say or do to them.

The world must be primed both religiously and politically to embrace the Antichrist when he suddenly rises to power. If "Christianity" is to be the official world religion (which must be the case if the Antichrist claims to be Christ), then it must become broad enough to accommodate all of the world's faiths. As for the political climate, the world must be united in the twin causes of global peace and ecological rescue when this man appears.

Through the many astonishing events of the past 24 months, political leaders have found themselves suddenly and almost miraculously transported into a new world where such a favorable atmosphere seems likely to prevail. Much credit must go to the initiative taken by Soviet President Mikhail Gorbachev. His unusual insight and courage have opened Eastern Europe to a previously inconceivable level of intercourse with the outside world, have ended the Cold War, and have begun a new era of mutual trust and growing partnership between the United States and the Soviet Union.

For the past 70 years we have lived in fear lest Communist totalitarianism move West to swallow the free world. But suddenly before our very eyes we see a surprising new picture emerging, taking even the most brilliant strategists completely by surprise: Democracy is moving East! Free elections are being held even in the USSR. Why the new freedom could play into the hands of the Antichrist will become clear as we proceed.

Yes, China has suppressed those seeking similar reforms. Yet even she must eventually succumb to world opinion or suffer increasingly costly isolation from an emerging and growing international community which has become remarkably united and outspoken. The Islamic world, too, remains tied to its own agenda and is still susceptible to the sudden call for a Holy War against the rest of mankind. But in Arab countries as well as the rest of the world there is a fermenting opposition to autocratic rulers, both religious and secular, and a great longing for democracy that cannot be denied much longer. There is a swelling international grassroots movement of great power that could well spread democracy worldwide, and perhaps do so in a shorter time than now seems conceivable.

In spite of periodic flare-ups of hostilities and serious political problems, the promise of peace on earth has never seemed more realistic than at the present. Within a surprisingly short time it may actually seem that mankind has at last united to eliminate the threat of major war from this planet. Global peace will have been achieved at last. Strangely enough, that may be the worst thing that could happen, as we shall see.

In the following pages we will trace the events and processes which appear to be moving the props in place for Antichrist's grand entry onto center stage. The curtain is about to rise for the final act of human history as we have known it. While God has deliberately hidden much from our eyes, He has told us what He wants us to know about the incredible face-to-face confrontation between Christ and Antichrist toward which events now hasten—and about the part that each of us must play.

Prophecy is a difficult subject, and many people have been disillusioned by the failure of false interpretations. Others feel that the subject is necessarily morbid and depressing and therefore to be avoided. But the true picture is not all gloom and doom, since prophecy also offers an unprecedented opportunity for those who understand the "signs of the times" and are willing to believe and act upon what the Bible declares for our day.

2 | *When They Say "Peace and Safety"*

A JUST AND LASTING PEACE! Such has been the universal longing of mankind since the dawn of history. *Worldwide* peace, the end of *all war for all time*! Nothing seems more desirable yet less attainable. Considering the spectacular advances that man has made in every other field, why has he not yet found a prescription for global peace? How is it that we have become nuclear giants while remaining moral midgets?

If only the shameful destruction of property and lives could be ended and the untold billions being spent upon armaments could be turned to constructive use, what an incredibly wonderful world science and technology could produce! And now, at long last, the prospect of a peace such as the world has never known before seems to have metamorphosed from an impossible dream to a realistic hope. In fact, the nations of the world will indeed establish an unprecedented international peace, and probably fairly soon. Of this we are certain, because it has been foretold in the Bible for thousands of years that it would occur in the "last days."

That time of peace is mentioned, however, not with joy but with sorrow, for the prophets declared that it would precede a holocaust that would threaten the survival of all life on this planet. Why? The answer to that question comprises the entire subject matter of the Bible, which in fact prophesies the coming of *two* periods of global peace: the first to be realized under the Antichrist, and the second to be established by the return

13

of Jesus Christ in power and glory to this planet where He was so cruelly rejected and crucified.

Earth's war-weary inhabitants will greet the first period of peace ecstatically, convinced that the millennium has dawned. And for a time it will appear that the world's economic, social, and ecological problems have been solved. It will, however, be a great delusion. Biblical prophets have warned that this false peace will usher in the great tribulation after Christ takes His church to heaven in the "rapture," and seven years later it will culminate in the most destructive war in earth's history—Armageddon! In somber revelation the apostle Paul declared:

> When they [the world, not true Christians] shall say, Peace and safety, then sudden destruction cometh upon them as travail upon a woman with child; and they shall not escape (1 Thessalonians 5:3).

On the one hand it seems incomprehensible that international peace at last attained should be the prelude to disaster. Yet it could not be otherwise, because the world's leaders pursue their negotiations among themselves in utter disregard for the essential role that must be played by the Prince of Peace, Jesus Christ. If mankind could by its own efforts establish a just and lasting peace, it would prove that the Bible—which declares that true peace can only come through Jesus Christ reigning upon earth—is not true. Therefore all such humanistic attempts are doomed.

Are we saying that the world's leaders shouldn't even try to achieve global peace? Of course they must try. But those who are not Christians don't realize the futility of their efforts, and are driven by necessity to use every possible means to establish peace. Christian leaders also are compelled to work for world peace. At the same time, however, they must declare solemnly and clearly to the rest of the world that the only true hope for global peace is to repent for having violated God's laws, to receive Jesus Christ as the Savior who has died for the sins of the world, and then to ask Him to come back to this earth to reign.

It may be objected that a Christian President of the United States would be ridiculed if he earnestly presented such a message to the United Nations. The question, however, is not how the proclamation would be received, but whether it is true to God's Word. Are we not compelled to speak the truth in love regardless of how the hearers respond to it?

The Bible is unequivocal: "There is no peace, saith my God, to the wicked" (Isaiah 57:21). Until man has repented of his sin and has been reconciled to God there can be no genuine peace on earth. The angels announced the birth of Jesus with these words: "Glory to God in the highest, and on earth peace, good will toward men" (Luke 2:14). The Prince of Peace had come through whom God's kingdom of peace would be established (Isaiah 9:6,7). There is no other way.

And how would this happen? Some would have us believe that peace can be established through educating the masses to rely on their inner potential for good. Others suggest that we must persuade everyone, for their own benefit and the survival of mankind, to follow the perfect example set by Jesus. Still others suggest that we must somehow convince world leaders of the futility of aggression. Still others are convinced that the message of the "universal Fatherhood of God and brotherhood of man" will bring respect for each other's rights and allow us to live together in peace. Yet all of the above have been tried repeatedly and failed.

Again the Bible is very clear. Peter explained to the first Gentile converts after Christ's resurrection that *peace* was to be *preached* through Jesus Christ (Acts 10:36). That is a radical thought to most of today's Christians. What pastor or evangelist on radio or television today is preaching *global peace* through Jesus Christ? Paul declared that this peace was both "to you which were afar off [Gentiles] and to them that were near [Jews]" (Ephesians 2:17)—and that this peace was only possible through Christ having died for the sins of the world:

> God . . . hath reconciled us to himself by Jesus Christ. . . .
> God was in Christ [on the cross], reconciling the world unto

himself... [forgiving] their trespasses... and hath committed unto us the word of reconciliation (2 Corinthians 5:18,19).

[God], having made peace through the blood of his [Christ's] cross, by him to reconcile all things to himself... in the body of his flesh through death... (Colossians 1:20,22).

The Hebrew prophets promised the attainment of perfect peace under the Messiah's rule, with corruption and pollution gone, sickness and death rare, and the earth a paradise. Of that millennial reign the Bible declares: "Mercy and truth are met together; righteousness and peace have kissed each other" (Psalm 85:10). There can be no real peace without the triumph of mercy, truth, and righteousness. Do we believe what the Bible says? Then Christians must declare that fact as part of the proclamation of the gospel of Jesus Christ.

There are those in the church today who keenly feel the lack of social concern on the part of many Christians. They are working for social justice, for the ecological rescue of our polluted planet, and for peace and harmony among earth's nations. These are good and legitimate concerns, but the goals will not be realized without submission to God's plan for this world.

Evangelicals tend to present the gospel exclusively as a remedy for personal sin and procurement of an eternal home in heaven. They generally neglect to proclaim it as God's means of bringing peace to this troubled planet, as did the angels at the birth of Christ and as did the early church. It is the duty of every Christian political leader, whether president, ambassador, or other official, to make very clear to the entire world that all human efforts to achieve peace are in vain unless Jesus Christ is invited back to this earth to reign in individual hearts and over all nations.

The Creator of the universe and of mankind, who is called "the God of peace" five times in the New Testament,[1] has a peace plan for planet earth—a plan that is contemptuously set aside in the very act of establishing a humanistic peace. The latter, in fact, will play into the hands of the Antichrist, who is necessarily embraced when the true Prince of Peace is left out of human plans. Indicting Israel's leaders for their hardness of heart, Christ explained the consequences of rejecting Him as Israel's Messiah—a rejection in which the entire world would one day join: "I am come in my Father's name and ye receive me not; if another shall come in his own name, him ye will receive" (John 5:43). Of that impostor, the Antichrist, the prophet Daniel warned: "By *peace* shall [he] destroy many" (Daniel 8:25).

It seems obscene even to question the current international optimism that was ignited so suddenly during the last few months of 1989 and has gathered momentum ever since. That period will surely be remembered as the most amazing epoch in modern times, if not in the entire history of mankind. However, it could very well mark a giant step toward that first deceptive time of peace which the prophets had in mind. The many reasons for believing this to be so will be explored in the following pages.

Day after day, through the marvel of television, the world watched in stunned surprise the sensational unfolding of events that had previously been considered impossible. Inexplicably the Iron Curtain between Hungary and Austria was drawn aside, allowing tens of thousands of East Germans to flee to the West. That astonishing event was followed by the dismantling of the Berlin Wall and a delirious floodtide of humanity pouring across it in both directions in a joyous reunion.

As if by supernatural command, Eastern Europe's seemingly invulnerable Communist dictatorships fell in rapid succession like so many dominoes. They were brought down not from without but from within, not by invading armies but by unarmed citizens marching through the streets in the hundreds of thousands to overwhelm their oppressors by sheer numbers. The only exception was Romania, where it took the army and much bloodshed to dislodge the evil regime. All of this without any interference from the Soviet Union—indeed, with its encouragement—which was further evidence, if any were needed, that a new era had dawned. The impossible had happened! From Vatican City Pope John Paul II announced that the world was at a "very special moment . . . as if awakened from a nightmare and opened up to a better hope."[2]

The unbelievable progression of events seemed to herald nothing less than the precipitous demise of Communism in Eastern Europe amid previously unthinkable public apologies from Communist leaders for past sins and shortcomings. It was useless to deny any longer that Marxism, the ideology they had preached as the world's salvation, had miserably failed. Seemingly from nowhere, and without rational explanation, a gale-force wind of freedom and democracy had suddenly begun to blow across Eastern Europe, sweeping everything before it. Russia and her satellites were undergoing a swift and radical transformation that caught even the most astute Kremlin watchers by surprise. As President George Bush would later declare in his January 31, 1990, State of the Union Address:

> The events of the year just ended—the revolution of '89— have been a chain reaction, a change so striking that it marks the beginning of a new era in the world's affairs. . . .
>
> Today, with Communism crumbling, our aim must be to . . . take the lead in forging freedom's best hope—a great and growing commonwealth of free nations. . . . And it's time to build on our new relationship with the Soviet Union—to endorse and encourage a peaceful process of internal change toward democracy and economic opportunity.[3]

As these stunning events unfolded, phone calls and letters began pouring in to me, reminding me of a book I had written seven years before titled *Peace, Prosperity and the Coming Holocaust*. "I've watched the scenario you laid out in that book unfold exactly as you described it," I was told repeatedly, "and now the incredible developments in Eastern Europe are like icing on the cake!" So it appeared. Exuberant talk of global peace was everywhere—and seemed at last to make good sense. To those who believed what the apostles and prophets had said in the Bible, however, it looked increasingly as though the curtain were about to rise upon earth's final drama. Surely Antichrist was waiting in the wings for his cue to take center stage—and then the *holocaust!*

In 1982, when I was writing that book, unemployment was at the highest level of the postwar period and still rising. A pall of gloom and doom hung thick over Wall Street. After months of weakness and pessimism, the market stood around 700 on the Dow and the experts were predicting a precipitous drop that would rival if not exceed the crash of 1929. Books by Christian authors predicting the demise of the dollar, an international banking collapse, and the imminent Soviet attack upon Israel, thereby precipitating World War Three, were selling briskly. There seemed little doubt that the Middle East could explode at any moment. Secular commentators agreed that the political and economic outlook was the worst since a devastated world had begun to rebuild itself out of the ashes of World War Two.

In that context, and based upon a straightforward approach to Bible prophecies, I presented "A Contrary Scenario"—the title of the first chapter. It suggested that, in contrast to popular expectations, if we were indeed in the last days preceding the rapture of the church, then we would see steady improvement in the world situation on all fronts. The stock market would go on to new heights, "Reaganomics" would seemingly work, the dollar would strengthen, and increasing prosperity, though not solidly based, would unfold before us. The leaders of the world would seemingly patch up differences, easing tensions and forging agreements that would bring new hope and apparent peace to our troubled planet.

The "coming new age of unprecedented peace and prosperity just over the horizon"[4] that was suggested in that book is well on its way to fulfillment. Events during the past eight years, by far the longest period in postwar history without a "recession," have followed to a remarkable degree the major

"Peace, Prosperity" thesis. Stock markets have risen to previously unthinkable heights, while unemployment has sunk to new lows. Soviet President Mikhail Gorbachev's *glasnost* (openness) and *perestroika* (restructuring), viewed at first with suspicion, have become household words to a grateful Western world. Increasingly genial Soviet-American summit meetings and arms negotiations have brought new hope for disarmament and lasting international peace. London's conservative news weekly, *Spectator*, summarized the remarkable situation:

> Europe is now living through the most fortunate epoch in its history. It has already enjoyed the longest period free from general war—45 years, 1945-90—since the concept of Europe was formed in the Dark Ages.
> West of the Iron Curtain, moreover—for the first time in history—every European state is a parliamentary democracy. And Europe west of the Iron Curtain is making steady progress toward creating common economic institutions [while] . . . all of the free European states are enjoying the highest living standards in their history. This holds out even better prospects in the 1990s.[5]

The "contrary scenario" presented eight years ago still has far to go in setting the world up for the ultimate holocaust. However, the unexpected and astonishing collapse of Communist regimes in Eastern Europe that occurred so swiftly during the last half of 1989 has suddenly moved the prospect of world peace—and thus the rapture of the church and the resulting revelation of the Antichrist—much closer, perhaps, than we suspect.

From the perspective of biblical prophecy, extreme caution is in order, rather than the popular euphoria, in appraising the recent introduction of new freedoms in Communist nations and improved relations with the West. We dare not neglect the guidance of Scripture in evaluating current events. And if we will heed God's Word, then we will see that what we have been witnessing recently around the world could well be leading not to the solution of mankind's problems but to history's greatest disaster.

Isn't it dangerous to attempt to correlate current events with biblical prophecy? Indeed it is. Nevertheless, if Bible prophecy concerning the "last days" is truly inspired of God, then the time must come when what the prophets have written describes current developments. In the following pages we will see that current newspaper and evening television news is now reflecting what biblical prophets have long ago predicted for the climax of human history.

We have been privileged to witness via news telecasts the mingled disbelief and jubilation reflected in the faces and voices of those newly liberated from oppressive Communist regimes. And we have in a measure shared in the rejoicing that has swept Eastern Europe. Would we dare suggest anything that would dampen present optimism? We must, for biblical prophecy requires it. History, as well, offers her wisdom to those who will hear.

We do well to remind ourselves that an optimistic confidence that peace was assured characterized Europe just before it exploded into World War Two. William Manchester's gripping biography of Sir Winston Churchill confronts us also with unpleasant and haunting reminders of Hitler—a man who came extremely close to being the Antichrist yet deceived the world with his promises of peace:

> Thomas Jones, who had been in and out of Whitehall for a quarter century, wrote in his diary: ". . . all sorts of people who have met Hitler are convinced that he is a factor for peace. . . . [He] does not seek war . . . [but] friendship." . . .
>
> Meeting the press after he had been closeted with Hitler for an hour, Lloyd George said he regarded him as "the greatest living German. . . ." A year later he wrote, ". . . I only wish we had a man of his supreme quality at the head of affairs in our country today." . . .
>
> Nazi goals were even applauded by Anglican clergymen, a group of whom expressed "boundless admiration for the moral and ethical side of the National Social programme, its clear stand for religion and Christianity, and its ethical principles. . . ."
>
> Sir John Simon, His Majesty's foreign secretary from 1931 to 1935 . . . [saw] in Hitler . . . not arrogance but a man "rather

retiring and bashful and . . . unconcerned with affairs in Western Europe." Later he described him to King George as "an Austrian Joan of Arc with a moustache." . . .

Arnold Toynbee . . . equally spellbound by the Reich chancellor, declared that he was "convinced of his sincerity in desiring peace in Europe and close friendship with England."[6]

Winston Churchill was not deceived by Hitler, but he stood almost alone in warning the world that the Fuehrer's real intentions would envelop Europe in war. Looking back with the clear view we now have, it seems incredible that the leading figures of the day were almost unanimous in their praise of the irrational demigod who had become Germany's leader, and in their confidence that peace was assured. The deception was well-nigh universal. Yet the hero whom everyone praised was a dangerous megalomaniac who would one day take his place with the most inhuman monsters in history. Moreover, he had frankly revealed his evil designs from the very beginning, yet the painful truth was overlooked by almost everyone.

As in the past, so today, international leaders can be both mistaken and misunderstood. Key events can be badly misconstrued. The assurance of peace and security can be never more certain than when the world, in fact, is teetering on the very brink of war. Yet today's optimism, in many respects, seems well-founded because of recent developments. Even the August 1990 invasion of Kuwait by Iraq became a new milestone on the road to global peace.

For the first time in history the nations of the world, almost without dissent, united against an aggressor and took swift and specific steps to force the return of sovereignty to a country that had been overrun by foreign troops. Russia and even China were both solidly in agreement with the United States. What could otherwise have eventually led to another world war became a lesson that the days when an aggressor nation can move with impunity against another have ended. A new day had apparently dawned. In a speech to the American people, President Bush declared:

We're beginning a new era. This new era can be full of promise, an age of freedom, a time of peace for all peoples. But if history teaches us anything, it is that we must resist aggression or it will destroy our freedoms. Appeasement does not work.[7]

Months before, Mikhail Gorbachev had already optimistically proclaimed: "We see a budding world order in which peaceful co-existence and mutually beneficial cooperation based on goodwill will be universal norms." Other world leaders are expressing the same confidence. Are they right? Everyone would like to believe so, but what is the truth?

Unfortunately, truth in politics is almost impossible to uncover—which makes it all the more important to discern what the Bible says. If ever there was a time when we needed to ask God for wisdom and seek to understand what His Word has prophesied for our own day, this is that time. In the following pages we will attempt—without detailed and complicated theological arguments—to ascertain how near we may be to the revelation of the Antichrist and to Christ's second coming.

3 | *Fulfillment in Our Day?*

I WELL REMEMBER, during my youth in the late 1930's, listening with growing conviction to the many traveling preachers who visited our small fellowship of believers to present from familiar Scriptures the prophesied "signs" that would herald the approach of Christ's second coming. Though not as prevalent as it is today, even in those days there was skepticism among some Christians concerning "last days" prophecy. Was it not a controversial topic with many diverse opinions? What could be the value of speculating about future events? Why not get on with living our lives faithfully in the present and leave the future to God? After all, whatever was going to happen would come to pass in its appointed time and way, so why worry about it prematurely?

There were those, however, who had implicit faith in Bible prophecy and believed that it was intended to present recognizable "signs of the times" to guide the attitudes and actions of a future generation that would be taken alive into heaven at Christ's return. Such was the view of my parents and the Christians of our acquaintance, who took the subject of prophecy very seriously. I remember the lively discussions about what place current developments had in the prophetic scheme. What was the significance of the 1929 stock market crash and the great Depression that followed it during the 1930's? Where did President Roosevelt's New Deal, with its innovative economic and banking measures, fit in? And what about Hitler, who was gathering increasing power in Germany and whose influence was growing abroad? Could he be the prophesied Antichrist? There was general agreement that *der Fuehrer* was certainly a prime candidate! Only time would tell.

There were several basic premises that evangelicals in those days generally considered essential to a proper interpretation of "last days" prophecies, but which seem to have been largely forgotten today. First of all, one had to differentiate between the *church* and *Israel*, each of which had a unique relationship to God and Christ. Failure to discern which of these two entities a prophecy pertained to would lead to great confusion in one's understanding of "last days" events. With proper understanding, however, prophecy would shed valuable light on the present and future, while prophecies already fulfilled, when recognized as such, would provide irrefutable evidence that the Bible was God's Word.

Secondly, one had to distinguish between the *rapture* and the *second coming* of Christ. These were viewed as two separate events. The *rapture* would be for the church, when Christ would catch her up to meet Him in the air and to take her, as His bride, to His Father's house of many mansions for a glorious heavenly marriage and honeymoon. The *second coming* would be for Israel seven years later, when Christ would come visibly in power and glory *with His church* to this earth to rescue His chosen people from the armies of the Antichrist and to begin His 1000-year reign from David's restored throne in Jerusalem.

Before the cross of Christ, mankind was divided into two groups: *Jews* and *Gentiles*. The Old and New Testaments both make very clear what caused this distinction: the everlasting covenants that God had made with Abraham, Isaac, and Jacob, and with their descendants through Moses. These covenants were *for Israel alone* and separated her from all other nations on the face of the earth (Leviticus 20:24-26), thereby making God's "chosen people" absolutely unique. Israel was segregated from other peoples by the Mosaic law and by her special relationship with the One who is pleased to call Himself "the God of Abraham . . . Isaac, and . . . Jacob" (Exodus 3:6) and who was so identified by Jesus Christ (Luke 20:37) and by Peter in his inspired and convicting sermon on the Day of Pentecost (Acts 3:13).

The important distinction between Jews and Gentiles is maintained consistently throughout the Bible, and Israel's special relationship with God is declared to be forever: ". . . so shall we be separated, I and thy people, from all the people that are upon the face of the earth" (Exodus 33:16); "What one nation in the earth is like thy people Israel, whom God went to redeem to be his . . . own people forever?" (1 Chronicles 17:21,22); ". . . ye [Gentiles] were without Christ, being aliens from the commonwealth of Israel and strangers from the covenants of promise, having no hope and without God . . ." (Ephesians 2:12).

After the cross a new entity was born: the *church* that Christ promised He would build (Matthew 16:18). As a result, there are now three divisions of mankind: *Jews, Gentiles,* and the *church.* Paul tells us that we are to "give no offense, neither to the *Jews,* nor to the *Gentiles,* nor to the *church of God*" (1 Corinthians 10:32). It is essential to understand that these three distinct groups exist side-by-side in today's world and will continue to do so until the end of the millennium. We must keep a clear distinction between them and recognize that God deals with each group differently. This is fundamental when it comes to interpreting prophecy.

The church was created through offering to both Jews and Gentiles a "new covenant" relationship with God. This did not bring Gentiles under the Jewish Mosaic law (as some erroneously teach), but delivered from it those coming into the church, both Jews and Gentiles, and placed them under a higher law, "the law of Christ" (Galatians 6:2). Paul explains that Gentiles who were "aliens . . . of Israel, and strangers from the covenants of promise" have been "made nigh [to God] by the blood of Christ." God has "broken down the middle wall of partition [between Jew and Gentile] . . . having abolished in his flesh the . . . [Mosaic] law of commandments contained in ordinances, for to make in himself of two [Jew and Gentile] one new man [the Christian]" (Ephesians 2:12-15).

These Scriptures (and many others) make it clear that the church did not replace Israel, but came into existence as a new and third entity comprised of both Jews and Gentiles and distinct from each. As surely as Gentiles continue to exist outside the church, so also does Israel, with all of God's promises and plans for her remaining in full force. In fact, most "last days" prophecies are concerned with Israel, for she will continue here upon earth to face the Antichrist and the "time of Jacob's trouble" (Jeremiah 30:7) after the church has been raptured to heaven. As for the church, God's plans for her are unique and different from His plans for either Israel or the Gentile nations.

In summary, prophecy becomes clouded in confusion if we fail to remember that the timing, manner, and purpose of the Lord's coming is different for "*Jews, Gentiles*, and the *church of God*." The use of vague or ambiguous terms such as "Jesus is coming again" or "the return of Christ" or "Christ is coming" can cause misunderstanding. Coming for whom? Returning for whom? For the church or for Israel and the nations? It makes a great difference.

Consider, for example, Matthew 24:29,30: "Immediately after the tribulation . . . shall appear the sign of the Son of man in heaven . . . and they shall see the Son of man coming in the clouds of heaven with power and great glory." This Scripture is commonly presented as absolute proof for a posttribulation rapture. That would be the case, however, only if it refers to Christ's coming to take the church to heaven. On the other hand, if it is describing Christ's second coming to rescue Israel, which indeed it is, then this Scripture is not teaching a posttribulation rapture at all.

We can have absolute confidence that, if we correctly understand prophecy, we can know the order of last-days events because God's Word is completely reliable. Those who deny the infallibility of the Bible are either blinded by prejudice or have relied upon faulty evidence. Among the world's religions there is no book like it. Certainly no other scriptures contain verifiable prophecies which have been fulfilled, much less specific and accurate prophecies that apply to the present or future. Nor are these other writings generally even historically valid.

Ancient Hindu or Buddhist sacred writings, for example, exist in many versions and offer contradictory philosophies and even conflicting accounts of alleged past events, which in fact never happened. Characters and their adventures in Hinduism's classic scriptures, such as the Baghavad Gita or Ramayana, are pure fiction. In contrast, the Bible is about real people, places, nations, and events which can be investigated and verified.

In contrast to the Book of Mormon, for example, in support of which not even a pin has ever been found, museums around the world contain mountains of evidence attesting to the historical accuracy of the Bible. In Israel today schoolchildren study their history out of the Old Testament, while the biblical description of terrain guides archaeologists to sites of ancient cities and even long-buried wells and trade routes. In *every case* where critics have challenged the Bible, when archaeologists have dug up the evidence the Bible has proved to be 100 percent correct and the skeptics wrong.

While this is not intended to be a treatise on biblical accuracy, we cannot ignore the fact that there has been an undermining of the authority of and confidence in God's Word. Peter testified that the apostles were presenting facts, not "cunningly devised fables" (2 Peter 1:16). There is no point in looking at Bible prophecy if one has lingering doubts about the Book's accuracy. It is therefore important to spend a few more paragraphs in establishing the fact that Bible prophecy is not in the same class with fortune-telling books such as the cryptic verse of a Nostradamus or the gropings of today's popular psychics.

The fact that already-fulfilled Bible prophecies have proved to be 100 percent accurate, and that not one prophecy has ever failed, gives strong reason for accepting the validity of its prophecies which are yet future. We will be referring to some of these prophecies as we proceed. In addition to prophecy, the Bible deals with all kinds of data that can be verified as evidence of its reliability in every respect.

Some of the most interesting verification was undertaken by former Princeton professor Robert D. Wilson, who was at home in more than 40 Semitic languages and whose book *Scientific Investigation of the Old Testament* is a classic. He testified: "For forty-five years continuously, since I left college, I have devoted myself to the one great study of the Old Testament, in all its languages, in all its archaeology, in all its translations, and as far as possible in everything bearing upon its text and history. . . . I defy any man to make an attack upon the Old Testament on the ground of evidence that I cannot investigate. . . . *I can affirm that there is not a page of the Old Testament concerning which we need have any doubt*" [emphasis in original].[1]

Wilson's years of study brought to light volumes of evidence, among which the following illustrates the precise accuracy of the Bible in a most unusual and interesting way. Wilson wrote:

> There are 29 ancient kings whose names are mentioned not only in the Bible but also on monuments of their own time. . . . There are 195 consonants in these 29 proper names. . . . in the Hebrew Old Testament there are only two or three out of the entire 195 about which there can be any question of their being written in exactly the same way as they were inscribed on their own monuments. Some of these [monuments] go back for 2,000 years, some 4,000. . . .
>
> Compare this accuracy with that of other writings. . . . take the list made by the greatest scholar of his age, the librarian at Alexandria in 200 B.C. He compiled a catalogue of the kings of Egypt, 38 in all; of the entire number only three or four are recognizable. He also made a list of the kings of Assyria; in only one case can we tell who is meant; and that one is not spelt correctly.
>
> Or take Ptolemy, who drew up a register of 18 of the kings of Babylon. Not one of them is properly spelt; you could not make

them out at all if you did not know from other sources to what he is referring.

If anyone talks against the Bible, ask him about the kings mentioned in it. There are 29 kings of Egypt, Israel, Moab, Damascus, Tyre, Babylon, Assyria, and Persia referred to, and ten different countries among the 29; all of which are included in the Bible accounts and those of the monuments [uncovered by archaeologists].

Every one of these is given his right name in the Bible, his right country, and placed in the correct chronological order. Think what that means![2]

In every test we can give the Bible—even to the proper identification of ancient kings and the correct spelling of their difficult names—it proves itself to be completely accurate. That being the case, we have every reason for believing it as well in those areas which are still beyond our ability to test. One of those areas, of course, concerns prophecies of events yet future.

Though it was a topic that for some years I avoided because so many modern "experts" were making contradictory interpretations, I was literally raised on prophecy. The memory remains vivid of sitting in meetings where Bible prophecy was systematically taught, often from large, colorful charts which some of the traveling preachers carried with them. I became convinced at a young age that there were a number of coming events which had been prophesied so clearly in Scripture that one could be absolutely certain they would take place. Foremost among these, of course, was the rapture of the church, an event which, as I have already explained, we believed could occur at any moment. I looked forward to it with dread in those early days because I had not yet received the Lord Jesus Christ as my personal Savior. I had no doubt that I would be left behind to follow the Antichrist and experience the great tribulation as God's judgment fell upon earth.

I well remember how convinced the old-time preachers of 50 years ago were that two extremely significant prophesied events related to the rapture were fast approaching: 1) Israel's return to her own land *in unbelief*, and her rebirth as a nation; and 2) the revival of the Roman Empire, uniting Western Europe to provide a base of power for the Antichrist. In those days there was nothing on the world scene to give anyone hope that either of these amazing prophecies might be true. Yet the first came to pass in 1948, setting the stage for further prophesied developments. And it would now appear, after the recent historic events in Eastern Europe, that the second of these prophecies is well on its way to fulfillment in our day.

Nothing conceivable by human imagination could exceed the miracle of Israel's astonishing rebirth. In the more than 40 years since then we have seen that nation's remarkable preservation in the face of overwhelming opposition. There is even a November 1975 United Nations resolution still standing that equated Zionism, the movement for a Jewish homeland, with racism. In effect, that resolution condemned the very existence of Israel—yet she will not be intimidated or die. She remains today one of the most phenomenal miracles in human history.

The hatred and persistent violence that has plagued the Jews has no parallel among any other peoples. Surely there is no ordinary explanation. And here we confront another evidence for the inspiration of Scripture. Even a cursory study of the attempts to annihilate the Jews throughout the centuries reveals a certain diabolical dimension that cannot be denied. Nor does one have to ponder long to find the reason.

Israel is the major topic of Bible prophecy, the preponderance of which pictures her back in her land once again in the "last days" with the Messiah reigning over her in righteousness. It is to *Israel* that Christ returns to conquer the Antichrist, establish His kingdom, and rule the world from Jerusalem. If there were no Jews left on earth to return to their land and their Messiah—or, if having arrived there, they could be destroyed—then God would have been proven a liar and Satan would have achieved a stalemate in his battle with God for control of the universe.

That the descendants of Jacob could be scattered throughout the world for 2500 years (since their captivity in Babylon) and remain an identifiable ethnic group is miraculous enough. But that this persecuted people, having survived the many attempts to annihilate them, would return to their own land at the end of 25 centuries to be established there once again as a nation is beyond the wildest imagination! Moreover, that this tiny piece of once-unproductive desert and swampland should now be, as the prophets foretold, burgeoning with modern cities and lush crops, should convince even the most hardened atheist. *Exporting food to Europe, technology to Japan, and flowers to Holland?* It's staggering!

There is more. Who would have dreamed a century ago—or even 50 years ago—that this insignificant piece of real estate, after the Jews had returned to it, would be the focus of the world's attention week after week, year after year, decade after decade? And not casual or ordinary attention, but fear of how to deal with this new nation in relation to its Arab neighbors, and of how to prevent war in that area from becoming a global holocaust. Yet what has happened is exactly what the Bible prophesied:

> Behold, I will make Jerusalem a cup of trembling unto all the people round about. . . .
> And in that day will I make Jerusalem a burdensome stone for all people: All that burden themselves with it shall be cut in pieces, though all the people of the earth be gathered together against it (Zechariah 12:2,3).

And who would have been so foolish as to imagine that after Israel's rebirth this Lilliputian nation's armed forces would rival in power and exceed in efficiency those of the United States and Russia! Tiny Israel, occupying about one-sixth of one percent of the land in the Arab world, has been more than a match for the surrounding Arab nations, though they outnumber it about 40 to 1 and have been given every possible help from the Soviets, from the latest arms to technical and strategic advisors by the thousands. After Iraq took over Kuwait in

August 1990 and threatened all enemies with poison gas, syndicated columnist George Will gave the following tribute to Israel's courage and military capabilities:

> ...the West should remember with gratitude recent history's single most effective and beneficial act of arms control, Israel's 1981 bombing of Iraq's embryonic nuclear weapons program.[3]

So far the periodic fighting that breaks out over Israel has been confined to the Middle East. Everyone knows, however, that sooner or later a battle over that miniscule land will explode into Armageddon! This too the Bible foretold 2500 years ago:

> I will gather all nations against Jerusalem to battle.... Then shall the Lord go forth and fight against those nations.... And his feet shall stand in that day upon the mount of Olives.... And the Lord shall be king over all the earth (Zechariah 14:2-4,9).

Modern Israel has many faults, which we do not excuse and for which she will yet taste God's judgment. She is back in her land not because of her own merit, but because God is fulfilling His promises to Abraham, Isaac, and Jacob as He swore that He would in the last days. We may be certain that the God who brought her back to her land in fulfillment of His promises, though she continues to reject her Messiah, will not allow Israel to be uprooted again. And woe to whoever attempts to do so! Jeremiah 30–32 should be sufficient (and there are many other similar Scriptures) to clear up any doubt on this subject. Typical is the following:

> O Israel...I am with thee, saith the Lord, to save thee; though I make a full end of all nations whither I have scattered thee, *yet will I not make a full end of thee*; but I will correct thee in measure....
> All they that devour thee shall be devoured.... Hear the word of the Lord, O ye nations. ... He that scattered Israel will

gather him and keep him as a shepherd doth his flock...
and they shall *not sorrow any more at all.* . . .

Thus saith the Lord, which giveth the sun for a light by day
and the ordinances of the moon and of the stars . . . if those
ordinances depart from before me . . . then the seed of Israel
also shall cease from being a nation. . . . Behold the days come,
saith the Lord, that [Jerusalem] shall not be plucked up nor
thrown down *any more forever.*

The importance of Israel in last-days events and of understanding the prophecies concerning her and her land cannot be
overstated. Even though Christ defeated Satan at the cross and
gave proof of His victory by rising from the dead, there could
be no final resolution of this battle if Satan could, by destroying the Jews, prevent God's solemn promises to Israel from
being fulfilled. So far all such attempts have failed. However,
the Antichrist will stage one massive final effort to effect a
permanent solution to what Hitler called the "Jewish problem." Christ Himself will personally return to earth at that
time to rescue those who have "endured to the end" (Matthew
24:13).

Nothing else in all of history even comes close to the miracle
of modern Israel and its impact upon today's world—all in
fulfillment of specific prophecies. Nothing more should be
required to convince even the most skeptical person of the
supernatural nature and complete reliability of the Bible. Yet
so few believe even in the face of such evidence! Thus the
rebirth of Israel has a further lesson for the world: that faith is
not the fruit of intellectual assent to overwhelming proof, but
the fruit of a heart that loves the truth and is eager to know and
do God's will.

We have also witnessed in recent years the formative stages
of the fulfillment of that other strategic prophecy that I heard
so much about in my youth: the revival of the ancient Roman
Empire prophesied for the "last days." It has been fascinating
to watch the concept of a loose union of six Western European
nations under the "Treaty of Rome" gradually expand to
include 12, which are scheduled to become the "United States

of Europe" in 1992. While many students of Bible prophecy have equated the European Economic Community (EEC or EC) with the revived Roman Empire, the Caesars controlled a far wider kingdom—the world of their day.

Formation of the EC has only been the first step, which students of Bible prophecy have been watching carefully. How could the same process extend throughout the entire territory that was once under the Caesars? That was the big question, which has now been answered at least in part. The collapse of Communism in Eastern Europe, beginning in the fall of 1989, has set in motion a process which promises to unite all nations on earth, thereby establishing the one-world government over which Antichrist will reign.

Already the door has been opened to include, in a United Europe, even the Soviet Union and her former satellites—a concept that was totally unthinkable only a few months ago. If this occurs, the very size, as well as the economic and military power, of the new united European Community (EC) that will stretch from the Atlantic to the farthest reaches of the USSR will force the remainder of the world to join as well. As one well-known analyst has written:

> Membership [in the EC] is already open to those European peoples who have embraced democracy and are willing to do a deal to enter. That being so, as Europe behind the Iron Curtain liberalizes, it seems right and inevitable that the EC should expand eastward. . . .
>
> In the very long term, the European structure will be considered the prototype for something much more ambitious. Talk of world government is at least a century old and has gone nowhere. But an ever-widening association, based on shared cultural values, is a more promising idea.
>
> The European cultural concept is not a conventional idea. It is a global one. We are taking the first steps toward an ecumenical community that will ultimately spread to all corners of our planet.[4]

This secular writer had no idea that he was reporting upon the fulfillment of one of the most important and amazing prophecies in the Bible. The "global . . . ecumenical community" to which he refers is none other than the revived Roman Empire over which Antichrist will reign. From the perspective of biblical prophecy, the current euphoria is hardly the right reaction to the recent introduction of new freedoms in Communist nations and improved relations with the West that have set the stage for these historic developments.

The revival of the Roman Empire presently underway is not merely the latest in the long string of prophecies fulfilled down through the centuries which demonstrate that the Bible, as it claims, is the Word of God. More than that, it is a most important sign of the nearness of the revelation of Antichrist, and of Christ's second coming, when He will confront that impostor face-to-face here upon planet Earth. And the rapture comes first!

By God's grace I have lived long enough to see much of what I learned in my youth as *prophecy* become *history*. It is awesome to watch events unfold in consummation of prophecies recorded in the Bible thousands of years ago. The most incredible events are yet to come, and the Bible has laid out the script for us in advance.

4 | *The Last of the "Last Days"?*

IS IT POSSIBLE THAT we could be living in the "last days"? And if we are, what does that mean—and what can we do about it? Or is there anything to do? Even to raise such questions in most secular circles causes politely raised eyebrows, smug smiles, scattered snickering, and perhaps some open ridicule. They've seen it all in apocalyptic films. Many Christians, too, have written the topic off as a scare tactic employed by sensationalist evangelists when all else has failed to "awaken the sinners." And there are those, both Christians and non-Christians, who angrily denounce any talk about the "last days" as negative gloom-and-doom defeatism that breeds pessimism and holds back progress.

One can understand such reactions. The topic is a most unpleasant one. The very phrase "last days" implies a disastrous end to human history, at least as we've known it—or perhaps even of the world. And nearly everyone, in spite of efforts to ignore the feeling, has a sneaking suspicion that just such a termination could very well happen, and would rather not think about it.

Whatever one's reaction to the subject, however, there is no escaping the fact that from Genesis to Revelation the "last days," "latter times," "end times," and other similar terms are used again and again to deal with what is clearly a major theme of the Bible. In the Book of Daniel alone, beyond the verses we have already considered, the subject comes up repeatedly. Daniel gives much insight into last-days events, some of which we will refer to later.

An interesting phrase—"the time of the end"—occurs five times, and the man Daniel is told that it means that God has appointed a particular time when the end will come. Human history as we have known it will indeed come to an end, brought about by man's rebellion and God's direct intervention here on planet Earth. God has intervened in the past—at the flood and at Babel—and He will do so again when the wickedness of man has reached such heights that He can no longer forbear. God knows exactly when this will occur, as well as everything that will lead up to the climax of present history.

How near to that time are we living today, or is it possible to tell? Unfortunately, there have always been enthusiasts who were convinced that they knew exactly when the end would come and who were able to persuade a multitude of followers to sell or give away their possessions and perch in trees or stand on hilltops to await the second coming. Apocalyptic theories flourish at the turn of every century, and especially at the end of a millennium. So it is only to be expected that the nearer we approach the year 2000 the more talk there will be concerning the end of the world, the second coming, and the dawning of a new age of peace and plenty (since not everyone expects God's judgment).

Skeptics argue that the early Christians and even the apostles, as well as countless others down through the centuries, all thought they were living in the last days, and that the term is therefore meaningless. It is true that in his sermon on the Day of Pentecost (Acts 2:17) Peter seemed to apply an Old Testament prophecy about the "last days" (Joel 2:28-32) to the outpouring of the Spirit upon the disciples at that time. However, reading carefully the context in Joel along with Peter's words makes it clear that Peter was not declaring that what was happening at that moment was the *fulfillment* of Joel's promise. Rather, it was a *sample* of what could have occurred if Israel had repented of her rejection of Christ: She could have experienced the millennial reign of her Messiah that Joel went on to describe. It was an offer that Israel refused (as it had been prophesied she would) but which she will accept at a future time, after God's judgment has been visited upon her.

The apostle John, writing in about 95 A.D., declared: "Little children, it is the last time; and as ye have heard that antichrist shall come, even now are there many antichrists, whereby we know that it is the last time" (1 John 2:18). Yet John was by no means declaring that the "last days" had fully come, as some assert. He made it clear that although there were already many antichrists, *the Antichrist* was to appear at a future time.

Elaborating upon the subject, Peter wrote that there would be "in the last days scoffers" who would ridicule the very idea (2 Peter 3:3,4) of the second coming. Implying that many years could elapse before "last-days" prophecies had all been fulfilled, he explained that to God "a thousand years [are] as one day" (verse 8). Yet God's judgment would indeed come, including the destruction of the entire universe, at some future time: "The heavens and the earth . . . are kept in store, reserved unto fire against the day of judgment and perdition of ungodly men" (verse 7). Peter's terminology makes it quite clear that he did not expect these "last-days" events during his lifetime.

Paul also spoke of "last-days" events as unmistakably future, referring to specifics that would not occur until after his death. He told Timothy, ". . . the time of my departure [death] is at hand. I have fought a good fight, I have finished my course" (2 Timothy 4:6,7). To the Ephesian elders he said, ". . . after my departing [death] shall grievous wolves enter in among you, not sparing the flock" (Acts 20:29). It is certain that neither John, Peter, nor Paul expected the "last-days" events of which they prophesied to occur within their lifetimes.

Let us be reminded that the *rapture* could have occurred at any moment. Indeed, then as now, the early church was watching and waiting in eager anticipation of being taken to heaven in that glorious event. There are no explicit signs to indicate that the rapture is about to occur. The "last-days signs" are not for the *church*, but for an unbelieving *Israel*. Nothing stands between the church and that "blessed hope" of being caught up to meet her Bridegroom in the air.

Those events that Christ prophesied when He was asked for signs of His coming are intended to warn *Israel* of Antichrist's appearance and that, after guaranteeing her peace, he would seek to destroy her. The signs also herald the coming of Israel's Messiah to rescue her from Antichrist's attacking armies, an event which Christians refer to as Christ's second coming in power and glory. Since the rapture comes first, however, certain signs that indicate the nearness of the second coming may cast their shadows far enough in advance to tell the church that the rapture must be soon. Nevertheless, we are always, regardless of any signs, to expect the rapture to occur at any moment and to live in that expectancy.

As for the second coming, it would have been premature for Israel to expect it when only a few of the signs were in evidence. Jesus declared: "When ye shall see *all* these things, know that it [the second coming] is near, even at the doors" (Matthew 24:33). Israel has been alerted so that she might know exactly when the moment of her Messiah's intervention to save her has come. How many of these signs will cast their shadows before them at the time of the rapture no one can say. We do know, however, that our generation is the first for which *any* of these shadows have appeared, and we now have *many*.

The New Testament writers seem to have understood the "last days" as a time that began with the ascension of Christ and would culminate with His second coming. That event would be preceded by specific signs indicating that the generation on earth at that time was living in *the last* of the "last days." It is exciting to note that *no generation* has ever had solid biblical reason for believing that it was living in the *last* of the last days preceding the second coming of Christ—*no generation until ours.*

Why could our generation as opposed to all previous ones be living in the *last* of the last days? Because so many of the major signs the Bible gives to warn of the nearness of Christ's second coming could not possibly have applied in the past, but have only recently become applicable. For the first time in history all of the signs heralding the second coming could occur at any moment. In fact, the present generation—*unlike any generation before it*—has more than sufficient reason for believing that the second coming is very near.

What are these signs that have recently become viable for the first time in history? Jesus gave a number of them. For example, in speaking of the events that would precede His second coming, He warned of a time of unprecedented destruction which would be so severe that "except those days should be shortened, there should no flesh be saved..." (Matthew 24:22). Such a statement was a puzzle to past generations: How could the destruction of all life on earth be threatened through bows and arrows, swords and spears, or even the conventional weapons of World War Two? Our generation, however, has developed and stockpiled arms unknown in the past and which actually have the potential to destroy all life on this planet. So we are the *first generation in history* for whom this particular prophecy no longer awaits some future development to make it possible. It could be fulfilled at any moment.

In the vision of the future given to Him by Christ, John saw a world ruler controlling the whole earth not only politically and militarily, but economically. No one would be able to buy or sell without Antichrist's mysterious "666" stamp of approval embedded in his hand or forehead to indicate his loyalty to him (Revelation 13:16-18). While past generations took this threat seriously, there was no way that all commerce and banking on earth could be controlled from a central location. Today there is. We have the computers, communication satellites, and worldwide electronic banking networks which make such control feasible. Moreover, everyone knows that it is only a matter of time until such a system will be in place and enforced. So once again we have a prophecy about the last days that no generation prior to ours could even imagine, much less understand, as applicable in its time.

John also saw that the entire world would worship Satan along with the Antichrist: "And they worshiped the dragon [that old serpent the Devil, or Satan—(12:9)] which gave power unto the beast [Antichrist]; and they worshiped the beast" (Revelation 13:4). Such a prophecy would have seemed unbelievable to previous generations, but not so in our day. Hard-core Satanism has been called "the fastest-growing subculture among America's teens."[1] Another analyst reports: "The alarming rise of Satanism and witchcraft are the dark side of the New Age revival of the occult. Certain types of rock music make free use of satanic imagery, and many troubled teenagers, both in the United States and in Europe, are attracted to satanic cults."[2] Satanists have their own chaplains in the U.S. Armed Forces and are protected under freedom-of-religion laws. The accelerating explosion of Satanism worldwide is a phenomenon peculiar to our time, making the thought of the world worshiping Satan far more plausible than in past generations.

While blatant Satanism may be looked upon as affecting only a fanatical fringe element, the more respectable segment of society is attracted to Satan under other names, such as Lucifer. The film *2010* was representative of the brainwashing now occurring. Near its conclusion the United States and the Soviet Union are about to engage in a nuclear exchange which would devastate earth, when suddenly a new sun appears in the sky. The event is so startling that it transforms consciousness worldwide, brings a halt to hostilities, and creates peace. In his novel *2010*, Arthur C. Clarke lets us know that the name of the new sun is *Lucifer*!

In a *Life* magazine interview of leading Americans on the purpose of life, the first person quoted proposed, "Our purpose is to...return to Eden, make friends with the snake [Satan] and set up our computers among the wild apple trees."[3] Such a statement in a leading magazine would have been unthinkable only a generation ago. The logo of one peace organization, Peace On Earth, shows the world with a huge dragon (one biblical identity of Satan) perched on top and guarding it. A brochure declares what previous generations would have found shocking, but which has recently become acceptable:

> . . . as we enter what has been described as the Aquarian Age, we are entering a time of cooperation between the spiritual and the material realms, so it is time for us to make peace with the dragon and work in partnership with the wisdom and the power of the earth that the dragon represents.[4]

At the same time that the world is being set up to worship the Antichrist, so is the professing Christian church. Paul's warnings concerning apostasy or a turning away from the faith in the last days are many. One of the specifics he mentions seems unbelievable: "The Spirit speaketh expressly that in the latter times some shall depart from the faith [apostatize], giving heed to seducing spirits and doctrines of devils" (1 Timothy 4:1). Such a prophecy is shocking: that a characteristic of the last days will be trafficking with evil spirits by those who call or have called themselves Christians! Yet our generation is experiencing this to a degree never known before in history.

There have always been attempts to contact the spirit world through seances, Ouija boards, and other divination devices. Very few participants were involved, however, and they rarely admitted the practice, which was generally conducted in semi-darkness and was always looked at askance by the average person. But today spiritism is practiced by scores of millions of people around the world, although under a variety of new forms and called by different names that make it widely acceptable. From kindergarten through graduate school, in the business world as success techniques, in psychotherapy and in medicine, "inner guides" are being contacted which are nothing less than seducing spirits. They bring a very consistent message that can only be described as "doctrines of devils." We have fully documented all of this in *America: The Sorcerer's New Apprentice*. Suffice it to say that this phenomenon is unique to our generation and is literally exploding.

In the church, too, there is a departure from the faith but in the name of faith. Seducing spirits are being contacted, but here they don't pose as "deeper levels of the psyche" or as "ascended masters" but as *Christ Himself*! The practice of visualizing "Jesus" (visualizing "Mary" works just as well for Catholics) is being used in "inner healing" and in order to enhance one's prayer life or to gain a deeper insight into what Jesus taught. That the "Jesus" who appears and takes on a life of its own is not the Lord Jesus Christ but a "seducing spirit" bringing "doctrines of devils" has again been thoroughly documented in books such as *The Seduction of Christianity* and *Beyond Seduction* and will not be dealt with here. The *explosion* of this phenomenon, however, so that it is becoming rampant even in the church, is unique to our generation and provides further evidence that we could be in the *last* of the last days.

Paul was given remarkable insights which are so uniquely applicable to our modern world that they could not possibly have come to him by any means except divine inspiration. He warned: ". . . in the last days perilous times shall come. For men shall be lovers of their own selves" (2 Timothy 3:1,2). Mankind has always been self-centered, selfish, and narcissistic. Our generation, however, is the first one in history that is being *taught* to love self. It is now widely accepted that we naturally dislike ourselves and must *learn* to love ourselves before we can love God or other people. The first commandment has become "Thou shalt love thyself," relegating "Thou shalt love the Lord thy God" to second place.

Christ would never have said "Do unto others as you would have them do unto you" if we all disliked ourselves. His command to "love your neighbor as yourself" obviously assumes that we already love ourselves and is not intended to encourage but to *correct* self-love. It urges us to give to our neighbors some of the loving care we naturally lavish upon ourselves. Yet a popular "gospel singer," who began her career with "Guide Us O Thou Great Jehovah" now croons "Loving yourself is the greatest love of all." Even evangelical churches hold seminars to teach members how to love themselves. It is like pouring gasoline on a fire already out of control. And once again the phenomenon has appeared for the first time in our present generation.

John also saw in his vision that not only the Dragon (Satan) would be worshiped, but that the Antichrist himself would be worshiped as God. Past generations would have thought it ridiculous to imagine that anyone, much less the entire world, would worship a *man* as *God*. In the last 30 years, however, the "god-men" from the East such as Bhagwan Shri Rajneesh, Baba Muktananda, Maharaji, and many others have come to the West and have been literally worshiped as God by thousands of their followers. While only a small minority of mankind currently follow the gurus, nevertheless worshiping a man as God has for the first time in history become commonplace in the Western world. Actors, actresses, sports heroes, and political leaders are among those now worshiping gurus.

The world of our day is unquestionably being prepared for the one who "as God sitteth in the temple of God, showing himself that he is God" (2 Thessalonians 2:4). This prophecy will have its primary fulfillment when the Antichrist sits in the Jewish temple yet to be rebuilt in Jerusalem. There is, however, a secondary application. The body of a believer becomes the "temple" of God through the indwelling of the Holy Spirit ("ye are the temple of God, and . . . the Spirit of God dwelleth in you"—1 Corinthians 3:16; cf. 6:19)—and so it should be with all mankind. Instead, the religion of the Antichrist exalts *self* as "God" within the human "temple."

Today, for the first time in history, not only a few Yogis and gurus but increasing millions of ordinary people worldwide are mystically looking deep within themselves. There, in what ought to be the temple of the true God, they seek to discover that their alleged "higher self" is "God." The practice of TM, Eastern meditation, and other forms of Yoga is widespread. The goal is "self-realization," to realize that one is "God." It is the very same lie with which the Serpent deceived Eve. Obviously the deification of self plays an important part in preparing the world to worship the Antichrist, giving us yet another indication that our generation could be living in the *last* of the last days.

One need not practice Eastern mysticism, however, to deify self. That philosophy is basic to humanistic psychology, which has gained prominence within the last 20 years. One of its leaders was Carl Rogers, who apostatized from Christianity while in seminary and turned to the study of psychology. Rogers offered students a substitute secular "born again" experience of being "baptized in the fluid waters of your own self." Declaring that "self in its unlimited potential is virtually a god," Rogers defiantly demanded, "Who needs a God above when there is one within?"

In spite of his determined anti-Christian stance, Rogers was honored with the 1967 Contribution Award by the American Pastoral Counselors Association. In contrast to Christ's command to "deny self" (Matthew 16:24; Mark 8:34; etc.) and Paul's admonition "Let each esteem other[s] better than themselves" (Philippians 2:4), a leading "Christian psychologist" writes without apparent shame:

> Under the influence of humanistic psychologists like Carl Rogers and Abraham Maslow, many of us Christians have begun to see our need for self-love and self-esteem. This is a good and necessary focus.[5]

Jesus warned that the major sign to herald the nearness of His return would be *religious deception*: "Take heed that no man *deceive* you." He went on to explain the elements of that last-days deception: "Many false prophets shall rise, and shall deceive many. . . . For there shall arise false Christs and false prophets, and shall show great signs and wonders, insomuch that, if it were possible, they shall deceive the very elect" (Matthew 24:4,11,24).

A secular analyst writing even 50 years ago would not have predicted the worldwide religious revival that Christ prophesied. Instead, he would have suggested that our day would be characterized by skepticism and atheism, and that science would have advanced so far that there would be little place for religion in the world. No educated person would give credence to "spiritual values," and materialism would have taken over completely.

How wrong such an analyst would have been! In contrast, how right Christ was in saying that *many* false prophets and false messiahs would arise and deceive *many*. The implication was clear: A revival of religion would sweep the world in the last days. It would not, however, represent the truth; instead, multitudes would be deceived by false prophets and false messiahs. The accuracy of this remarkable prophecy from 1900 years ago cannot be denied.

We have seen a surprising resurgence of interest in spiritual experiences—an interest so significant that Soviet President Mikhail Gorbachev was forced to adjust his plans and to negotiate with the Pope. As for false messiahs, they number in the hundreds if not thousands. One of the many is Korean Sun Myung Moon. Having previously only hinted that he was the Messiah, Moon stated his claim clearly at the opening session of an Assembly of the World Religions held in San Francisco in mid-August, 1990. As the *San Francisco Chronicle* reported: "Surrounding himself with an eclectic collection of swamis, scholars, lamas and imams, the Rev. Sun Myung Moon on Thursday declared himself the new world Messiah."[6]

And *false prophets*? They are among the most popular figures seen and heard in Christian media today. In December 1989 Oral and Richard Roberts mailed to potential donors packets containing two small candles, one red and the other green. Recipients were instructed to return the red candle along with their prayer requests and, of course, the inevitable "seed faith offering," which would allegedly "release" their faith. On Christmas eve each person was to light his green candle while Oral and Richard lit the thousands of red candles sent back to them. The simultaneous lighting of candles, it was suggested, would empower the prayers said at that time and generate "miracles." Behold a standard witchcraft technique adapted to "Christian" fund-raising!

About the same time Robert Tilton sent out to his mailing list a packet containing paraphernalia for getting money and healing from God by practicing similar sorcery. Again a vital part of the process was first of all to send an offering. Then one was to step into the magic circle provided and place one's feet on the outline of Tilton's feet encircled in red. "As a divine point of contact place your feet on mine every morning for 21 days," read the instructions. On the front of the envelope in large print was the declaration "MAN RECEIVES $5000 in 14 days after stepping into circle!" On the back of the envelope: "Woman gets HEALED OF CANCER after stepping into circle!"

That Tilton has become wealthy through such practices is not as shocking as the fact that so many professing Christians are taken in by him and others like him. Only a few years ago such obvious witchcraft would not have been countenanced in the church. Yet today it is heralded on Christian television and supported by presumed believers. Surely we have here another sign of the times.

The situation in the church today is reminiscent of the last days of Israel's kingdom. Instead of heeding God's Word, God's people consulted spirit mediums (Isaiah 8:19). Israel had sunk into the mire of occultism, astrology, and idolatry (Jeremiah 19:4,5,13; 32:29). Immorality was rampant even among the priests (Ezekiel 16:15-59; Hosea 6:9). God's righteous judgment was about to fall, as it is upon today's church and world. Nebuchadnezzar's army would be the instrument, and the long Babylonian captivity for God's chosen people would begin.

Israel desperately needed rescue from a merciless, invincible invading army, but deliverance could only come through repentance and submission to her Lord. God had patiently sent prophet after prophet to indict Israel with her rebellion, idolatry, wickedness, and occultic practices and to plead with her to repent, but she would not. She needed to face the truth, but turned instead to the numerous false prophets who lulled her to sleep with their soothing lies. Their "positive" message was far more appealing than the "negative" pronouncements of those who spoke for God. In the face of misleading assurances that all was well, Jeremiah gave solemn notice: "For I have taken away my peace from this people saith the Lord" (16:5).

Earnestly Jeremiah warned of God's impending judgment against the positive-thinking false prophets who promised Israel "Peace, peace, when there is no peace" (6:14; 8:11). Calling such deceitful assurances "vain vision" and "flattering divination" (12:24), Ezekiel declared:

> Therefore thus saith the Lord God: Because ye have spoken vanity and seen lies . . . I am against you . . . mine hand shall be upon the prophets that see vanity and that divine lies. . . .
> Because . . . they have seduced my people, saying, Peace; and there was no peace . . . (13:8-10).

We live in a similar twilight of history. This time it is settling over the entire world. Once again those who warn of God's soon-coming judgment are accused of being negative. The cure-all magic of a Positive Mental Attitude (PMA) is widely taught in the secular world of business, psychology, education, medicine—and also in the church. As Volkswagen recently advertised in *Time* magazine, "Thought is the most powerful force in the universe. . . . We have the ability to turn any thought into form with the power of mind."[7]

Many Christians now assume that our thoughts and words, not God, control our destiny—that we are little gods under Him capable of creating our own world.[8] One seminar by a well-known Christian success/motivational speaker promises: "How To Get What You Want."[9] A popular booklet by another Christian leader is titled *How To Write Your Own Ticket With God.*[10] Such a philosophy seems at obvious odds with Christ's prayer in the Garden of Gethsemane:

> Father, all things are possible unto thee; take away this cup [of the cross] from me; nevertheless not what I will, but what thou wilt (Mark 14:36).

Presumably, if Christ had only understood and practiced the "principles of success" that are now being taught in the church, the New Testament would have had a different story to tell. Had He only taken a Dale Carnegie course in "How to Win Friends and Influence People," He could have won the rabbis and Romans over to His side and wouldn't have been crucified. Instead of making enemies by His negative pronouncements, His goals could all have been worked out peacefully by the principles of Positive Thinking.

While guaranteed by today's "prophets" that we are in the "greatest revival ever," the church is sinking deeper into the last-days apostasy foretold by Christ and His apostles. New Age occultism of every variety is exploding not only in the secular world but also in the church in what is indeed the greatest worldwide revival of paganism ever known. The "last-days signs" indicating that God's judgment is soon to fall are everywhere.

Rampant homosexuality, pornography, abortion, and other forms of gross immorality are becoming the norm for the church as well as for the world. Fornication and divorce are running at almost the same rate among evangelicals as they are in secular society. The lifestyle of students in most Christian colleges and universities differs little from their humanistic counterparts. More than 30 years ago A.W. Tozer preached that rather than "revival" the church desperately needed *reformation*. Conditions are now far worse, making his prophetic warning even more apropos today:

> It is my considered opinion that under the present circumstances we do not want revival at all. A widespread revival of the kind of Christianity we know today in America might prove to be a moral tragedy from which we would not recover in a hundred years.[11]

Yet the prospects of a humanistic world peace grow ever brighter. Man seems on the verge of solving his problems without God. "Peace and safety" is the swelling cry. It is the greatest of delusions, the deceptive calm before the storm.

Mankind is about to reap the full wrath of God for its rejection of His Son, who Himself is poised to return in vengeance. Surely the signs which herald the second coming are already casting their shadows to signal that our generation is living in the *last* of the last days.

When each of the events we have so far considered stands alone, its value as a "last-days sign" may not seem too impressive. But when we see the convergence of these events all together within the same time frame—and particularly the swiftness of the recent developments in Eastern Europe and internationally as well—the pieces of the puzzle begin to fit together. The significance of this convergence cannot be overstated.

World leaders are growing excited at the prospects for peace. There is much talk about entering a "new era" and about the establishment of a "new world order." For students of prophecy the interpretation is much more grim. And for those who truly belong to Christ, though they mourn for the delusion and disaster they see coming upon the world, there is the joy and excitement of knowing that it cannot be long until they will hear that shout from Christ Himself calling them to meet Him in the air.

What motivation that realization gives both for holy living and for declaring with clarity God's message to mankind! And what is that message? The standard "evangelistic" approach has long been to promise healing and joy and blessing for those who come to Christ, but a world that imagines it is in the process of achieving peace and prosperity has little motivation for heeding such a gospel.

The message that is needed is one of *conviction of sin and the fear of God.* Until men and women realize that they have violated God's laws and that this world is ripening to reap His wrath, they will not see their need for the forgiveness which Christ bought with His blood. That message will be increasingly difficult to deliver in the days ahead, but it is the only one that will prevent "converts" from coming to Christ for the wrong reasons and thereby being set up to follow the Antichrist when he appears. It is both awesome and thrilling to realize that our responsibility and privilege is to rescue as many as possible from the wrath to come.

5 | A United Europe: Stepping-stone to Global Peace?

WE HAVE NOW EMBARKED upon the last decade of the *second millennium* since Christ's birth. Already the 1990's are being hailed as the most exciting and encouraging period in human history. Never before has the prospect of world peace and prosperity seemed so promising—and never before has the tide of international public opinion taken such a dramatic turn from near despair to joyful hope as it did just before entering this new decade. How quickly the unbelievable events of the last few months of 1989 accelerated and fed upon one another! Even the most astute political observers and media commentators were taken totally by surprise.

An astonished world watched as unbelievable changes swept Eastern Europe. Words failed to describe what was happening. One journalist simply said, "The party's over—the Communist Party!" Even to suggest such a possibility only a few short months before would have seemed ludicrous. How abruptly everything had changed! The seemingly permanent Iron Curtain mentality was suddenly transformed into candid openness and cooperation between East and West. Winston Churchill had coined the phrase with his famous statement in 1946: "From Stettin in the Baltic to Trieste in the Adriatic, an iron curtain has fallen across the Continent." It had become a fixture, part of the harsh reality of life that no one anticipated would ever change. Then, with surprising ease, 43 years and many deaths and desperate escapes later, the evil curtain was no more.

The "absolutely impossible" continued to unfold day after day in breathtaking progression. As one TV commentator (who was covering the historic meeting between Soviet President Gorbachev and Pope John Paul II, and the Gorbachev-President Bush summit which immediately followed) said with awe: "Astonishing changes are completely transforming the world at such a rapid pace that we can hardly keep up with them!" Francis Fukuyama of the U.S. State Department called it "not just the end of the Cold War . . . but the end of history as such." The front cover of the December 11, 1989, *Time* magazine, reporting on the Bush-Gorbachev summit, displayed their pictures with this auspicious caption: "BUILDING A NEW WORLD."

Gorbachev's *glasnost* and *perestroika*, viewed with considerable suspicion in both East and West, had been fermenting for months. After the historic summit with President George Bush, *perestroika* suddenly exploded with irresistible force in the Soviet Union and all across Eastern Europe. The impossible was actually happening! Oppressed citizens ecstatically dancing on top of the Berlin Wall and brazenly tearing it down, while border guards stood back and observed it all with approving smiles? Unbelievable! Yet there it was on TV for the incredulous world to witness! Gorbachev declared:

> Things are truly changing, and in the most radical way. People are having an impact on politics . . . and if anyone thinks they want changes only in one region, they are very much mistaken.[1]

In rapid succession oppressive, totalitarian Marxist regimes, seemingly invulnerable, collapsed in the face of peaceful demonstrations. Hundreds of thousands of students joined by citizens from all walks of life, who until that heady moment had been afraid even to *imagine* themselves in such a role, took to the streets, waving banners and demanding freedom. They were not to be denied, and the results were dramatic beyond comprehension.

Picture the spectacle: top leaders of Communist parties across Eastern Europe, which had for decades condemned capitalism and pretended to represent equality for all, being exposed at last for shocking criminal corruption. Totalitarian tyrants, who had ruled by terror and intimidation, were suddenly being arrested by non-Communists taking over the leadership of heretofore Communist countries! Fresh evidence of the basic selfishness and hypocrisy of the human heart, though hardly needed, was carried in newspapers around the world:

> WANDLITZ, East Germany—Massive iron gates seal off the luxurious quarters here where senior officials of the East German government and Communist Party have made their homes for years. . . .
>
> Throughout the country, the old leaders are being angrily condemned for . . . plundering public accounts and socking away their illicit fortunes in foreign banks . . . of building lavish [personal] retreats with public money.
>
> Since the party's grip on East Germany began to unravel in October, previously unimagined luxury has been disclosed. New reports of scandalous activity surface almost daily, and they have had a powerful impact on ordinary East Germans. For, under state socialism, everyone was supposed to have lived more or less on the same scale.
>
> The reaction has been fierce. . . . The newspaper of the National Democratic Party commented that "millions of people in this country feel that they have been seduced and victimized. . . ." A university graduate student complained: "The question of corruption means the dissolution of the Communist Party . . . we are seeing reality as it is." A worker in East Berlin said: "It's disgusting the way [the party leaders] lived— and meanwhile they were preaching to us to work harder for socialism." . . .
>
> In the village of Rottleberode, in the Harz mountains, former Mayor Edeltrout Tielo was brought before an ad hoc court, stripped of her title and charged with personal enrichment at public expense. She is now taunted and threatened in the streets. Such situations are said to be commonplace in much of the country.[2]

Picture the Warsaw Pact meeting in mid-December, 1989, following the Bush-Gorbachev summit, its representatives being told by the Soviet President that all of the rules were now changed: They were free to go their separate ways. Most of the "old guard," solidly entrenched in leadership positions for decades, were missing at that historic gathering. Those few remaining who were present knew they were on the way out.

Head still held high, Nicolae Ceausescu, Romania's despotic ruler for 24 tragic years, sat in that Moscow meeting, scowling at the newcomers, hiding his bewilderment and fear behind a fragile mask of business-as-usual bravado. A few days later he would ruthlessly order his troops to machine-gun citizens peacefully begging for democracy, killing thousands in his desperate bid to retain his tyrannical rule. Within 36 hours, however, toppled from power by his own army, Ceausescu fled by helicopter from his flaming palace, was captured, and with his wife, Elena, was executed by firing squad on Christmas day 1989, the last Warsaw Pact dictator to fall.

All across Eastern Europe the seemingly impossible events that millions imprisoned behind the now-shredded Iron Curtain had scarcely dared even to dream about had come to pass, and with a swiftness that was breathtaking. Democracy was invading the Communist world! Toward the end of 1989, in response to pleas for advice from the emerging new leadership, Paul Weyrich led a team of experts to Eastern Europe to provide training in "the fine points of Western-style politicking." Often called "one of the ablest nuts-and-bolts political operators active in the conservative movement," Weyrich and his team encountered in Moscow what he calls "the most incredible experience of our lives" when they worked with members of the Inter-Regional Group in the Supreme Soviet. Said Weyrich:

> These deputies made no bones about their preference for private property, free markets and the restoration of religion...[and] asked penetrating questions about the techniques of political action in the United States.[3]

The destiny of earth's 5 billion-plus inhabitants was taking a dramatic and gigantic leap in an unforeseen direction. Apparently, by some mysterious decree, "the time had come" for such transitions to occur. Or was there perhaps a more sinister explanation?

Some analysts were convinced, and many still are, that *glasnost* and *perestroika* were a deliberate ploy to set up the West for its final destruction. *The McAlvany Intelligence Advisor* warns that "Gorbachev and his brilliant KGB script writers and military planners have decided to trade 'nominal' control over the Eastern bloc satellites for the neutralization of Western Europe and the destruction of the NATO military alliance . . . the script calls for America and Western Europe to be allowed to take over the financial burdens of Eastern Europe." Sounding an alarm that Alexander Solzhenitsyn and others have also voiced, Donald S. McAlvany argues:

> From Lenin to Gorbachev, the communist leadership has talked of the necessity of using wealthy finance capitalists (e.g., like the Armand Hammers, the David Rockefellers) to help finance their world revolution. . . .
>
> So, the communist leadership . . . is willing to go along with the . . . reunification of Germany and then Europe . . . to grovel before their Western benefactors, and smile, and bow, and humbly admit their mistakes . . . and ask for financial and industrial help to change their ways.
>
> But at a point in time (this writer believes in the mid-90's), the Soviets, the greatest masters of deception in history, will . . . double-cross their liberal Western capitalist benefactors, and will attack the United States. . . .[4]

McAlvany goes on to assert that the reunification of Germany and the neutralization of Western Europe through a great peace offensive have been on the Kremlin's drawing boards for years. The apparent democratization of Eastern Europe is the Soviets' master ploy to deceive the West into disarmament and thus to set up their final move for world domination. This theory is given further plausibility by no less an authority than John Lenczowski, who was director of European and Soviet affairs at the National Security Council from 1983-87. Lenczowski brings the following disquieting facts to our attention:

> While the West looks with wonder and astonishment at the ostensible breakdown of one communist regime after another in Eastern Europe, this observer confesses to having a certain sense of unease....
>
> In 1984, Anatoly Golitsyn, one of the most prominent defectors ever to leave the KGB, predicted a false liberalization in Eastern Europe and the Soviet Union, whose reforms would be so dazzling that the West would be incapable of retaining a consensus in favor of a strong defense.
>
> Among the scenarios Golitsyn envisioned (Gorbachev was then a faceless Politburo apparatchik): the demolition of the Berlin Wall; a coalition government in Poland involving Solidarity and the church; Alexander Dubcek's return to government in Czechoslovakia; a Soviet Dubcek succeeding Leonid I. Brezhnev; amnesty for dissidents and the return of exiles and a place for Andrei Sakharov in government.
>
> A deception the magnitude of Golitsyn's scenario is well beyond the scope of the Western imagination. But so was the deception performed by Moscow's "trust" operation in the 1920s, which involved the creation of a false opposition and which succeeded in deceiving 11 Western intelligence agencies for several years.[5]

Let us suppose that Golitsyn was right and the democratization of Eastern Europe began as an incredible deception. It would nevertheless appear that events have gone far beyond the point where any human agency is any longer in control. Communism's Humpty Dumpty would seem to have fallen so far and shattered so badly that even the fabled KGB will not be able to put it back together again. We will have to wait and see.

One thing, however, is certain: Much of Lenin's evil empire has gone up in flames, and the unlikely arsonist who struck the match was none other than the presumed leader of world

Communism, the Soviet president himself. It is not unlikely that Gorbachev used the Kremlin's long-standing plan for a "false liberation of Eastern Europe" as a cover for his own scenario. Otherwise it is inconceivable that he could have lasted so long without being ousted by the other members of the politburo.

Could it be that Gorbachev's real plans involve personal ambitions far beyond the office he now holds? Already a poll reveals that if an election were held today, Gorbachev would be voted in by a wide margin as head of a united Western Europe. It is not unlikely that his ambitions go beyond even that exalted position.

The skeptics remain convinced that it's all a trick. It would seem, however, that events have gone too far for the Kremlin ever to turn the clock back, even if Gorbachev were ousted from power. And who would want to take over his job under present conditions! With the Pope at his side, the Soviet president bravely and resolutely pledged the unthinkable:

> We have now decided, firmly and irrevocably, to base our policy on the principles of freedom of choice. . . . Having embarked upon the road of radical reform, the socialist countries are crossing the line beyond which there is no return to the past.[6]

The ironfisted rule of Soviet Communism, which held its subjects by force, is metamorphosing into a free society. No longer need the world tremble for fear of Marxist totalitarianism moving West. Suddenly, mysteriously, and contrary to all of the experts' forecasts, *democracy is moving East!* Not only have the oppressive regimes of Eastern Europe fallen, but one by one they are moving as fast as they can in the direction of Western-style democracy.

More significant, perhaps, than even their public pledges of cooperation, was the air of brotherly love and trust that Bush and Gorbachev exuded toward one another in the joint news conference after their historic eight hours of talks together at Malta early in December 1989. Newspapers around the world blazoned the headlines: "New Trust Infusing U.S.–Soviet Relations—Friendship, Hope Replacing Suspicion." Andrei V. Nikiforov, editor of the influential Soviet journal *USA*, summed it up:

> ...the ideological confrontation is over. That in itself is a historic shift of immense importance for our two countries.... We now act, in fact, from the premise that we have common interests with the United States on many issues...problems remain from the era of confrontation...but they are not the obstacles they once were.[7]

That trust seems to have grown with each summit meeting that Bush and Gorbachev have had since then. Many former Cold War antagonists on both sides are confused. A Kremlin official remarked, "Some of the old-timers left at the Foreign Ministry wander up and down the halls, shaking their heads and mumbling to themselves about all the changes.... What is changing is not just our relations with the United States or the West, but our whole understanding of the world, of our place in it, of our own country and of ourselves."

The significance for the fulfillment of Bible prophecy of the remarkable historic events we have just outlined and which continue to unfold should be clear. With the coming of democracy to Eastern Europe the door is now opened to something that no one could have even imagined: the possibility that former Communist nations could now join their onetime enemies from the West to form a much larger united Europe than previously envisioned. Such a union could end the threat of the repeated wars that have ravaged that continent since it was first inhabited by primitive tribes. That this development could also represent a giant step toward the false peace under the Antichrist is at least a very strong possibility.

Furthermore, the expansion of the EC to include Eastern Europe would appear to necessitate a revision of the most widely accepted prophetic interpretation concerning the revival of the Roman Empire. In the next chapter we will consider one of the most amazing prophecies in Scripture: Daniel's interpretation of Nebuchadnezzar's vision of the great image. The ten toes on the image's feet of "iron mixed with miry clay" (Daniel 2:43) have generally been interpreted to signify that the revived Roman Empire would consist of ten Western European nations.

Already in trouble because the EC includes 12 nations, with the possibility of others from the West joining, the addition of yet more countries from Eastern Europe would effectively scrap the "ten nations in Western Europe" theory. In fact it never did make sense to equate the *revived* Roman Empire with Western Europe because that was only a fraction of the *ancient* Roman Empire. The door seems to be opening to a *global* unification of nations and thus *global peace*. If the entire world is united, then we may be certain that the Antichrist will not rule over only a small part of it. So we move another step closer to understanding that the only sensible interpretation is a literal one of John's declaration concerning the Antichrist:

> ... and power was given him over all kindreds, and tongues, and nations. And all that dwell upon the earth shall worship him, whose names are not written in the book of life of the Lamb slain from the foundation of the world (Revelation 13:7,8).

While we dare not be dogmatic, it would appear that the prophesied revival of the Roman Empire actually does signify a *worldwide* empire to be ruled by the Antichrist. We will give further reasons for that assumption later. According to the Bible the Antichrist will exercise his power ruthlessly, destroying three nations (Daniel 7:8), devouring and breaking in pieces (7:19). It certainly won't be a worldwide "love-in." Yet his kingdom will also have the elements of a voluntary association and democracy at first, and he will be worshiped, which certainly indicates some affection and trust. The whole picture remains a mystery.

Of course a multitude of questions arise. One wonders why this *revival* of an ancient empire must occur at all. And why the *Roman* Empire rather than one of the others? What are the characteristics of ancient Rome that are so important that they must be present in the world of the last days?

The answers to these and other questions will become apparent only as we examine the relevant Bible prophecies and take a brief look at related history and current events. In that process we will discover that the revival of the ancient Roman Empire *of the Caesars and Popes* is one of the most important events prophesied for the last days. It is no less significant than the return of Israel to her land and the rapture of the church. In fact, without it Christ's second coming could not occur at all.

6 | *Daniel's Remarkable Prophecy*

IN GENESIS 11:6 WE FIND one of the most staggering statements in the Bible: "Behold, the people is one, and they have all one language . . . and now *nothing will be restrained from them which they have imagined to do*." The occasion was God's visit to the Tower of Babel, and this declaration was the reason He gave for inflicting its builders with many languages so that, unable to understand each other, they would be forced to abandon their diabolical project. Why *diabolical*? Because it so obviously echoed Satan's ambition: "I will ascend into heaven, I will exalt my throne above the stars of God" (Isaiah 14:13).

God had only recently destroyed earth's inhabitants with a flood because man's imagination was "only evil continually" (Genesis 6:5). And now so soon after that great judgment the descendants of Noah, whom God had spared so that mankind could make a fresh start upon earth, had focused the incredible power of imagination upon accomplishing the ultimate rebellion: to build a tower that would give them access to the very throne of God and thereby make them equal to Him.

History has proved that God's appraisal of the power of imagination was accurate and that His judgment was just. While man, unlike God, cannot create out of nothing (just try imagining a new prime color for the rainbow), his imagination is free to explore the most incredible utilization and manipulation of the forces innate within the universe which God has made and put at his disposal. And whatever he imagines, he will eventually find a way to perform! That man can ultimately develop whatever science, technology, or mad scheme he can imagine has been proved all too true. Yesterday's science *fiction* is today's *fait accompli*. And who would deny that man's imagination has repeatedly led him ever deeper into evil, so that wickedness thrives and earth's very survival now hangs in the balance?

Abandoned under God's judgment and left to crumble into ruin, Babel was rebuilt centuries later to carry on once again, from its summit, the worship of the stars and pagan deities. Around the tower was constructed the city of Babylon, capital of the *first world empire*. It became the center of astrology and sorcery, the epitome of false religion, and pursued the old Babel passion of reaching heaven through human ingenuity in partnership with occult principalities and powers. Under the brilliant leadership of Nebuchadnezzar II, not only Babylon's fabled hanging gardens but the entire city, covering more than 100 square miles, became one of the wonders of the ancient world. It was surrounded by a wall more than 100 feet high and 90 feet thick, upon the top of which four chariots could race abreast around the spectacular city.

God used the mighty power of this empire to punish His people Israel for their idolatry. He even refers to Nebuchadnezzar as "my servant" and declares that He has given Israel to him (Jeremiah 25:9; 27:6). Jerusalem was destroyed, its once-invincible warriors killed or scattered, its proud people reduced to scavengers and its nobility carried captive. And so it was, in the first deportation of Jews, that Daniel and his three companions, Shadrach, Meshach, and Abednego of fiery furnace fame, were brought to Babylon in about 605 B.C.

These four quickly distinguished themselves for their unflinching loyalty to the God of Israel. They absolutely refused to be corrupted in any way with Babylon's enticements, even to the food they ate. For this resolve God blessed them. In skill, knowledge, and wisdom they were found to be "ten times better than all the magicians and astrologers" (Daniel 1:20) in the royal court of advisors, among whom they too served the king.

That service put them in jeopardy of their lives. Unknown to them, Nebuchadnezzar had demanded that his inner circle of advisors reveal to him a dream he had had, along with its interpretation. The magicians and astrologers told the king that such an unreasonable request had never been made by any ruler. If he would tell them the dream, then they would give the interpretation. But the king had forgotten the dream, and now for the first time he saw through the charlatanry of his advisors. If they could not tell him the dream, then why should he believe their interpretation—or anything else they had been passing off as the secret knowledge to which they alone were privy? Enraged, Nebuchadnezzar gave the order for *all* the wise men in Babylon to be slain.

When Daniel learned of the execution decree and the reason for it, he promised the king that he would show him the dream and its interpretation if the king would only give him time to pray to his God. That night God revealed it all to Daniel in the first of many visions he would later receive. The next day he told the king:

> There is a God in heaven that revealeth secrets, and maketh known to the king Nebuchadnezzar *what shall be in the latter days.*
>
> Thou, O king, sawest . . . a great image . . . and the form thereof was terrible.
>
> This image's head was of fine gold, his breast and his arms of silver, his belly and his thighs of brass, his legs of iron, his feet part of iron and part of clay.
>
> Thou sawest till that a stone was cut out without hands, which smote the image upon his feet . . . and broke them to pieces.
>
> Then was the iron, the clay, the brass, the silver, and the gold broken to pieces together, and became like the chaff of the summer threshingfloors; and the wind carried them away . . . and the stone that smote the image became a great mountain, and filled the whole earth (Daniel 2:28,31-35).

Then Daniel gave the interpretation which God had revealed to him. He explained that Nebuchadnezzar, represented by the head of gold, was the ruler of the first *world empire*. The three other parts of the image, made of silver, brass, and iron, foreshadowed three more *world empires* that would follow Babylon as its successors. In a later vision Daniel would be given the name of the second world empire, Medo-Persia, and details concerning the third kingdom which clearly identified it as the Grecian empire. The fourth world empire, of course, would be Rome. That much is history.

So accurate was Daniel that skeptics who deny that the Bible is inspired by God have tried to prove that Daniel was not the author of this book, but that it was actually written centuries later. Of course it must have been written *after* these kingdoms had come and gone, they claim, for no one could so accurately foretell the future of world events of such magnitude. Unless, of course, he was inspired of God, as Daniel claimed and the evidence proves.

In fact, it has been demonstrated that the Book of Daniel was written during the Babylonian captivity, before the last two world empires came into existence. However, it was not the anticipation of these kingdoms that was the most outstanding part of Daniel's interpretation of the dream. It was the prophecy that the fourth, the Roman Empire, would be revived in the "last days." If that indeed occurs, it is one of the most remarkable prophecies in the Bible. Its great importance will become clear as we proceed.

The image revealed other insights as well that simply cannot be explained away. For example, the Roman Empire was represented by the two iron legs. Would it, in fact, be divided into two parts? Indeed it was, both politically and religiously, between East (Byzantium and the Eastern Orthodox Church) and West (Rome and Roman Catholicism) in the middle of the fourth century A.D. Early in the fifth century the empire disintegrated politically under the onslaught of the barbarians. It remained united religiously in the West, however, under the Roman Catholic popes, who continue to rule from Rome to this day and who must play a vital part in the revived Empire as well.

How do we know that it must be *revived*? Why couldn't the ten toes represent some aspect of the *original* Roman Empire? There are a number of reasons. In explaining the ten toes, Daniel made one of his most startling and important disclosures:

> In the days of these kings shall the God of heaven set up a kingdom which shall never be destroyed; and the kingdom shall . . . break in pieces and consume all these kingdoms, and it shall stand forever (Daniel 2:44).

Obviously, what the toes represent has not yet come to pass. God's kingdom was not established "in the days of these [ten] kings." In fact, there never were such kings in the Roman Empire, not even during the Middle Ages. Although there were periods of division between rival emperors, there were never ten at one time. When a division finally came it was into *two* parts, as we have just noted, and not ten.

Furthermore, the Antichrist never appeared to take the reins of the ancient Roman Empire. Therefore it must be revived in order for him to do so. In a later vision the angel Gabriel told Daniel that after the Messiah would come and would be "cut off" (i.e. killed), "*the people of the prince [i.e. Antichrist] that shall come* shall destroy the city [Jerusalem] and the sanctuary [temple] . . ." (Daniel 9:26).

In fulfillment of this amazing prophecy, and more than 600 years after Daniel wrote it, the Roman armies under Titus destroyed Jerusalem and its temple in 70 A.D., thereby identifying the "people" of the Antichrist. Nor can this be interpreted as simply meaning that the Antichrist would be born somewhere within the territorial boundaries of what used to be the Roman Empire. Once again we have a compelling reason why that Empire must be *revived*.

Of course Daniel did not use the term *revived*. He saw the feet and toes as a continuation of the empire represented by the legs, which in turn was a continuance of the three empires that preceded it. It would be the "people" of the fourth empire who would (and did) destroy Jerusalem. But the "people" of this empire are also said to be the Antichrist's "people" in his capacity as "the *prince* that shall come." Since he obviously didn't reign over ancient Rome, that empire must be revived in order for Antichrist to reign over a "people" who are identified with it. In fact, he will be the new emperor over a world empire that has its roots in, and in many ways will resemble, the Roman Empire of the *emperors and popes*, as we shall see.

Some writers have attempted to show that Nero was the Antichrist. He ruled, however, *before* Jerusalem was destroyed, whereas Antichrist's coming is said to be after this event. He would still be "the prince that *shall come*" at the time of Jerusalem's destruction. Nor did God destroy the Roman Empire during Nero's reign, or at any other time, in the manner depicted by the "stone cut out without hands": in one sudden, irremedial blow. And certainly God did not set up His own eternal kingdom either during the days of Nero or at any other time during the existence of the ancient Roman Empire. Therefore we can only conclude that the Roman Empire *must be revived* so that these remaining elements of Daniel's remarkable prophecies can be fulfilled—including Christ's second coming to "break in pieces and consume all these kingdoms [represented by the ten toes]" (2:44) and in their place set up His own millennial kingdom.

As for the ten toes, we have already expressed the opinion that they do not represent ten nations in Western Europe. It seems more likely that the toes of the image represent ten global regions into which the world will be divided under the Antichrist. These regions will probably be determined for computer convenience in controlling all banking and commerce under the new economic system that we read of in Revelation 13:16-18. They may also coincide with the "Regional Security Councils" that have been proposed since the Iraq-Kuwait crisis as the means of dealing with such emergencies in the future.

It is beyond the scope of this book to deal with Daniel's prophecies in any depth. He predicts the very date of Christ's triumphal entry into Jerusalem as coming 69 heptads ("weeks") of years (483 years) after "the going forth of the commandment to restore and to build Jerusalem" (9:25). Archaeologists have discovered and dated the letter of Artaxerxes Longimanus giving Nehemiah the authority to rebuild Jerusalem (Nehemiah 2:4-8). It just "happens" to have been written exactly 483 years to the day before the event now celebrated as Palm Sunday! This fact was investigated and verified by Sir Robert Anderson, for many years head of the criminal investigation division of Scotland Yard and an outstanding Christian. He provides the evidence in his book *The Coming Prince*.[1]

In the midst of these details we must be careful not to lose sight of the big picture: It is not just a *kingdom* or even a *world empire* that is being revived, but everything represented by *Babel*, in which all of the kingdoms depicted by Nebuchadnezzar's image had their roots. Not only the Roman Empire, but Babylon itself (where Babel was first resurrected) will also be revived. Thus in the vision given to the apostle John of the last days, Rome is called "MYSTERY, BABYLON THE GREAT, THE MOTHER OF HARLOTS AND ABOMINATIONS OF THE EARTH." Further discussion of that "mystery" must be deferred until Chapter 10.

As we have seen, Babel became Babylon, the center of occult religion, sensuality, opulence, and worldly power. Down through the centuries it has represented man's rebellion against God through attempting to play god by his own genius and psychic power in partnership with Satan. The Bible reveals that this entire Babylonian religious/political system will reach its zenith in the last days under the Antichrist and that God will judge and destroy it. That judgment was first pronounced by Isaiah with these words:

> Babylon, the glory of kingdoms, the beauty of the Chaldees' excellency, shall be as when God overthrew Sodom and Gomorrah.

It shall never be inhabited, neither shall it be dwelt in from generation to generation; neither shall the Arabian pitch tent there; neither shall the shepherds make their fold there (Isaiah 13:19,20).

For years the above Scripture was read in churches around the world (accompanied by slides of the ruins of ancient Babylon) as "proof" that, just as Isaiah had prophesied, Babylon had not been rebuilt and never would be. Unfortunately for that interpretation, ancient Babylon is now in the process of being rebuilt by none other than the infamous Saddam Hussein, whose megalomania required that his name be stamped on every one of the millions of bricks used in its reconstruction. Hussein imagines himself to be the new Nebuchadnezzar who will lead a united Arab confederacy, the revived Babylonian kingdom, and once again destroy Israel. The logo for the 1987 and 1988 festivals held in Babylon contained two faces in profile: Nebuchadnezzar's on the left and Hussein's on the right. The theme for both festivals was: "From Nebuchadnezzar to Saddam Hussein, Babylon undergoes a renaissance."

So has the Bible been proved wrong after all? No, the above Scripture has simply been misinterpreted. Isaiah puts this destruction in "the day of the Lord" when God will "punish the world," and his description (13:9-11) sounds like the great tribulation of Matthew 24. He was foretelling *the destruction of a Babylon in the last days*—the future destruction that John describes in Revelation 18. That the Bible is not referring to a reconstructed city of Babylon in Iraq as Hussein is foolishly attempting to do should be clear. Something far more important is involved.

God is foretelling His final judgment upon a great evil which began at the Tower of Babel and which has only grown as politics, religion, and science have become more sophisticated—until finally the whole world is united in the pursuit of Satan's ancient lie. This is the Babylon, revived and headquartered in Rome, that will be destroyed, never to be inhabited again. This world system that has usurped the place of Jerusalem in attempting to rule the world must be demolished. Then Jerusalem will be restored to its rightful place, with Christ reigning there over His millennial kingdom.

God's solution at the original Babel was to confound the languages and scatter mankind in order to prevent the very disaster that the world now hastens toward. Paul explained that one of the purposes of God's judgment at Babel was to set bounds upon the nations, keeping them apart, in order to encourage them to seek Him according to truth (Acts 17:26,27). Instead, still bent upon rebellion and the desire to play God with the universe and to establish himself independently of his Creator, modern man declares that he is going to undo what God did at Babel. He is going to unscramble earth's languages through simultaneous translation techniques and communications satellites and unite as one the nations of the world once again.

Not only is Babel being revived, but a trend is developing to boast in that fact, as though daring God to oppose it this time. It is remarkable how many times Babel is being associated with modern efforts to unite the world once again in a common purpose and language. The official poster of the Council of Europe, representing the EC, is a case in point. It depicts the EC as the Tower of Babel under construction, with 12 stars above it representing the 12 nations of the new United Europe. The caption reads, EUROPE: MANY TONGUES, ONE VOICE.

Others are picking up the same theme. In its special insert in the European Edition of the *Wall Street Journal* for the second quarter of 1990, IBM also depicted the new united Europe as the Tower of Babel under construction and transmuting into the skyscrapers of modern cities. Lockheed Aircraft Corporation, too, has taken up the same thesis. Advertising its capabilities in magazines such as *Scientific American*, Lockheed declares that its computer systems are designed to "combat the Babel effect" and to get everyone back together in a global understanding once again.

Is this sudden focus upon rebuilding Babel merely a coincidence? Whether it is or not, the fact remains that the projects represented by that theme fulfill Bible prophecy in a way that has never been done before. The scenario becomes macabre when one notices that the 12 stars representing the members of the EC on the Council of Europe poster are not ordinary stars, but upside-down pentagrams, the symbol of the Goat of Mendes, or Satan. Coincidence again? Interesting question.

7 | *Two Great Mysteries*

$\mathbf{A}$MONG THE ENDLESS RECITAL of crimes of all kinds in the daily news, all too frequently appear those shocking stories too horrible to believe. Yet the seemingly inhuman monsters who are guilty of these outrages—be it a Charles Manson or a Richard Ramirez, the Los Angeles "Night Stalker"—are embarrassingly human, members of our same species. It is deeply troubling to realize that criminals, no matter how infamous, were generally, once-upon-a-time, apparently normal children whose births brought great joy to their parents and whose childhoods held out wonderful, and sometimes exceptional, promise of good things to come as life unfolded.

What went wrong? Whence this overwhelming outpouring of *unmitigated evil*? How could it remain hidden behind a facade of seeming normality? How could such loathsomeness be practiced secretly while family and friends saw nothing to betray the awful truth? Some of the most horrifying crimes, including mutilation and even eating of the victims, have been perpetrated by those who seemed, to friends and neighbors, to be the most kindly, humane persons they knew. No wonder, then, that the Bible presents good and evil as two great *mysteries* and goes to some pains to reveal what is behind them.

In sentencing Richard Ramirez to death on November 7, 1989, Los Angeles Judge Michael Tynan said that there were "no mitigating factors." He reminded the court that Ramirez, who had even gouged out the eyes of one victim, had shown not the slightest remorse, and that in his crimes he had displayed "cruelty, callousness and viciousness beyond any human understanding." Ramirez's only response was to deliver a chilling final statement to the court:

> I don't believe in the hypocritical, moralistic dogma of this so-called civilized society.... You maggots make me sick. Hypocrites one and all....
> You don't understand me. You are not expected to. You are not capable of it. I am beyond your experience . . . I am beyond good and evil. I will be avenged. Lucifer dwells in us all....
> Legions of the night. Night breed. Repeat not the errors of the night prowler and *show no mercy!*[1]

There is no psychological explanation for a Richard Ramirez—or for any one of us. Human behavior cannot be reduced to a formula. Psychologists' "criminal profiles" may seem to fit in general terms in many cases, but freedom of choice and human ingenuity make it impossible to predict the individual's next move. God declares, "The heart is deceitful above all things, and desperately wicked; who can know it?" (Jeremiah 17:9). The shameful recital of human wickedness that marks the history of our race bears witness to that judgment.

It has been ironic to see the juxtaposition of the news in papers across America. Alongside the reports of the sensational blossoming of freedom in Eastern Europe have been other articles far more numerous detailing the horror of what years of that seemingly desirable freedom have produced in the West: a raging epidemic of murder, rape, robbery, sodomy, pornography, child abuse, and Satanism; organized crime as big business, with drug cartels downing commercial planes and bombing banks, public buildings, and innocent civilians to protect their "right" to reap their fortunes at the cost of millions of ruined lives; gangs of teenagers terrorizing neighborhoods and even cities; random shootings on freeways; an AIDS epidemic that could decimate and bankrupt the West— the horrifying list goes on and on.

For all of the disadvantages of life under oppressive dictatorships in Eastern Europe, at least there was far less crime than in the West. There was plenty of alcoholism, child abuse, and divorce, but heroin and crack were not being pushed on street corners, and there were no knifings and student rebellion in the schools. Communism has been the enemy of freedom, but it has also been tough on crime. One could safely walk the streets of Moscow or Leningrad or any other city, large or small, in Eastern Europe at any hour of the day or night. One need have no fear of being mugged or raped or set upon by a gang of young toughs or shot at random by some thrill killer. Will such benefits of oppression vanish when Western "freedom of expression" has fully come to the East? Already crime, including murder, is escalating in the Soviet Union.

Yes, evil is rampant in our world, not only in the crimes that shock us but in the "legal" entertainments that Western prosperity supports so well. Large portions of Stockholm, Copenhagen, Amsterdam, Frankfurt, Paris, London, New York, Los Angeles, San Francisco, and scores of other major Western cities have become shameless cesspools of iniquity. Sodom and Gomorrah would envy the gross wickedness protected by "freedom of speech and expression" throughout the Western world and the modern techniques for promoting and enjoying evil that it has developed. Can we doubt that this moral decadence will now spread rapidly and efficiently with the freer flow of people, goods, and influences across once-closed borders? In an interview upon his arrival at Budapest airport in July 1989, Billy Graham "applauded removal of trade barriers" and other freedoms coming to Eastern Europe, but warned:

> The issues which face our world are fundamentally moral and spiritual, and they cannot be satisfied by economic or political solutions alone.
> How tragic it would be if Hungary fell into the same trap as many in my own country, and gained the whole world, but lost its soul. . . . All too often economic progress and expanded

freedom have been accompanied by moral and spiritual decay. . . .[2]

Is it possible that the West has so long prided itself upon human rights and freedom that it is not willing to face the horror of its own corruption? Western technology has created a paradise of materialism that has become the envy of Eastern Europe. It has also contributed to the explosion of drugs, pornography, abortion, child abuse, and organized and petty crime that will now spread eastward with democracy. As Robert Benne of the Center for Church and Society in Salem, Virginia, has pointed out:

> The "victory" of democratic capitalist ideas [in Eastern Europe] should be greeted by no more than one cheer. For the moral foundations of the West, which make both democracy and capitalism viable, are eroding. [3]

In late 1988, Bill Moyers did one of his television specials on the subject of *evil*. It was an example of a humanistic approach that is hopelessly inadequate to come to grips with a basic fact of human existence. There was much erudite discussion by articulate and even compelling speakers with impressive credentials—none of whom had anything to offer except the hopeful but obviously specious suggestion that through education mankind would eventually overcome this problem. Though at times intellectually stimulating, the discussion failed to answer the real questions. One was left with the impression that one could feel good about oneself for having engaged in "honest probings" of this unpleasant subject and especially for having admitted that there is "some good and evil in us all," even though we still couldn't define or explain good and evil. Ramirez's horrifying declaration that "*Lucifer* dwells in us all" seemed closer to the truth.

Lucifer! Yes, there is where it all began. God inspired Isaiah to pull the veil aside briefly to give us a glimpse into the incredible origin of evil:

How art thou fallen from heaven, O Lucifer, son of the morning!...

For thou hast said in thine heart, *I will* ascend into heaven, *I will* exalt my throne above the stars of God, *I will* sit also upon the mount of the congregation....

I will be like the most High.

Yet thou shalt be brought down to hell, to the sides of the pit (Isaiah 14:12-15).

An evil and secret ambition transformed God's highest angel, "the anointed cherub" (Ezekiel 28:14), into "that old serpent, called the Devil, and Satan" (Revelation 12:9). Lucifer's burning passion expressed in those five "I will's" was the epitome of self-assertion, now seen as one of the secrets to success in our modern world. Can it be true? Yes, the fall of the wisest and most beautiful creature that God had made came about through attitudes that are avidly cultivated and considered commendable in today's society and which form the basis of success seminars and bestselling books! Can there be any doubt that Lucifer is "the god of this world" who has "blinded the minds of them which believe not" (2 Corinthians 4:4)?

Take note also that his rebellion was not provoked by a poor environment, a deprived childhood, or the negative influence of society, for Lucifer lived in the very presence of God. Nor could the triggering of this evil behavior be blamed upon some traumatic experience of childhood buried in Lucifer's deep unconscious. He had not been raised in a ghetto nor had he been abused as a child. The problem was not that his parents had been too strict or had forced religion down his throat.

None of the theories of sociologists and psychologists could account for this sudden break with divine order and this ruthless obsession with power. Nor would any amount of psychotherapy have taken care of the problem by helping Lucifer to understand himself and get in touch with his feelings. Today's specious theories of human behavior, which have impacted the church as well as secular society, fail to effect real cures because they do not and cannot deal with the evil that has enslaved the human mind and emotions. Medical causes aside,

any theory that does not fit the case of Lucifer can hardly be
expected to explain aberrant human behavior, since he is the
moral "father" of mankind. As Jesus so poignantly put it: "Ye
are of your father the devil, and the lusts of your father ye will
do" (John 8:44). Small wonder, then, that we need to be "born
again" by the Spirit of God into God's family! Unfortunately,
that expression has become almost a meaningless cliché today.

Let it also be clear that Lucifer's downfall was not due to a
bad self-image or low self-esteem, which we are told today are
the cause of everything from drug addiction to pornography
and homosexuality. It was not that Lucifer thought too lowly of
himself—not at all. Pride and self (*I will*) were at the root of
this rebellion—a cosmic anarchy in which, tragically, the
entire race of mankind has joined. The Devil was determined
to be like God so that he could set his own standards of
behavior and do his own thing. Is that not the world of today?

Lucifer was cast out of heaven, though he still has limited
access there. A cosmic warfare ensued between God and
Satan, which is still in process and approaching its climax. If it
were a matter of raw power, God could have finished off Satan
in a moment. Instead it is a battle of truth against the lie, a
deadly conflict for the minds and the loyalties of angels first of
all, and now for the hearts of mankind as well, since Satan
seduced Eve into joining his side. The struggles in our individual lives are but a microcosm of the larger conflict between
God and Satan, and are intimately related to it. Each of these
master strategists has a plan, and our eternal destiny depends
upon which one we follow.

God loves us and wants to win us back, but He will not force
Himself upon anyone. Each person must be free to repent of his
sin against God and believe in Christ as his Savior, or to reject
Him and to follow Satan. Moreover, God's adversary must
have full liberty to tell his lies, offer his false gospel, and
restore this earth to be a paradise once again if he can.

How many angels followed Satan we are not told. We do
know, however, that they, like Satan himself, are "reserved in
everlasting chains under darkness unto the judgment of the

great day" (Jude 1:6). This does not mean that they are locked up in some *place*, but that their minds are in darkness, without hope of ever being rescued from the final doom awaiting them. Satan, though brilliant beyond our wildest imagination, is a self-deluded megalomaniac who really believes, to this moment at least, that he will emerge victorious in his rebellion against God. His followers, both from the realm of angels and from our species, eventually come under the same delusion, though for many it no longer matters who is going to win, since rebellion has become an end in itself.

Karl Marx presents a profound example of the mysterious enslaving power of evil—the hopelessness of one who has become a disciple of Satan and knows that he faces God's judgment, yet cannot repent. That Marx was a knowing follower of Satan can hardly be doubted. Richard Wurmbrand, a Communist prisoner for 14 years in Romania, has documented this fact in his booklet *Was Karl Marx A Satanist?*[4] Other writers have come to the same conclusion.

Professing to be a devout Christian in his youth, Marx *never renounced his belief in God*. Instead he became God's bitter enemy. It is important to understand that Marx, like his master, Satan, was not an atheist. Like the demons who "believe and tremble" (James 2:19), Marx also trembled, yet continued to hate and oppose the God he believed did indeed exist. In one of his poems Marx wrote: "I wish to revenge myself against the One who rules above . . . nothing but revenge is left to me!"[5] In another he lamented:

> Thus heaven I've forfeited,
> I know it full well.
> My soul, once true to God,
> Is chosen for hell.[6]

Marx's virulent hatred for God, and especially Christianity, has long been the hallmark of the socialist system he founded. Communism has been openly anti-God and anti-Christ. That blatant approach, however, has failed. Mankind remains incurably *religious* and, above all, *self-righteous*. The ultimate seduction of this present world can only be accomplished through a false *religion*, not through overt *atheism*, and Satan is well aware of that fact. Thus the Antichrist will be the head not only of a new world *government* but of a new world *religion* as well. Certainly the new face of Communism now being presented to the West under the leadership of Mikhail Gorbachev, which offers "freedom of conscience" to practice all religions, is a necessary step toward the rise of Antichrist.

How long Satan and his demonic disciples in revolt have been allowed to challenge God, and what colossal battles have been fought across the galaxies in ages past, we don't know. It is clear, however, from what God has chosen to reveal in His Word, that Satan's rebellion seeks nothing less than the complete overthrow of God Himself. As a vital part of his strategy, Satan intends to set up his own global kingdom here upon earth with the Antichrist at its head as world ruler. The time is coming when it will suit God's own purposes to allow the Antichrist to take over the world. That day could be upon us sooner than we think.

None of the above *explains* evil. It cannot be explained any more than can any other facet of human behavior. And every theory that presumes to *explain*—for example, in terms of past abuse suffered—why people behave the way they do is really *explaining away evil* and providing a convenient *excuse*, not a solution.

The Bible speaks of evil as a *mystery* because it involves puzzling questions for which there seem to be no rational answers. How could Lucifer, the most wonderful creature God ever made, become Satan, the personification of evil? Why would God allow this to occur? Why does He endure the continued rebellion that defies Him daily on planet Earth? Yes, God seeks to win us with His love, and love cannot be forced: It must be free to respond willingly, so we must have the option to reject as well as to accept, to hate as well as to love. But that only raises more questions: Why do some believe and others doubt, some accept the pardon God offers and others refuse it—and how can love so quickly turn to hate?

Painful though the admission may be, we must confess that there is a deep current of evil coursing in each of our hearts. Paul referred to it as "the mystery of iniquity" that is at work in the world like yeast in a lump of dough. It is being restrained by God, but the day is coming when that restraint will be removed so that evil can bear its full fruit, the mask be ripped off, and evil be exposed for what it really is. Having begun with Lucifer, *evil* will reach its zenith and full revelation in *a man*, the Antichrist, who is also called "the man of sin, the son of perdition" and "that wicked one." Paul's description of that future rampage of uninhibited moral depravity reinforced by psychic power is overwhelming:

> Let no man deceive you by any means, for that day [of Christ, or the Lord, which begins with the rapture] shall not come except there come a falling away [apostasy] first, and [subsequently] that man of sin be revealed, the son of perdition, who opposeth and exalteth himself above all that is called God, or that is worshiped, so that he as God sitteth in the temple of God, showing himself that he is God. . . .
>
> And now ye know what withholdeth [hinders], that he might be revealed in his time.
>
> For the mystery of iniquity doth already work; only he who now letteth [hinders or restrains] will restrain until he be taken out of the way.
>
> And then shall that wicked one be revealed, whom the Lord shall consume with the spirit of his mouth, and shall destroy with the brightness of his coming, even him whose coming is after the working of Satan with all power and signs and lying wonders, and with all deceivableness of unrighteousness in them that perish, because they received not the love of the truth that they might be saved (2 Thessalonians 2:3-10).

The mystery of iniquity fermenting in our world is destined to explode in naked revelation under the Antichrist—yet it will not seem horrifying or even evil at first. Many who have eventually been swept up in the raw, malignant perversity of full-blown Satanism testify that in the beginning they were

wooed (as so many involved in the New Age have been seduced) by an appealing "white magic," with its promises of
psychic powers. They wanted to use the "light" side of the
Force for good—and, incidentally, to fulfill their every desire
as well. That was the first step, followed by many more in
directions that were not at first fully understood. Gradually the
downward momentum accelerated until the victims were irresistibly sucked into a maelstrom of evil which, though it now
held an overpowering fascination for them, would have been
repugnant had they been exposed to it too soon. So it will be
with the entire world when Satan's power to deceive is loosed
without restraint under the Antichrist.

One of Christ's most frightening statements to His disciples
was "One of you *is a devil!*" He referred to Judas, who would
betray Him, and in so doing would betray his very humanity.
Some of the most awesome passages in Scripture indicate that
those who refuse to repent of their rebellion will, in the
unfolding of the *mystery of iniquity*, be drawn irresistibly by
their own lusts and in preparation for hell, to become (like
Judas) the embodiment of the very evil with which they have
been obsessed and finally possessed. Such is the terrifying
judgment that God pronounces upon those for whom there is
no longer any hope:

> He that is unjust, let him be unjust still; and he which is
> filthy, let him be filthy still [i.e. eternally!] (Revelation 22:11).

Alongside of evil another mystery is at work in today's
world: "the mystery of godliness." Just as the manifestation of
evil in human flesh is mysterious beyond comprehension, so is
the manifestation of goodness. "Why callest thou me *good?*"
Jesus demanded of someone who had addressed Him as "good
master." "There is none good but one," He remonstrated,
"and that is God" (Matthew 19:17). Far from denying that He
was God, Christ was asserting that fact. His deity was proved
by His intrinsic goodness, which separated Him from every
other person. In reference to Jesus, Paul declared:

Without controversy great is the mystery of godliness: God was manifest in the flesh, justified in the Spirit, seen of angels, preached unto the Gentiles, believed on in the world, received up into glory (1 Timothy 3:16).

Why did God forbid Adam and Eve to partake of the tree of the knowledge of *good* and *evil*? Why would it be the tree of death for them? Because man is incapable in himself either of knowing or doing good. Therefore, desiring to know good and evil from within oneself and to be able to do good and refrain from evil through one's own resources was aspiring to be independent of God and thus like God. It was the ultimate act of rebellion. Asserting that he didn't need God in order to be good, man cut himself off from his only source of goodness and became the slave of evil.

Having joined the wrong side, there was no escape for mankind. Even those who had a change of heart and wanted to defect were held hostage by Satan. There was only one solution: God Himself must become a man to pay the debt that His justice demanded for man's sin, giving mankind the opportunity to repent of rebellion against God and His laws and to receive Christ as Savior and Lord. God's goodness could then be united with humanity once again, but this time in a bond that could never be broken. That's who Jesus Christ is and what He came to do. To the Christians Paul exclaims in triumph that the great mystery of godliness has now become "Christ in you, the hope of glory!" (Colossians 1:27).

Satan also has a man representing him in this battle upon earth: the Antichrist. As the man Christ Jesus is "God manifest in the flesh," so Antichrist will be Satan manifest in the flesh. When he is revealed, as we have already seen, Satan's man will pose as God's man, the Antichrist will pretend to be Christ, and the majority of mankind will believe and follow him. He offers an alternate plan of rescue—not from sin, for that concept is rejected, but from ecological disaster and war. He promises peace and prosperity, the good life here and now rather than "pie in the sky in the sweet bye-and-bye."

The mystery of godliness ultimately involves Christ turning men from self to God and indwelling them in preparation for heaven. The mystery of lawlessness ultimately involves Satan turning men from God to self and indwelling them in preparation for hell. Satan's is a gospel of self and ambition that caters to human pride. It promises that we each have within ourselves the means of our own salvation. That something has gone wrong with mankind is not denied, but Satan's diagnosis absolves man of any explicit moral blame. We are not separated from God by sin; we are alienated from ourselves and our environment through ignorance of who we really are. We imagine ourselves to be weak mortals when in fact we are gods. We do not need a "Savior" external to ourselves, but simply need to learn to tap the infinite potential that lies within. It is the same appealing lie that seduced Eve.

Everything that occurs in human history is moving the pieces on the chessboard that much closer to the final conflict between Christ and Antichrist and the inevitable defeat of Satan. Human history as we have known it will culminate in this face-to-face encounter between God's man and Satan's man. When will that take place? No one can say, but we do know that certain events must occur first.

Among the most important happenings which set the stage for the second coming is the *revival of the Roman Empire*, to which we have already briefly referred. Ancient Rome was intimately involved in Christ's *first* coming, and it must likewise be involved *in revived form* both in His *second* coming and the coming of the Antichrist. This is a fascinating fact both of history and prophecy and a key element in understanding the rise of the Antichrist.

8 | *The Revived Roman Empire*

S OVIET PRESIDENT MIKHAIL GORBACHEV is driven by a passion: to see the Soviet Union and its former satellites become part of a new United Europe—and then a united socialist world of freedom and peace! How long this incredible and un-Marxist dream had obsessed Gorbachev before he at last felt the time was ripe to make it public in his 1987 book, *Perestroika: New Thinking for Our Country and the World*, we do not know. Emboldened by that book's enthusiastic reception, he vigorously expressed and updated his dream in his historic speech to the General Assembly of the United Nations in December 1988. It was the first time a Soviet President had addressed that world body in 25 years. The cultured and convincing delivery by *Time* magazine's 1980's "Man of the Decade" was a far cry from Khrushchev's crude tirade before that same body when he emphasized his points by pounding the lectern with his shoe.

Gorbachev's speech was a public relations masterpiece. He caught everyone off-guard by announcing a unilateral reduction of Soviet troops stationed in Eastern Europe and appealing for a renunciation of the use of military force in international relations. Warning that closed societies would fail, he called for the democratization of every nation and the universal recognition of basic human rights and full freedom for every individual.

Most Westerners thought Gorbachev was just spouting more of the same old propaganda. The Soviet leader, with a straight face, calling for "*democratization* of every nation"? Stop joking! And condemning "closed societies" to failure? Wasn't that a description of his own country? Few of his listeners that day would have believed that the "closed societies" of Eastern Europe would indeed all have failed and fallen within a year of that prophetic pronouncement, but nearly everyone has since then become a believer in Gorbachev and in his revolutionary proposals, which do not stop with Europe but extend to the entire world.

How I wish that some of the old-time preachers from my youth could be alive today! They would be thrilled to see the developing revival of the Roman Empire of which they spoke with such confidence 50 years ago. They would also, I believe, see their mistake in interpreting the "ten toes of Nebuchadnezzar's image" (Daniel 2:31-45) as ten nations in Western Europe. We have already noted that both recent events and the facts of history require a much larger view of what those "ten toes" represent.

At the peak of its power ancient Rome controlled territories far beyond Western Europe. In addition there were Greece, Turkey, and parts of what used to be East Germany as well as much of Hungary, Romania, Yugoslavia, Albania, Bulgaria, Soviet Armenia, and other parts of the Soviet Union around the Black Sea. The Caesars' ancient Empire also took in Syria, Lebanon, Israel, Jordan, Egypt, and the Mediterranean coastal areas of North Africa all the way to the Atlantic Ocean.

It was simply a mistake ever to equate the revived Roman Empire with a theoretical ten-nation confederacy in Western Europe. What is the justification however, for extending this Empire of the Antichrist far beyond the actual area controlled by the Caesars? There are many reasons.

The Caesars ruled the world of their day, so it would make sense that the Antichrist, heading a revived form of the Caesars' empire, would rule the world of his day, which now includes all nations. But isn't it presumptuous to leave out the largest portion of the earth, including the great ancient civilizations in India and China, in referring to the Roman Empire as the world of its day? Again, there are good reasons for doing so.

The Bible itself refers to the four kingdoms represented by Nebuchadnezzar's image as "rul[ing] over all the earth" (Daniel 2:39). So we must view ancient Rome as a *world empire* if we are to adopt the biblical perspective. It then follows that the revived Roman Empire will be a *world empire* also. What that means in the world of the last days is stated very clearly: "... power was given him over *all kindreds and tongues and nations. And all that dwell upon the earth* shall worship him..." (Revelation 13:7,8). As we have already pointed out, these verses state explicitly that the Antichrist will rule over and be worshiped by the entire world.

There can be little doubt, for reasons already given, that the nations of the world will eventually all unite. As we have also noted, it makes little sense, particularly in light of the plain statements of Scripture, that the Antichrist would rule over only a small part of a united world. Furthermore, as Vaclav Havel, newly elected President of Czechoslovakia, pointed out in a major article written early in 1990 for *U.S. News & World Report*:

> Europe has been the cradle of a civilization that has shaped the history of the world for the last 2000 years. The spiritual impulses of antiquity, Judaism and Christianity, merged into a force that has forged the world as we know it.
>
> European civilization discovered, explored, conquered and dominated other continents, other civilizations. It has brought European thinking, enterprise and inventions to the remotest corners of the earth....[1]

These colonial nations not only spread European culture and ideas around the globe but also "Christianized" their colonies. Thus the foundation was laid worldwide for the apostate "Christian" church that will follow the Antichrist, thinking that he is Christ. It is this "spiritual impulse," as Havel calls it, which more than anything else links the entire world back to ancient Rome. This is the most important connection, as we shall see.

The revival of the Roman Empire begins with the uniting of Europe and moves out from there, following the pattern of ancient Rome in her conquests and then that of the colonial era. We can see this pattern emerging now in one of the most important developments in this century for the fulfillment of last-days prophecies. The "democratization" of Eastern Europe now underway is following Gorbachev's scenario, and it has opened the door for East and West to be united in a new and much larger Europe than almost anyone else had dared to envision. It was in *perestroika* that he first proposed what at that time seemed either an insane fantasy or pure propaganda: a Europe that would be united *"from the Atlantic to the Urals!"* [2]

The one other leader who shared Gorbachev's incredible vision in those days was none other than Pope John Paul II. In 1987, while performing a mass for 55,000 people outside Speyer, Germany's massive 900-year-old cathedral, he too appealed for a united Europe *"from the Atlantic to the Urals!"* After the Berlin Wall crumbled and Communism collapsed in Eastern Europe, others also began to take up the same theme. Early in 1990, about two weeks after reestablishing ties with the Vatican, following a break in relations of 40 years, Hungary's Foreign Minister, Gyula Horn, proposed that Eastern European nations "join NATO's political councils"—an idea that was utterly unthinkable in the past. He went on to say:

> I would like to stress that a united democratic Europe is our goal. We need to act on this. To that end, a lot of things have to be rethought. [3]

In the same article quoted above, Vaclav Havel went on to state:

> For more than 40 years, there has been not one Europe, but at least two. One is the Europe of the West, the land of democracies and relative prosperity. The other is the Europe of the East, of totalitarianism until recently unchallenged, the Europe that has finally awakened. . . .

Then the tide turned . . . pav[ing] the way for the enormous changes in Eastern Europe that we have recently witnessed. . . .
   Europeans in the West have made clear their intention to
overcome national, political and geographical barriers, and to
enter the next millennium as a single community. Europeans in
the East have made equally clear their interest in joining this
community of free nations.[4]

To Gorbachev must go most of the credit for the "enormous
changes in Eastern Europe." The infamous Berlin Wall is no
more; there is no longer any barrier between what used to be
East and West Germany. They have become one again, something that most analysts could not have foreseen for at least 100
years, if ever. But this is only the beginning. Not only is Europe
changing, but the entire world as a result. All of this, and so
much more that the future now holds in store, is the result of
one man's vision and one man's astonishing courage to stand
up against the fierce opposition within the Soviet hierarchy to
his innovative *perestroika* and *glasnost*. The amazing result
was the end of the long-standing Cold War and the new hope
for peace that world leaders now express.
   Yes, much credit must go also to President Reagan for
keeping the U.S. military machine strong in spite of heavy
domestic opposition and for standing firm on equitable disarmament. Much credit is also due to President Bush, not only for
continuing to negotiate with the Soviets from strength rather
than weakness, but also for being quick to recognize the
changes that Gorbachev was seeking to effect and for responding with friendship and trust. Without Gorbachev at the helm
of the Soviet Union, however, the Kremlin might well have
decided that because of its economically hopeless situation its
only option in its rivalry with the West was war. Instead,
we now have a new and previously unbelievable partnership
between the United States and the Soviet Union—a partnership that is working for the mutual interests of worldwide
peace and unity.

There now seems little doubt that the division between East and West Europe has ended and that it is only a matter of time and implementation until Europe will indeed be united "from the Atlantic to the Urals." But that isn't all. Something much larger is in process. With the Eastern bloc joining the West and receiving an influx of investment capital and business and farming expertise, the resulting European Community will have the power to dominate the world. At some point everyone will want to join for economic and security reasons. After the church has been taken to heaven and his power has been consolidated, the Antichrist will use force to maintain his rule. His kingdom will eventually explode in war between rival factions at Armageddon, but first the foundation must be laid, which current events seem to be doing.

The new united Germany has called for the United States and Canada to form a " 'new trans-Atlantic partnership' bolstered by a treaty to complete the work of ending East-West divisions in Europe." Japan and other Asian nations are preparing to negotiate their relationship to the new Europe. Again Gorbachev turns out to be a prophet, for in that same United Nations speech he had called for the adoption of a new economic system as the key to *a new and united world of peace and prosperity.*

The first Moscow envoy to speak at a U.S. college commencement, departing Soviet Ambassador Yuri V. Dubinin, told the May 1990 graduates of George Washington University's Elliott School of International Affairs that the Cold War is obsolete and that now the Soviet Union and the United States "think of each other not as adversaries but as partners." Dubinin told the graduates that they must participate in "shaping a *new international order.* . . ."[5] We have already quoted the *Spectator*, London's conservative weekly, in reference to the new larger Europe that promises to unite East and West: "We are taking the first steps toward an ecumenical community that will ultimately spread to all corners of our planet."[6]

Globalism! The very thought used to evoke in thinking Christians the horrifying image of the Antichrist ruling the world. But now such a reaction is looked upon, even in many Christian circles, as a paranoid carryover from an "Antichrist phobia" that inhibited progress. It is now generally taken for granted that the world must be united under some form of binding association that supersedes national boundaries and loyalties. The necessity for this new unity grows more urgent each day not only to prevent World War Three with its inevitable global destruction but to rescue the entire planet from the brink of ecological collapse.

There are also economic and banking reasons for unifying the world which are equally compelling. Unless one is a Christian and really believes that either Christ or Antichrist must rule the world, nothing makes better sense than a one-world government in some benign form. Consequently, we may expect an increasing and less subtle promotion of "one-worldism" throughout our society, from the highest levels of government to the classrooms of our youngest children. As the National Education Association has said:

> It is with . . . sobering awareness that we set about to change the course of American education for the 21st century by embracing the ideals of global community, the equality and interdependence of all peoples and nations, and education as a tool to bring about world peace.[7]

Even forgetting the Antichrist, there are obvious moral consequences to making the world one. An integral part of the new global education is, as Allan Bloom warns in *The Closing of the American Mind*, "to force students to recognize that there are other ways of thinking . . . [in order] to establish a world community and train its members—the person devoid of prejudice."[8] Bloom's use of "prejudice" is tongue-in-cheek, for in the new community there can be no moral absolutes. It must be labeled "prejudice" to suggest that one point of view might be right and another wrong, particularly with regard to religion. There must be *absolutely* no absolutes, for such dogmatism would destroy global unity. So Lynda Falkenstein of Northwest Regional Educational Laboratory argues:

Black-and-white answers probably never really existed, but the time is long past when even the myth can endure. Competent world citizens must act in the large zone of grays where absolutes are absent.[9]

The most dangerous part of global education is its teaching about religion. It is especially in this area that the planners realize they must eliminate "prejudice" and introduce tolerance for all beliefs. Thus the new curriculum in American public schools calls for teaching not religion, which is forbidden, but "about" it in a comparative study of the world's religions. Soviet schools, also, where atheism once reigned, plan a similar "religious studies" program. Evangelical leaders have joined liberals and atheists in endorsing such globalist education programs as The Williamsburg Charter. Its curriculum in public schools across America, which is calculated to make global citizens for the new world order, will teach students that all religious beliefs are to be tolerated. It is an easy step, especially in a child's mind, from tolerance to acceptance.

Teachers, of course, cannot even suggest that one religion might be wrong and another right—much less that only one could be right. It will be only logical for the students to conclude that all must be equally valid. Therefore one's choice of religion doesn't really matter, since there is no such thing as right and wrong—a concept they have been taught for years in the area of morals through such programs as "Values Clarification." It is the perfect preparation for the Antichrist's ecumenical world religion. Forming a partnership between all religions is, of course, foundational to the creation of global citizens and the Antichrist's world government. Political unity is impractical when religious barriers still divide.

In *Learning for Tomorrow: The Role of the Future in Education*, Wendell Bell makes it clear that the "demise of superstition and cultural 'absolutes' " is necessary in order to "unshackle humankind" for the new world of the future.[10] To create the new world citizen it is necessary to remove all "prejudice" against the beliefs which other people may hold.

This fact is forgotten by Christians in their excitement over the new "freedom of conscience" being offered. *Focus On The Family Citizen* enthusiastically reports that "Gorbachev has publicly admitted to Pope John Paul II that his nation needs Christian moral values."[11] But what does he mean?

Gorbachev's promotion of "spiritual values" must be taken in the context of his warnings against "outmoded dogmas." In an obvious affront to the One who is the Alpha and Omega (Revelation 1:8), he stated at his June 1990 reunion with Ronald Reagan in San Francisco (where tolerance has borne such deadly fruit as AIDS):

> Everything must change. Tolerance is the alpha and omega of a new world order.[12]

Evangelical Christianity is already recognized as the enemy of the new "freedom of conscience" and must either change or be outlawed because it expresses what is considered to be the ultimate intolerance: that Jesus Christ is the *only* Savior of the world, and that all must believe in Him or be eternally lost. Yet church leaders, both Protestant and Catholic, are jumping on the "one-world" bandwagon, which can only be held together by tolerance for all beliefs. As early as 1970, the Lutheran Church in America adopted an official position statement titled "WORLD COMMUNITY—Ethical Imperatives in an age of interdependence." Under the heading "Toward a Global Civil Order" it advocated the establishment of "world and regional institutions" to implement a new world order. The National Conference of Catholic Bishops similarly expressed its support for globalism in a recent Pastoral Letter:

> ... we are now entering an era of new global interdependence requiring global systems of governance to manage the resulting conflicts ... these growing tensions cannot be remedied by a single nation-state approach. They shall require the concerted effort of the whole world community.

If the Catholic Bishops, the Pope, and many Protestant leaders as well are in favor of it, then why not join all nations together in one global brotherhood? Why should a world government be evil in and of itself—and why must the Antichrist rule over it? With the threat of a global Communist takeover removed, it would appear that the uniting of the world will not, as was once thought, come about by the forceful imposition of an ideology, but by a voluntary association of those who are tolerant of one another's differences.

It sounds like the fulfillment of Daniel's prophecy that the revived Roman Empire would be iron mixed with clay. Indeed, the clay of democracy emerging out of Communist dictatorships to form the new international socialism adds an element of persuasion that plays an important part in the deception. The "iron" of fading totalitarianism must be mingled with the "miry clay" of democracy for the Roman Empire to be revived. It is happening.

So what is the significance of the revival of the ancient Roman Empire? Why *this* empire instead of another? What function will *Rome* play, if any? The answers to those questions bring us to the heart of the matter. Here again is where the plot thickens.

It is fascinating, first of all, to notice that ancient Rome did indeed serve more than one function concerning Christ's first advent. For example, it was Roman execution by crucifixion that caused Jesus to die in the manner prophesied by David: ". . . all my bones are out of joint [characteristic of crucifixion] . . . they pierced my hands and my feet . . . they part my garments among them, and cast lots upon my vesture" (Psalm 22:14-18). As in His death, so in His birth Rome played an integral part as well:

> And it came to pass in those days that there went out a decree from Caesar Augustus that all the world should be taxed. . . . And all went to be taxed, every one into his own city.
> And Joseph also went up from Galilee . . . unto the city of David, which is called Bethlehem (because he was of the house and lineage of David) to be taxed with Mary his espoused wife, being great with child. And so it was that while they were there . . . she brought forth her firstborn son . . . (Luke 2:1-7).

Interesting! It was a decree of the Roman Empire (which therefore had to be in existence for Christ to come to earth) that put Joseph and Mary in Bethlehem at just the right time for Jesus to be born there in fulfillment of the prophecy that every rabbi had to acknowledge was Messianic: "But thou, Bethlehem Ephratah, though thou be little among the thousands of Judah, yet out of thee shall he come forth unto me that is to be ruler in Israel, whose goings forth have been from of old, from everlasting" (Micah 5:2).

Yet Jesus Christ, in spite of being born in Bethlehem and fulfilling all other criteria which the Hebrew prophets had set forth concerning the coming Messiah, did not rule over Israel when He came 1900 years ago. His people rejected Him as their king, and instead crucified Him, an event which was also foretold by the Hebrew prophets. Obviously Jesus Christ must return to this earth to sit on David's throne in Jerusalem and reign over Israel and the world if biblical prophecies are to be fulfilled.

When will that be? *In the days of those kings,* said Daniel—the "kings" that are represented by the ten toes of iron and clay who comprise the revived Roman Empire. It is only fitting that Christ should return when the Empire which played such an important role in His first advent has been revived to become the world Empire of its day once again. It is also fitting that He should return to destroy the Empire that crucified Him and destroyed Jerusalem, and which in its revived form will seek to destroy Israel totally.

Moreover, the Roman Empire must be revived for the Antichrist to rule over it. His subjects, "the people of the prince that shall come," would crucify Christ again if they could. Indeed, their armies not only seek to destroy Israel but will knowingly fight against Christ (Revelation 19:19) when He returns for a face-to-face confrontation with the Antichrist, destroys his counterfeit world empire, and begins His millennial reign of righteousness.

There is another element that must not be overlooked. The

Roman Empire was not only a political, economic, and military entity—it was highly *religious* as well. In fact, religion played a dominant role both before and after Rome was Christianized. Therefore, if that ancient Empire is indeed to be revived, then its religion must be revived as well, for it has a vital role to play in causing the world to accept and worship the Antichrist.

To fulfill the prophesied last-days criteria, the revived Roman Empire must include two vital religious elements from its past. First of all, it must be ruled by a new pagan "Emperor" who will be worshiped as god. Such was the case in the days of the early church. During periodic waves of persecution against Christians, all who refused to worship an image of the Emperor as god were killed. The Bible leaves no doubt that even this seemingly extreme aspect of ancient Rome's religion will be revived:

> . . . that they should make an image to the beast, [Antichrist] . . . and cause that as many as would not worship the image of the beast, should be killed (Revelation 13:14,15).

That there must also be a restoration of the close working relationship that existed between the popes and the emperors seems to be clear from the same passage. It is the miracle-working second beast in Revelation 13, clearly a religious figure and commonly known as "the false prophet," who "causeth the earth and them which dwell therein to worship the first beast [Antichrist]" (verse 12). He is the one who makes the image of the first beast and decrees the death of those who refuse to worship it.

The false prophet must be the head of the World Church, identified in Revelation 17 as "mystery Babylon." Even Catholic apologist Karl Keating admits that Babylon signifies Rome. The current Pope, John Paul II, is working feverishly to merge all faiths. He obviously understands that not only Protestants and Catholics but all mankind must unite in a new world religion.

9 | *Emperors and Popes*

S OMETHING ASTONISHING IS HAPPENING. It is not only that the Cold War has ended and that former antagonists in that war now work together with a new sense of mutual trust. Nor is it only that Communism has collapsed in Eastern Europe and that we are seeing the unbelievable formation of a new European community stretching from the Atlantic to the Soviet Union's easternmost shores on the Pacific. Nor is it just that a new era of peace seems to have dawned in which aggressors immediately find themselves confronted by the rest of the world rising up as one to make them behave. All of these developments border on the miraculous—but there's something more.

In addition to all of the above, and far more remarkable, is the exploding worldwide interest in *religion* and *spirituality*. We have already pointed out that Jesus and His apostles foretold the coming of a time of apparent peace that would lead to Armageddon, and also prophesied a religious revival involving deception that would prepare the world for the Antichrist. Most amazing is the convergence of all of these events at one time, thereby setting the stage for the fulfillment in our day of the prophesied revival of the Roman Empire. If this is indeed the case, then we are witnessing one of the most important events of all time and one that will precipitate both the rise of Antichrist and the second coming.

In the last chapter we saw that because the Roman Empire was a highly religious entity with an official world religion,

99

therefore the revival of that Empire would necessitate a restoration of that same religion to its former status once again. If that should occur, it would be even more significant than any political or military developments. The question, then, is whether we are witnessing merely a revival of religion in general, or moving toward the restoration of the official religion of the ancient Roman Empire.

The political summit at Malta between U.S. President Bush and Soviet President Mikhail Gorbachev in early December 1989 undoubtedly played a major role in establishing a new working relationship of mutual trust between these two world leaders and the superpowers they represented. It could only be properly evaluated, however, in the context of the religious summit which preceded it. The meeting between Gorbachev and the Pope on December 1, 1989, changed all the rules of the international game.

In 1945, in response to the suggestion that the Vatican might object to some of his policies, Stalin had sneered, "How many divisions did you say the Pope had?" It was in obvious admission of the power of nearly 900 million Catholics worldwide that 44 years later Gorbachev journeyed to Rome to make his peace with the current Pope. In the opinion of Joseph Sobran, syndicated columnist and senior editor of *National Review*:

> The real summit—the one that deserves to be called historic—occurred not in Malta but in Vatican City. There Rome and Moscow met. Moscow was on its knees....
>
> Mr. Gorbachev, a baptized Christian, referred to the pope as "Holy Father"... praised the Pope and the influence of all faiths....
>
> ...men such as John Paul II, Lech Walesa and Michael Gorbachev... are the founding fathers of a new [world] order.[1]

Why did the Soviet President make his unprecedented pilgrimage not to the World Council of Churches headquarters in Geneva, but to the Vatican in Rome? Let Gorbachev explain. After his audience with the Pope, he took his wife Raisa's hands and greeted her, an atheist professor of "scientific Marxism," with these words: "We have visited the highest religious authority in the world. . . ."[2] *Authority*—and the power that goes with it—that is what Gorbachev understands and wants to use.

In contrast to previous Kremlin leaders, Gorbachev had been making clear for a number of months the great importance he placed upon religion. And well he might, considering the estimated 70 million professing Christians in the Soviet Union plus 74 million in the six satellite nations of Eastern Europe—to say nothing of the swelling numbers of Muslims and Buddhists. Religion's role in shaping the new world would obviously be a major one, and the leader of world atheism had plans to exploit that fact.

Inviting Russian Orthodox Church leaders into the Kremlin for a highly publicized meeting, Gorbachev "promised greater religious tolerance, sought support for his drive for domestic change [and] condemned past repression of religious activity." The unusual meeting, "reported by the official news agency Tass, was the lead item on the evening news program 'Vremya' and a front-page story in that day's editions of *Pravda* and other Soviet dailies."[3]

Gorbachev's attitude toward religion, and particularly Christianity, has been an astonishing departure from official Kremlin policy. As the leader of a country whose official religion is "scientific atheism," his sworn duty has been to destroy all other faiths. Yet in his book, *Perestroika*, Gorbachev had boldly revealed a sympathy for religion and his recognition of the vital role it must play in bringing peace and creating the new world order. That as a child he was baptized into the Russian Orthodox Church as Mikhail Sergeyevich means little if anything. Christianity is important to Gorbachev only because of its *function* as an essential ingredient for uniting his own country, Europe, and then the world.

In fact, the Soviet President has surprisingly appealed a number of times to Russia's "Christian" roots as justification for its inclusion in the new united Europe. Those statements have boggled Western Soviet experts. Gorbachev appears to be willing to allow a revival of "Christianity" in the USSR because he sees it as an essential step toward membership in the EC! In *Perestroika* he wrote:

> Some in the West are trying to "exclude" the Soviet Union from Europe. . . . Such ploys, however, cannot change the geographic and historical realities. . . .
>
> We are Europeans. Old Russia was united with Europe by *Christianity*, and the millennium of its arrival in the land of our ancestors will be marked next year [1988].[4]

Something of incredible importance is happening! The leader of world Communism/atheism, which has sworn to destroy all religion, now claims that the Soviet Union is a *Christian* country and is encouraging the growth of Christianity! No one in his right mind would have even dreamed of such an impossible scenario. Yet it is unfolding before our eyes. Indeed it had to for Bible prophecy to be fulfilled. That fact is what makes these developments so significant and exciting to the Christian!

Pope John Paul II showed remarkable agreement with Gorbachev long before their historic meeting in December 1989. In spite of Eastern Europe's domination by atheism for more than 70 years, the Pope sensed, along with the Soviet leader, the vital role that would be played by religion, and especially by Christianity, in creating the new world order. As *Newsweek* reported:

> The jewel in the Pope's international design is a Utopian vision of a unified—and re-Christianized—Europe stretching from the Atlantic Ocean to the Ural Mountains.
>
> Phase one would be an end to the divisions between Eastern and Western Europe. Phase two: reconciliation between Roman Catholics and the Orthodox Christians of the Soviet East.[5]

That this "dream," as the first step toward a new world order, is shared both by the Pope and the President of the

Soviet Union must be more than coincidence. What went on in their secret meeting in Rome when they spoke Russian together without interpreters present we can only guess. What we do know is that their mutual "dream" began to take on substance shortly after that meeting.

In a "groundbreaking speech in Rome" two days before his audience with the Pope, Gorbachev "depicted religion as a powerful moral force that is helping *perestroika*." He candidly declared that he was "openly seek[ing] the moral force of organized religion as an ally for his sweeping restructuring of an alienated Soviet society." That staggering announcement from the head of the Soviet Union was a pragmatic acknowledgment that atheism, Russia's official faith, had utterly failed to capture the masses, while religion, cruelly suppressed and derided for the past 70 years, had multiplied its adherents. As the astonished press reported:

> Confirming the new official view of religion in a nation that has long been aggressively atheistic, Gorbachev told the Pope that believers of many faiths, Jews to Buddhists, Christians to Muslims, live in the Soviet Union today.
> "All of them have a right to satisfy their spiritual needs," he said. "Shortly, a law on the freedom of conscience will be adopted in our country."[6]

In turn, the Pope "gave his blessing to the restructuring of Soviet society proceeding under Gorbachev's revolutionary program of *perestroika*...." That "restructuring" had already brought about the unprecedented television broadcasting of worship services, the opening of 3000 churches in the previous nine months, and the celebration of the Orthodox Eucharist in the fifteenth-century Assumption Cathedral inside the Kremlin—the first time since 1918.[7] The Religion Newswriters Association named Gorbachev the number one "religion newsmaker" of 1989, and called his meeting with Pope John Paul II "the year's top religious news story."

The two leaders, described in news reports as "the two most compelling figures on the world stage today," agreed to restore diplomatic relations and official ties between the Holy See and the Kremlin, a relationship that had been broken during the Revolution in 1917. There can be no doubt that this new partnership between John Paul II and Mikhail Gorbachev has as its goal a new world united not only politically and economically but *religiously*. The significance of this development cannot be overstated.

The Pope and Gorbachev are not the only world leaders who see "religion," and especially "Christianity," as playing a key role in forming the new world order. As we have already seen, Czechoslovakian President Vaclav Havel is another. Robert Muller, recently retired Assistant Secretary General of the United Nations, has stated: "I have come to believe firmly today that our future peace, justice and fulfillment, happiness and harmony on this planet will not depend on world government but on divine or cosmic government . . . my great personal dream is to get a tremendous alliance between all major religions and the U.N." Referring to the deep economic problems that have plagued the USSR in spite of repeated "five-year plans," Soviet economist Stanislav Shatalin suggested that a "spiritual and moral renewal is necessary for workers to care about their jobs."[8] *World Press Review* declared:

> For Russia to be ready to join the [European] community, it will have to . . . allow the Christian religion once more to occupy the forefront of life. For Russia is at heart a profoundly *Christian* country, and *that is its chief title deed to European status* [emphasis added].[9]

Suddenly secular leaders are declaring that not just religion but "Christianity" is the key to uniting Europe! Why is this so? Since the Antichrist pretends to be Christ, his followers must be "Christians" and his world religion must be a perverted form of "Christianity." Not only the Pope calls for a "spiritually united Europe,"[10] but numerous other leaders voice the same novel opinion. Orthodox dissident leader Alexander Ogorodnikov predicts a "second Christianization" of

Russia. That process seems to have already begun under Gorbachev's bold leadership, as indeed it must. It does not mean, however, what most Christians imagine.

Evangelicals are encouraged by the new freedom of religion introduced into the Soviet Union by Gorbachev. And indeed every effort ought to be made to take advantage of the liberty to preach the gospel while it lasts—which may not be long. Many evangelical leaders are equally enamored with Pope John Paul II. America's alleged "foremost Christian expert on the family" regards the Pope as "the most eminent religious leader who names the name of Jesus Christ."[11] Others believe that his is an evangelistic message to turn the world to Christ.

In actual fact, neither the Pope nor Gorbachev has the least sympathy for "born-again" evangelical Christianity, which John Paul II openly derides and warns his flock against. While encouraging dialogue with Buddhists, Muslims, and Hindus, the Pope warns Catholics "not to be seduced by Protestant fundamentalist sects. . . ."[12] In fact, by "Christianity" both Gorbachev and the Pope mean *Roman Catholicism*. That just happens to have been the official world religion of the Roman Empire—the very religion which must recover that status in preparation for the Antichrist.

At the same time that the foundation is being laid for the political revival of the Roman Empire something else of equal significance is happening. The church and "Christianity" of ancient Rome are being resurrected before our very eyes with the blessing of the leaders of the world's religions and leading Protestants as well. A brief look at history will help us to understand that what happened to Christianity under Constantine is recurring today.

The ancient Roman Empire was a pluralistic society such as both Gorbachev and the Pope hope to create. Any religion was tolerated. There was, however, one exception: Christianity, which by its very claims condemned all other religions. Christians were hated and persecuted and often killed, not because they believed in Christ, but because they believed *only* in Him. This was the faith which Peter had boldly expressed to the rabbis in Jerusalem and which made the Jewish religious leaders so furious that they determined to kill the apostles:

> Be it known unto you all, and to all the people of Israel, that by the name of Jesus Christ of Nazareth, whom ye crucified, whom God raised from the dead, even by him doth this man stand here before you whole [healed].
>
> Neither is there salvation in any other, for there is no other name under heaven given among men whereby we must be saved (Acts 4:10,12).

That same belief aroused the hatred and loathing of the pagan leaders as well. The Romans were convinced that the Christians' "atheism" (i.e. rejection of pagan deities) brought the wrath of the gods upon the whole Empire. Christians had "abandoned the religion of their forefathers... accepted 'Jewish myths' at their face value, and made a criminal [Jesus] into a cult-hero."[13]

Just as the Roman Emperors ultimately realized in their day, so Gorbachev, too, has recognized that the persecution of Christians is futile. Tertullian's saying, "The blood of the martyrs is the seed of the church," was all too true. The Emperor Constantine decided that, to unify the Empire, Christians should be given the right to worship as they pleased. Gorbachev has obviously come to the same conclusion with regard to the USSR and the world. Soviet Christians need to remember history!

A brilliant military commander, Constantine also understood that there could be no political stability without religious unity. Yet to accomplish that feat would require a union between paganism and Christianity. How could it be accomplished? The Empire needed an ecumenical religion that would appeal to every citizen in a multicultural society. Giving Christianity official status was not enough to bring internal peace to the Empire: Christianity had to undergo a transformation so that pagans could "convert" without giving up their old beliefs and rituals.

Constantine himself exemplified this expediency. He adopted Christ as the new god that had given him victory in the crucial battle at Milvian Bridge in 312 A.D. and brought him into Rome as its conqueror. Yet, as Caesar, he continued to function as the *Pontifex Maximus* of the Empire's pagan priesthood, known as the Pontifical College. Even as he endowed Christian churches, Constantine continued to support the construction of pagan temples. As a "Christian" Emperor, he automatically became the de facto civil head of the Christian church and seduced her with promises of power. Thus began the destruction of Christianity and the process that created Roman Catholicism as it is today.

Satan offered to give Jesus the kingdoms of this world if only He would bow down and worship him. Jesus, of course, refused. Constantine offered, for his own reasons, to share his kingdom with a church that was weary of persecution, and she succumbed to the temptation. As historian Will Durant explains:

> Constantine aspired to an absolute monarchy; such a government would profit from religious support. . . . Perhaps that marvelous organization of bishops and priests could become an instrument of pacification, unification and rule? . . .
>
> Throughout his reign he treated the bishops as his political aides; he summoned them, presided over their councils, and agreed to enforce whatever opinion their majority should formulate. A real believer would have been a Christian first and a statesman afterward; with Constantine it was the reverse. Christianity was to him a means, not an end.[14]

"Christianity" became a *means* for nearly everyone. Being a "Christian" was soon essential to anyone who wanted to advance in business, politics, or even the military. Thus many became "Christians" for the accompanying advantages—a problem the church had been spared when being a Christian meant persecution and possible martyrdom. Ecclesiastical posts, from priest to bishop, cardinal, and even Pope, went to the highest bidder. Augustine lamented the debilitating effect upon the Christian church:

The man who enters [a fourth-century church] is bound to see drunkards, misers, tricksters, gamblers, adulterers, fornicators, people wearing amulets, assiduous clients of sorcerers, astrologers. . . .

He must be warned that the same crowds that press into the churches on Christian festivals also fill the theatres on pagan holidays.[15]

So the "Christianity" of the Roman Empire, which became known as Roman Catholicism and of which the Pope is the head today, was not the same as the biblical Christianity of the early church and of the martyrs. Instead, it was the old paganism of Rome surviving under a thin veneer of Christian terminology and form. Says Durant:

When Christianity conquered Rome the ecclesiastical structure of the pagan church, the title and vestments of the *pontifex maximus*, the worship of the Great Mother and a multitude of comforting divinities, the sense of supersensible presences everywhere, the joy or solemnity of old festivals, and the pageantry of immemorial ceremony, passed like maternal blood into the new religion, and captive Rome captured her conqueror.

While Christianity converted the world, the world converted Christianity. . . .[16]

As head of the church, Constantine claimed two new titles in addition to paganism's *Pontifex Maximus: Vicar of Christ* and *Bishop of Bishops*. The title "Vicar of Christ," is most interesting. *Vicar* comes from the Latin word *vicarius*. The Greek equivalent would be *anti*, as in Antichrist. Using the Greek, then, Constantine, as Vicar of Christ, was an Antichrist, and so are the Popes, for they bear the same title. Antichrist will be the new Constantine, the head of the revived Roman Empire worldwide, while the Pope will be his assistant, the second beast of Revelation 13.

Early Protestant creeds unanimously called the Pope Antichrist—not only because of Rome's heresies but because the lives of many popes exemplified Antichrist's evil. More than one Pope vacated "Peter's throne" when killed by a furious husband who caught him in bed with his wife. Even Catholic historians admit that many of the popes were among the most inhuman monsters to walk this earth. In *Vicars of Christ*, Jesuit Peter de Rosa reminds us that Pope after Pope engaged habitually on a grand scale in wholesale mayhem and murder, pillage, rape, incest, simony, and corruption of the worst sort. Their evil lives are a blot upon the pages of history. It is a travesty to refer to such shameless perverts and master criminals as "His Holiness" or "Vicar of Christ," as they *all* are in official Roman Catholic dogma and documents.

Even if the popes had all been paragons of virtue, it would still be a mockery to claim that they represent an unbroken chain of "apostolic succession" back to Peter. Such a concept is unknown in the New Testament. And even if it were, it would have been necessary for each "Pope," as the possessor of an authority allegedly passed down from Peter, to have passed it on personally to his successor. Yet the popes did not choose their successors (and still do not to this day), much less lay hands upon and pass on any authority to them. It became the custom for the popes to be voted in by the populace of Rome— a populace which had its own selfish reasons for desiring one candidate above another. Such a majority vote could hardly be called "apostolic succession" and in fact is not acceptable by Rome today. Some popes were deposed by angry mobs in protest of their unbearable evil. Some were installed and/or deposed by kings and emperors. Political expediency along with the wealth and influence of the candidate as often as not determined who would be Pope. "Apostolic succession" indeed! (See Appendix A.)

As their reward for doing his bidding, Constantine endowed his three religious titles upon the popes, an office which he created, the better to use the church for the imperial good. It was Constantine who decreed that since Rome was the capital of the Empire, its Bishop should be the ecclesiastical head of the church. Prior to that time there had been no "Pope," but bishops of equal authority presiding over the regions surrounding

Rome, Antioch, Alexandria, Jerusalem, and Constantinople. Thereafter the popes worked closely with the emperors in the administration of the Empire. The three titles bestowed by Constantine upon them are still retained by the popes, known as Roman pontiffs, to this day.

While the Roman Empire was thoroughly pagan in the beginning, "Christianity" had become, in the end, its official faith. It was "Christianity," in fact, which gave the Empire a unity and continuity that held it together culturally and religiously. When the Empire later disintegrated *politically* under the onslaught of the Barbarians, it was held together *religiously* by the all-pervasive presence of the Roman Catholic Church with its ingenious ecumenical blend of paganism and Christianity still headquartered in Rome.

Consequently, it was to the popes, successors of the pagan emperors, that the world of the Middle Ages looked for leadership in the long-awaited *revival* of the Roman Empire, which nearly everyone longed for as a return to the "good old days." No one seemed aware, however—not even the popes and Roman Catholic theologians—that the Empire's revival was prophesied in the Bible as something *evil* that would occur in the "last days" and upon which God's judgment would fall. Ignorance of Bible prophecy still prevails among Catholics, and there seem to be decreasing numbers of Protestants as well who understand that subject today.

The parallels between Constantine and Gorbachev are, in the very least, fascinating. Gorbachev has shown his fellow Communists the better way to destroy the church: Give it the same freedom it has enjoyed in the West and take it in as a partner in solving the pressing problems of state. Share the kingdoms of this world with it just as Constantine did. In place of deliberate atheistic brainwashing, the new tactics are far more subtle and effective.

Gorbachev seems to have in mind the same use of "Christianity" as did Constantine, and for basically the same purpose. He does not need to create a new "Christianity," however, for it already exists, having been created by Constantine

1600 years ago. And today the influence exerted by the head of Rome's "Christianity" extends far beyond the confines of the ancient Roman Empire, making the Pope once again the ideal partner for the Antichrist in ruling what will be a worldwide kingdom of darkness.

This is not to proclaim that Gorbachev is the Antichrist and John Paul II the false prophet—but that pattern is definitely emerging, whether it is to be played out in the final act of history by these two men or some others. The pieces of the puzzle begin to fit together in line with biblical prophecy.

According to *U.S. News & World Report*, Pope John Paul II discusses world affairs weekly with U.S. President George Bush and also with Soviet President Mikhail Gorbachev.[17] That the Pope is almost universally recognized as the religious leader of the world takes on great significance as we see the revival of the Roman Empire underway. Other world leaders are adding their voices to the call by former U.N. Assistant Secretary General Robert Muller for the Pope to come "to the United Nations [to] speak for all the religions and spiritualities on this planet. . . ."[18] The picture becomes ever clearer and more ominous.

10 | *The "Whore of Babylon"*

ISLAM'S HUGE DOME OF the Rock is built over the place where Muhammad allegedly ascended to the seventh heaven on a winged horse that had the cosmetically made-up face of a woman. Occupying the very center of Temple Mount in Jerusalem, its towering gold dome dominates the panoramic view of the old city from the Mount of Olives, and its presence effectively blocks Israel's desired reconstruction of Solomon's temple. Stepping inside, the visitor is left breathless by the beauty of polished matching marble pillars and the profusion of handcrafted inlaid art in intricate Arabic patterns. One never ceases to be overwhelmed by the sheer enormity and beauty of this third-holiest of Muslim shrines.

Recently, after spending some time in Israel we flew directly from there to Rome. As we passed along the colonnade skirting the vast open square in front of the cathedral, I realized that the image I had retained in my mind from a past visit did not do justice to the vast dimensions and classic beauty of this place. Jerusalem's Temple Mount was dwarfed by Roman Catholicism's New Jerusalem. Here was the headquarters of the church which, claiming to have replaced the seed of Abraham and to be the new kingdom of God on earth, refused to give the State of Israel official recognition.

Entering the basilica I found myself comparing it with the Muslim shrine we had just visited. In surprise I realized there was no comparison. Half-a-dozen Domes of the Rock could fit inside St. Peter's immense interior! And as for beauty, the countless statues by such masters as Michelangelo, the endless dazzling mosaic depictions of biblical stories, the huge sunlit stained-glass windows—it left one gasping in awe. Gazing around me in stunned awe at the incomparable wealth that was beyond calculation, I understood something of what the apostle John expressed when he was given a vision of the power and wealth of this church: "When I saw her, I wondered with great admiration" (Revelation 17:6).

It was not only the materialism and sensuality that staggered John, but even more so it was her inconceivable spiritual corruption. That first-century Christians, hated and persecuted by the world, could metamorphose into a centrally controlled empire of religious perversion under the pretense of representing Jesus, was a revelation that left John reeling in shock. His vision was amazingly accurate, as the following brief excerpt reveals:

> I will show unto thee the judgment of the great whore that sitteth upon many waters, *with whom the kings of the earth have committed fornication....*
> And I saw a *woman* sit upon a scarlet-colored beast, full of names of blasphemy, having seven heads and ten horns....
> And upon her forehead was a name written: MYSTERY, BABYLON THE GREAT....
> And I saw the *woman* drunken with the blood of the saints, and with the blood of the martyrs of Jesus....
> The seven heads are seven mountains [or hills], on which the *woman* sitteth....
> And the *woman* which thou sawest is that great city which reigneth over the kings of the earth (Revelation 17:1-3,5,6, 9,18, emphasis added).

God has always called unfaithfulness to Him by His people spiritual adultery. Bowing down to idols and worshiping any gods except the one true God is the gravest of sins. Jeremiah's indictment of Judah with having "committed adultery with stones and with stocks [idols]" (Jeremiah 3:9)—an indictment echoed by other prophets—reveals God's view of paganism.

That standard is violated by John Paul II's praise of Hinduism, Buddhism, and other pagan religions, just as it has been for centuries by the mixture of paganism and "Christianity" within the Roman Catholic Church which he heads.

That the woman is called a "whore" guilty of *fornication* identifies her as the false church in contrast with "the bride, the Lamb's wife" (Revelation 21:9). The true church would be committing *adultery* if she engaged in the illicit relationships with ungodly kings of which the false church is guilty. That this gorgeously dressed woman is even called a "whore" indicates that she professes to be the true church. Yet she has sold herself, bartering a pretended spiritual authority and relationship with Christ for a share in the kingdoms of this world.

The identification of this "whore" is unmistakable: She is a *city* located upon *seven hills*. While Rome is not the only city so situated, she has been traditionally known as the city built on seven hills—and she is the only city that meets the other criteria: *with whom the kings of the earth have committed fornication* and which *reigneth over the kings of the earth*. It is not political Rome but Vatican City whose worldwide power and influence sways kingdoms even to this day. Much of the incalculable wealth in the Vatican Museum and the Sistine Chapel was given to the popes by the heads of numerous nations with whom the Papacy has repeatedly entered into unholy relationships. That fornication will play an important role in setting up the world for the Antichrist.

Only the Roman Catholic Church could possibly be in view. No other church exists that has enjoyed anything even approaching her influence with worldly rulers. The Pope receives and blesses a steady stream of visiting dignitaries, including terrorists such as the Palestinian Liberation Organization's Yasser Arafat and advocates of violent revolution such as South Africa's Nelson Mandela. The Pope is obviously the most influential leader on earth.

On the eve of his meeting with Gorbachev, the Pope "suggested establishing permanent ties with the Kremlin."[1] The head of Christendom's "one true church" initiated "permanent ties" with the leader of world atheism and Communism? Surely ecumenical delusion knows no bounds! The Pope was demonstrating once again that the Roman Catholic Church is the "great whore." What could "ties" with the Kremlin on the part of the Catholic Church be called except "fornication with the kings of the earth"! The extent of the delusion on both sides is seen in the following statement of Kremlin spokesman Gennady I. Gerasimov in the course of expressing Soviet enthusiasm for a partnership with the Vatican:

> Christian values are human values, and they are the same as socialist [Communist] values.[2]

Why do world leaders want to get into bed with the Vatican? The heads of state in today's world all recognize that the Pope wields a power which in many ways is even greater than their own. It is not only Catholicism's 900 million subjects and enormous wealth that causes the world's most powerful governments to cultivate friendly relations with the Roman Catholic Church; it is because Vatican City's citizens are found in great numbers in nearly every country. They constitute an international network that reaches into the inside circles of the world's power centers.

Are these millions of Roman Catholics of every nationality loyal? While some may criticize their clergy, deep down in his soul every Catholic still believes that the Church holds keys to heaven and that without her favor only hell awaits. Thus the power that Rome holds over its subjects is far greater than that of any secular government over its citizens. When the time comes to make a choice concerning where one's real loyalty lies, there is little doubt of the outcome for the Catholic of whatever citizenship.

It is not surprising, then, that all the major nations in the world, including the United States, have ambassadors to the Vatican just as they do to other nations. When he wanted to make his peace with the West, one of the first moves Gorbachev made was to journey to Rome on a mission of conciliation to reestablish Soviet ties with the Vatican. That fact speaks volumes. Will Durant is unable to hide his admiration as he explains how the Church inherited its power from a disintegrating Roman Empire—a power which will be even greater when that Empire is revived:

> The reins and skills of government were handed down by a dying empire to a virile papacy . . . the armies of state were replaced by the missionaries of the Church moving in all directions along the Roman roads; and the revolted provinces, accepting Christianity, again acknowledged the sovereignty of Rome.
>
> Through the long struggles of the Age of Faith the authority of the ancient capital persisted and grew, until in the Renaissance the classic culture seemed to rise from the grave, and the immortal city became once more the center and summit of the world's life and wealth and art.
>
> When, in 1936, Rome celebrated the 2689th anniversary of her foundation, she could look back upon the most impressive continuity of government and civilization in the history of mankind. May she rise again.[3]

Durant doesn't realize that the Bible says Rome *will* "rise again" to be ruled by Antichrist, thus bringing God's judgment upon mankind, and culminating in Armageddon. That this MYSTERY BABYLON will embody the same marriage of Babel/Babylonian paganism and "Christianity" that ancient Rome developed under Constantine is clear.

The church which Christ founded was called the *ekklesia* in New Testament Greek, meaning the "called-out ones"— called out of the world for heavenly citizenship. "If ye were of the world," Christ told His disciples, "the world would love his own; but because ye are not of the world, but I have chosen you out of the world, therefore the world hateth you. . . . If they have persecuted me, they will also persecute you" (John 15:19,20).

Christ's promise of persecution by the world for faithfulness to Him proved to be all too true during the first three centuries of Christianity. Yet the church grew strong in spite of martyrdoms, and comprised about 10 percent of the population. Then came Constantine, giving Christians a worldly status that corrupted them. The church that had been espoused to Christ as a chaste virgin (2 Corinthians 11:2) to await His return to take her to His Father's house for that heavenly marriage began to play the harlot with the world. Soon she became the very evil to which she had given herself: "MYSTERY, BABYLON THE GREAT, THE MOTHER OF HARLOTS...." For centuries that would be the "Christianity" visible to the world!

When Rome fell to the barbarians the church mourned, but for selfish reasons. The popes whom Constantine had installed often needed the protection of larger armies than they could muster. The hope of Christ returning to rapture the church to heaven had long since been swallowed up by earthly ambitions that could hardly be gained by "turning the other cheek." Forgotten were Christ's words, "My kingdom is not of this world; if my kingdom were of this world, then would my servants fight" (John 18:36). The popes' kingdom was of this world and required armed conflict. They missed their partners, the emperors, and longed for a revival of the Roman Empire so that "God's kingdom" could be enlarged upon earth. Expressing what that partnership could accomplish, Pope Innocent III declared:

> The state of the world, which is falling into ruins, will be restored by our [Emperor's and Pope's] diligence and care . . . for the pontifical authority and the royal power . . . fully suffice for this purpose. . . .[4]

Hoping to usher in that long-awaited imperial revival, Pope Leo III, who had had his eyes torn out by a mob seeking revenge for his unbearable tyranny and wickedness, groped his way to the side of Charlemagne, placed on his head a crown, and declared him to be "Emperor!" It was Christmas day 800 A.D. The King was attending mass at Rome's cathedral. Abjectly pledging his loyalty, the Pope knelt before Charlemagne, whose protection he desperately needed.

In bowing before Charlemagne, however, the Pope was at the same time asserting his own authority to make him the Emperor. Although Charlemagne despised Leo, he accepted his new title and spent the next 40 years leading his marauding armies in extending the "kingdom of God" through military power. In a letter to Leo, Charlemagne expressed the arrangement between Emperor and Pope: "It is our part . . . to defend by armed strength the holy Church of Christ everywhere from the outward onslaught of the pagans and the ravages of the infidels. . . . It is your part, most holy Father, to help our armies with your hands lifted up to God like Moses. . . ."5

No one doubted in those days the claim that outside the Roman Catholic Church there was no salvation. Without the sacraments administered by her priests no one could enter heaven. Civil rulers, no matter how great, trembled when threatened with excommunication. Thus Rome's Vatican City, as John saw in his prophetic vision, ruled over the kings of the earth—and still does to this day, though much more subtly, as Gorbachev has implicitly acknowledged.

Who could have imagined at the end of the first century, when John wrote the Revelation, that the church which was hated and persecuted to the death at that time would one day rule the Empire? Yet it happened. Here we have another remarkable prophecy, the fulfillment of which gives further evidence of the reliability of the Bible. Not until the Reformation would anyone seemingly notice the obvious fact that the Roman Catholic Church was acting out the vision Christ had given to the apostle John.

We have noted some of the growing evidence that ancient Rome's Empire is being revived. It is no less apparent that the Roman Catholic Church is regaining her past importance and will play a major role as the "last-days" scenario unfolds. In John's vision it is, at least for a time, *the woman who rides the beast,* which represents both the revived Roman Empire and the Antichrist.

Some Bible scholars argue that the woman is Iraq's rebuilt Babylon. They suggest that Iraq will "ride the beast" by controlling the bulk of the world's oil and thus exercising economic power over the Antichrist's European-based empire. On the contrary, the Antichrist is so strong that no one can make war with him (Revelation 13:4-7). If he wants the Arabs' oil, he has the power to take it. And he will be worshiped by everyone on earth, including the Arabs (verse 8). Incredible? We shall see how that could happen.

Certainly the rebuilt Babylon in Iraq, Hussein's Disneyland in the desert, does not fit John's description of the *woman.* She is "drunken with the blood of . . . the martyrs of Jesus" (Revelation 17:6) and "in her was found the blood of prophets and of saints and of all that were slain upon the earth" (Revelation 18:24). Nearly a million martyrs died in the Catholic Inquisition in Spain, France, and Holland alone. Yet the phrase "all that were slain upon the earth" indicates again that John is seeing the wickedness and idolatry that came from Babel and culminates in the false church of the last days. It will encompass all religions under the leadership of the Pope in Rome.

That this "last-days" Babylon is described as a *woman* again identifies her as the Roman Catholic Church, for whom a *woman*—"the Virgin Mary"—is the dominant deity. Though many Catholics would deny it, she has taken the place of God and Christ. If it seems extreme to suggest that "Mary" is Catholicism's chief deity, consider the following from the classic book, long accepted by the Vatican, *The Glories of Mary,* by Cardinal Alphonsus de Liguori:

> He falls and is lost who has not recourse to Mary. . . .
>
> We shall be heard more quickly if we have recourse to Mary and call on her holy name, than we should be if we called on the name of Jesus our Saviour. . . .
>
> Many things . . . are asked from God, and are not granted; they are asked from Mary, and are obtained [for] she is even Queen of Hell. . . .

All power is given to Thee [Mary] in heaven and on earth that at the command of Mary all obey, even God. Thus . . . God has placed the whole church . . . under the dominion of Mary.[6]

When asked why they pray to Mary, most Catholics will deny that they do so and will insist that they only ask her to intercede in the same manner that Protestants would ask a friend to pray for them. Yet prayers are addressed *to* Mary for everything from safety to forgiveness of sins and eternal salvation. Official prayers to Mary can be found in such imprimatured booklets as *Devotions in Honor of Our Mother of Perpetual Help*. Its back cover declares, "No true child of Mary is ever lost." How does one become a *child of Mary*? Is that better than being a *child of God*? The following is typical of the booklet's prayers and praise to Mary:

> O Mother of Perpetual Help, thou art the dispenser of all the goods which God grants to us miserable sinners. . . . Come, then, to my aid, dearest Mother. . . .
> *In thy hands I place my eternal salvation and to thee do I entrust my soul.* . . . For, if thou protect me, dear Mother, I fear nothing: not from my sins, because *thou wilt obtain for me the pardon of them*; nor from the devils, because thou art more powerful than all hell together; *nor even from Jesus, my Judge himself, because, by one prayer from thee, he will be appeased.*
> But one thing I fear, that, in the hour of temptation, I may neglect to call on thee, and thus perish miserably. Obtain for me, then, *the pardon of my sins* . . . [emphasis added].[7]

Such is the false and idolatrous "Mary" of Catholicism—an insult both to God and to the Mary of the Bible. She is looked to for the very pardon of sins and salvation that Christ procured with His own blood, and which He freely dispenses by grace to all who believe in Him. He is depicted as an adversarial Judge who would condemn us were it not for Mary's intercession! What an abomination! Yet Protestants in growing numbers are joining with the Catholic Church to "evangelize the world" by the year 2000.

Catholic dogmas about Mary cannot be found in Scripture, but were developed through the centuries as the Church evolved its extrabiblical teachings. "Mary" has been progressively exalted ever higher, while Christ has been made less important in proportion. No rejection of Christ by the world is as diabolically cunning as the calculated downgrading of the Savior by Roman Catholic tradition *in the name of true Christianity.* A typical Catholic newspaper late in 1990 reminds parishioners:

> Mary, as the litany says, is "the Refuge of Sinners" and "the Gate of Heaven." And she is "the Gate of Heaven" as well for the poor souls in Purgatory; surely we should pray to her for them. . . .
> St. Bernard wrote, "No sinner, however great, is lost, if Mary protects him." Words worth meditating on for weeks. . . .
> The Church prays, "Through the Virgin Mother of God, may the Lord grant us salvation and peace. . . . We should pray daily to the Queen of Peace for peace in our strife-torn world." . . .
> We need her hand to guide us along the dark road of life.[8]

In relation to Catholicism's "Mary," Jesus Christ is a subordinate figure. He is almost always depicted as either a helpless babe on His mother's breast, a small child at her side, or a lifeless victim of the cross being held across her knees, as in Michelangelo's famous Pieta. Yes, He was a babe and child in the *past*—but Catholicism depicts Him as such in the *present.*

This false presentation of Jesus Christ is not only found in official Catholic art and literature, but in alleged "appearances." The visions of "Mary" at Fatima, Portugal, for example, that have meant so much to all of the popes since then and especially to John Paul II, are very explicit in their diminishing of Christ and elevating of Mary in His place. On several occasions the "child Jesus" accompanied its mother "Mary" when she appeared as "Our Lady of Fatima." The official account of the apparitions declares:

On the 10th of December, 1925, the Most Holy Virgin Mary appeared to Lucia, with the *Child* Jesus by Her side, elevated on a cloud of light.

Our Lady rested one hand on Lucia's shoulder, while in the other hand She held a heart surrounded with sharp thorns. At the same time the *Child* Jesus spoke:

Have pity on the Heart of your Most Holy Mother. It is covered with thorns with which ungrateful men pierce it at every moment, and there is no one to remove them with an act of reparation [emphasis added].[9]

How can Catholics blindly accept such obviously false teaching? Both the "Mary" and the "Jesus" that appeared at Fatima were betrayed as masquerading demons by the heresy they taught. On February 15, 1926, "the *child* Jesus" again urged Catholics to "spread this devotion of [and] reparation to the Immaculate Heart of His Holy Mother," declaring that *reparation must be made to the Immaculate Heart of Mary for mankind to be saved!*[10] What a perversion of the simple gospel of salvation by grace through faith in the redemptive work of Christ, yet it is promoted by "the one true Church," thus proving the remarkable accuracy of John's vision.

That this apparition of "Jesus" was a seducing spirit should have been obvious by its appearance as a small child. Jesus Christ was about 33 years old when He was crucified. Having conquered Satan, death, and hell, He is at the Father's right hand in heaven—a mature man whose resurrected and glorified body still bears the marks of His crucifixion. The apostle John saw Christ as He is now and described Him in Revelation 1:13-18. Such was His majesty that John "fell at his feet as dead." Yet Catholicism persists in still depicting Him today as a helpless babe or a small child dependent upon its mother Mary, who is now the "Queen of Heaven."

If we credit those who saw these apparitions with telling the truth, then two spirits must have appeared to them, one in the form of a *woman* and the other as a *child*. Mary and Jesus? Obviously not. They could only have been demons spreading

Satan's lies. The many appearances of "Mary" around the world, and the fact that millions believe her promises, are a fulfillment of Paul's prophecy:

> Now the Spirit speaketh expressly that in the latter times some shall depart from the faith, giving heed to seducing spirits and doctrines of devils; speaking lies in hypocrisy, having their conscience seared with a hot iron . . . (1 Timothy 4:1,2).

No one is more convinced of the authenticity of the Fatima visitations than the present Pope. Nor is anyone more devoted to "Mary." John Paul II, who has "dedicated himself and his Pontificate to Our Lady,"[11] bears the M for Mary in his coat of arms; his personal motto, embroidered on the inside of his robes in Latin, is *totus tuus sum Maria* (Mary, I'm all yours). The Pope has unusual personal reasons for his special devotion to Mary. While recovering from the assault upon his life it occurred to him that the assassination attempt on May 13, 1981, had taken place on the anniversary of the Virgin Mary's first appearance, May 13, 1917, at Fatima, Portugal.[12] In a vision she appeared to him to declare that she had spared his life for a special mission he was to fulfill.[13]

John Paul II made a solemn pilgrimage to Fatima on May 13, 1982, where he "prayed before the statue of Our Lady of Fatima. Thousands heard him speak and consecrate the world to Mary as she had requested." On at least three other occasions, "on October 16, 1983; on March 25, 1984; and on December 8, 1985 . . . he consecrated the world to our Lady"[14] with "special mention" of the Russian people. She had promised that if the popes and bishops would consecrate the world and Russia to her Immaculate Heart, ". . . My Immaculate Heart will triumph, Russia will be converted, and there will be peace!"[15]

Such a statement is in the fullest opposition to the clear teaching of the Bible, which offers "peace with God through our Lord Jesus Christ" (Romans 5:1) as a free gift of God's grace—a peace that was bought "through the blood of his cross" (Colossians 1:20). Individual peace comes by faith to all who believe the gospel. Global peace will only be established when Christ returns to reign from Jerusalem as the prophets have foretold. Yet "Mary" has taken the place of Christ as the one through whom peace will come, and the present Pope and his church support this heresy.

In only partial obedience to "Our Lady of Fatima's" request, an imposing series of popes consecrated the world, but not the Russian people to the Immaculate Heart of Mary. This partial consecration was performed by: Pope Pius XII on July 7, 1952; Pope Paul VI twelve years later; and Pope John Paul II on May 13, 1982, and again on May 13, 1984, and the other dates mentioned above. Declaring that the Lord had "confided the peace of the world to her," the apparition that appeared as the Virgin of Fatima offered its own peace plan in the place of Christ:

> Say the Rosary every day to obtain peace for the world. . . . Pray, pray, a great deal, and make sacrifices for sinners, for many souls go to Hell because they have no one to make sacrifices and pray for them. . . .
>
> God wishes to establish in the world the devotion to MY IMMACULATE HEART. If people do what I tell you, many souls will be saved and there will be peace.[16]

"Say the Rosary every day to obtain peace . . ."? A popular Catholic television program advertises, "There is no problem that cannot be solved with the Rosary," and gives an 800 number to call for further information. To say the Rosary one must repeat The Lord's Prayer and "Glory be to the Father . . . Son . . . and Holy Spirit" six times each. The "Hail Mary, full of grace," however, must be repeated 53 times. The closing prayer of the Rosary begins: "Hail, holy Queen, Mother of Mercy! our life, our sweetness, and our hope! To thee do we cry . . . to thee do we send up our sighs, mourning and weeping. . . ." Yes, the *woman* dominates.

It is blasphemy to claim that "many souls go to Hell because they have no one to make sacrifices and pray for them." There is only one sacrifice that can be made for sin and which can deliver the soul from hell, and that sacrifice was completed once for all by Christ upon the cross more than 1900 years ago. Obviously a major purpose of these "apparitions" is to undermine what the Bible teaches concerning salvation by grace through faith in the finished sacrifice of Christ and His glorious resurrection.

Yet every Pope in the last 60 years has attested to the genuineness of the apparitions at Fatima.[17] John Paul II has said, "The message of Fatima is addressed to every human being and is more relevant and more urgent than ever.[18] Padre Pio, one of the present Pope's heroes (and who, in order to deliver souls from purgatory, allegedly bled from his palms in a stigmatic simulation of Christ's suffering), was convinced of Fatima's authenticity.

News articles are now crediting "Our Lady of Fatima" with holding back war,[19] bringing down the Berlin Wall, and reconciling East and West. Yet John Paul II is convinced that failure to dedicate the Russian people by the time limit set means that severe judgment is coming upon the world. He also believes that "Our Lady of Fatima" has given him a crucial role to play in bringing peace.[20] We'll come back to that later.

Devout Catholics, of whom more than 20 million belong to the International Fatima Rosary Crusade, are convinced that it was Mary who appeared at Fatima, Portugal. Faith in what these demonic apparitions declare makes Roman Catholics susceptible to the false peace which the Antichrist will establish. In order to play upon this superstition, the Antichrist may very well incorporate something similar into his new world religion, which Catholics along with the followers of all other faiths could embrace.

Similar appearances of the "Virgin Mary" have occurred at Lourdes, France, and in many other places around the world (and still continue). The message they bring is consistent, and is so contrary to the Bible that it could not be uttered by the biblical Mary. Claiming for itself the authority and attributes of Christ, the apparition of "Our Lady of Fatima" declared:

I will never leave you. [This is the promise of Christ to His disciples, and it presupposes omnipresence, an attribute of God alone.] My Immaculate Heart will be your refuge and the way that will lead you to God. ["God is our refuge" (Psalm 46:1, 7,11) and Christ claimed to be "*the* way" to the Father.] . . .

Sacrifice yourselves . . . for the conversion of sinners [only Christ's sacrifice avails for sinners], and in reparation for the sins committed against the Immaculate Heart of Mary. . . . [All sin is against God, and Mary is one of those sinners, whose heart was not "Immaculate," for "*all* have sinned" (Romans 3:23).]

I promise to assist at the hour of death with all the graces necessary for salvation all those who, on the first Saturday of five consecutive months, go to Confession and receive Holy Communion, recite five decades of the Rosary and keep me company for a quarter of an hour while meditating on the mysteries of the Rosary with the intention of making reparation to me.[21]

"Mary's" offer of "the graces necessary for salvation" and to "lead you to God" constitutes one more denial of Christ's finished work upon the cross, a denial which is implicit in Catholic dogma and rituals. It is to *Mary's* heart that the world must make *reparation* for the evil it has done *against her*— another blasphemous teaching. David said, "Against thee, *thee only*, have I sinned" (Psalm 51:4). Sin is against *God*, not against any of His creatures. Thus to teach that *reparation* must be made to Mary for *sins against her* is to put her in the place of God. This elevation of the woman not only fits John's vision but also makes this blend of paganism and "Christianity" appealing in a time when the women's movement has gained such popularity and power.

Further clinching the identification of the Roman Catholic Church as the "whore," no other church has even come close to committing the spiritual "fornication" of which she has been guilty. Since Catholicism as it developed beginning with Constantine was paganism disguised as Christianity, it has consistently accommodated itself to the pagan religions of those peoples which it "Christianized." In Haiti, for example, every Voodoo ceremony begins with Catholic prayers. There is a saying that Haiti is 85 percent Catholic and 110 percent Voudun. The frightening spiritist cult of Santeria exploding across America is also a blend of African paganism and "Christianity" carried on in the name of Catholic saints who front for demons. Visit the cemeteries in Rio de Janeiro on any religious holiday and you will find the Catholic faithful there petitioning the spirits of their ancestors along with the Catholic saints.

Catholic retreat centers around the world mix "Christianity" with Hinduism, Buddhism, and all manner of New Age beliefs and practices. Typical is the Ashram Ya Azim, a Franciscan Sisters' Center for Meditation in Willard, Wisconsin, that seeks to reach "Christ consciousness" through various New Age techniques. In its defense, Virginia Barta, president of the Franciscan Sisters in the USA, explains: "We can be Catholic and at the same time open beyond dogma and doctrine to recognize the mystical truth in all religions."[22]

While we may appear to be spending too much time on pointing out the heresies innate within Catholicism, we must be careful and thorough in our identification of the false religious system that will seduce not only the world of the last days but multiplied millions who consider themselves to be Christians. It is especially important in view of the increasing acceptance of and joint evangelism with Catholics by Protestant leaders, including some evangelicals who once considered Rome to represent the Antichrist system.

Do Catholics believe their images have power? Recently at St. Peter's Basilica, John Paul II declared: "A mysterious 'presence' of the transcendent Prototype seems as it were to be transferred to the sacred image. . . . The devout contemplation of such an image thus appears as a real and concrete path of purification of the soul of the believer. . . because the image itself, blessed by the priest. . . can in a certain sense, by analogy with the sacraments, actually be considered a channel of divine grace."[23] Such idolatry the Bible repeatedly condemns as spiritual adultery or fornication!

The entire May/June 1988 issue of *The Catholic World* was devoted to Buddhism. The articles were all sympathetic, including favorable quotes from the Pope. One article was even titled "The Buddha Revered As A Christian Saint"! John Paul II takes a broad-minded view of Buddhism and all other religions. He considers the Tibetan Buddhist Deity Yoga of his good friend the Dalai Lama, along with the prayers of witch doctors, spiritists, and every other "faith," to be generating "profound spiritual energies" that are creating a "new climate of peace."[24] Similar examples could be multiplied. According to a *Los Angeles Times* news report:

> Pope John Paul II slipped off his shoes to sit quietly and solemnly with the supreme patriarch of Thailand's Buddhists at a Buddhist monastery in Bangkok....
>
> The Roman Catholic pontiff later praised the "ancient and venerable wisdom" of the Asian religion.[25]

Spiritual fornication? Try to imagine Peter attending a Buddhist temple ritual and praising Buddhism's wisdom! Or the apostle Paul telling audiences of Hindus, as John Paul II did during his visit to India, that he had not come there to teach them anything but "to learn from [their] rich spiritual heritage"! The early Christians would never have been martyred had they taken a similar approach to Rome's pagan practices. In fact, they died rather than compromise, as John Paul II does in his role as Christ's "Vicar."

Mindful of the mission that "Our Lady" has given him, the current Pope maintains contact with the world's leading religions. He accepts them as worshiping the same God and their prayers as being as effective as those of Christians. Nor has he attempted to convert any of them. He simply wants everyone of every religion to acknowledge him as the moral and spiritual leader of the world.

Although the "whore" is the Catholic Church, all religions will be gathered together under the Vatican. Already we are

seeing leading Protestants working together with the Roman
Catholic Church and adopting its ecumenism. A new spirit of
compromise is sweeping the "Christian" church and the entire
religious world today. The Pope's avowed respect for Buddhism is carried the next step by Newark's Episcopalian
Bishop John S. Spong, who testifies:

> In the fall of 1988, I worshipped God in a Buddhist temple.
> As the smell of incense filled the air, I knelt before three
> images of the Buddha, feeling that the smoke could carry my
> prayers heavenward. It was for me a holy moment... beyond
> the words and creeds that each [religion] uses, there is a divine
> power that unites us. . . .
>
> I will not make any further attempt to convert the Buddhist,
> the Jew, the Hindu or the Moslem. I am content to learn from
> them and to walk with them side by side toward the God who
> lives, I believe, beyond the images that bind and blind us.[26]

Such "unity" will prevail among all religions under the
Antichrist. Even many "Prayer Breakfasts" bringing political
and religious leaders together across America and patterned
after the one which began in Washington D.C.—originally
conceived by evangelicals as opportunities for a clear witness
to Jesus Christ—have largely deteriorated into ecumenical
platforms for the acceptance of all religions. "Participating
groups" at Los Angeles's annual Interfaith Prayer Breakfast,
for example, "range from the Board of Rabbis and the Buddhist Sangha Council to the Greek Orthodox Church and the
Bahai faith."[27]

At such gatherings it would be in very bad taste, if not
forbidden, for Jesus Christ to present Himself and declare, "I
am the way, the truth, and the life; no man cometh unto the
Father but by me" (John 14:6). Such dogmatism is not to be
tolerated by those who preach tolerance for all beliefs. Yet who
is the more dogmatic—the One who made this true statement,
or those who refuse to allow it to be repeated in their presence?
One would have to be blind not to see that the foundation is
being laid for worldwide religious unity.

The proper Christian attitude toward ecumenical gatherings is easily ascertained. Try to imagine the apostle Paul's reaction if he learned that Timothy was sponsoring an "interfaith" prayer service to which he invited participation by the Jewish Sanhedrin, excommunicated "Christian" heretics, and priests from the various pagan temples. Imagine Peter apologizing to Jewish leaders for having been so dogmatic and negative as to preach "Neither is there salvation in any other [than Jesus], for there is no other name under heaven given among men whereby we must be saved" (Acts 4:12). Imagine him now subscribing to the view that "we're all taking different roads to get to the same place"!

Yes, it is the *woman* who rides and thus controls the Beast, which is obviously much more powerful than she. The Antichrist needs the false church, just as Gorbachev needs the help of religious leaders in the Soviet Union today. The time will come, however, John was told, when "the ten horns which thou sawest upon the beast, these shall hate the whore, and shall make her desolate and naked, and shall eat her flesh and burn her with fire" (Revelation 17:16).

God will use the Antichrist and his lieutenants to execute His judgment at last upon the apostate church. The one religion remaining will be the worship of the Antichrist and of Satan who empowers him. As that awful day is revealed, John hears a voice from heaven saying, "Come out of her, my people, that ye be not partakers of her sins, and that ye receive not of her plagues."

11 | *Communism, Catholicism, and World Destiny*

COMMUNISM! WHAT A SCOURGE it has been, responsible for the deliberate killing of more than 120 million persons, to say nothing of the torturing and imprisoning of untold millions of others! Militantly atheistic, it has been especially antagonistic toward Christianity, which Communists understand is their principal enemy, and the belief system they hope to replace worldwide. That ambition seemed to be going according to plan as the followers of Marx and Lenin took over country after country in the years following President Roosevelt's gift of Eastern Europe to Stalin.

Small wonder that since its inception Christians have regarded Communism as their great enemy. Entire ministries were devoted to opposing Communism. Newsletters analyzed what Marx, Lenin, Gus Hall, and Mao Tse-tung had written to show that their dastardly plan was to destroy Christianity—and so it was. Other ministries were devoted to smuggling Bibles and financial aid behind the Iron and Bamboo curtains. Those tactics are no longer necessary in Eastern Europe. Though Gorbachev's motives for posing as the champion of religious liberty are no less pragmatic than were Constantine's, one can bring in Bibles and preach the gospel on the streets, activities unthinkable just a few months ago. The same may eventually be true even in China, Cuba—everywhere.

Unfortunately, truth is no more the issue now than it ever was. Gorbachev knows that the Soviet people must have *something* to *believe in* beyond themselves and their dismal circumstances.

134 ◆ Dave Hunt

Such a "faith" is essential to carry them through the extremely difficult transition from Marxism to some form of democracy and market economy in the crucial transition period that lies ahead for the entire world. The already overly-extended West will have to share its wealth not only with the failed economies of Communism but with the other underdeveloped countries as well. And the Western powers dare not be ungenerous lest *perestroika* fail.

The Communist Revolution began in Russia and spread from there around the world. For more than 70 years the Soviet Union has been the support base of this contagious plague—a support base which has now collapsed. Having openly admitted that Communism doesn't work, the Soviets are abandoning it and passing laws for private ownership of property, studying business methods in order to establish free enterprise, and seeking to join the capitalist West. It seems reasonable to expect that just as Communism spread from Russia around the world, so will its rejection spread as well.

Is Christianity, then, being miraculously delivered by God from its nemesis in order to usher in a great, worldwide revival? Certainly there is much cause for thanksgiving, and the church must take advantage of the new liberties to spread the gospel as quickly and effectively as possible. At the same time, however, we must be certain that it is the genuine gospel and not a false one that is being proclaimed. Unfortunately, once-closed borders have been opened to error as well as to truth.

Although the church in Eastern Europe is benefiting from the new freedom, it is at the same time being corrupted by heresies coming in from the West. Soviet national television is now showing its first Christian video, airing just before the evening news. It is a children's cartoon called *Super Book* produced by the Christian Broadcasting Network. Unfortunately, a viewer could see no difference between the occult power used by the heroes in other programs and the "power" emanating from this miraculous book. The Soviets are being misled by a false presentation of Christianity.

The first televangelist to be allowed on national Soviet TV explained that he was chosen not only because of the influence of wealthy friends like Armand Hammer but because "his nonsectarian approach is what appealed to Soviet officials... his message will not be evangelistic despite his strong religious convictions." He said he would present "his longtime message of 'possibility thinking'[1]... a self-esteem message not heavily laden with 'Jesus talk.' "[2] His humanistic gospel masquerading as Christianity, which draws America's largest Sunday morning TV audience, will now seduce the Soviets, too—another step along the road to Antichrist's new world religion.

Again we find the pervasive influence of Catholicism, which this preacher considers to be perfectly compatible with his Protestant beliefs. Before building his multi-million dollar Cathedral he went to Rome with an artist's sketch of the building to obtain the "blessing of the Holy Father." Martin Luther would weep! So should we—and pray—as we see the pieces of the puzzle fitting together.

This man's influence is enormous. On the occasion of his one-thousandth television broadcast, those who appeared in taped interviews congratulating him included President Bush and the four living ex-presidents of the United States.

The Roman Catholic and Russian Orthodox Churches, which the Pope hopes to merge, will be by far the major "Christian" presence and power in Eastern Europe to step into the spiritual vacuum left by Communism's failure. The fact that Catholicism is taking over from Communism is hardly cause for rejoicing; it is a strategic and necessary move. The Roman Empire cannot be revived without Catholicism recovering its dominant role. That recovery is now taking place with the support of Protestant and political leaders.

Though it has suppressed, imprisoned, tortured, and killed millions of Christians, Communism has actually not been the worst enemy of true Christianity. That distinction belongs to the "whore of Babylon," which claims to be "Christian" yet has sent far more souls to hell than Marxism, with which it has much in common. Ironically, the Roman Catholic Church is as totalitarian as Communism ever was.

It would be laughable, were the results not so tragic, to see Gorbachev meeting with the Pope and pledging to this spiritual despot that the Soviet Union is going to respect freedom of religion for all of its citizens. There is something sinister about such a spectacle—especially of the Pope going along with the game and posing before the world as the champion of "freedom of conscience." This is deceit of the highest order. Such freedom is explicitly denied by the Roman Catholic Church to its members, who must accept its teachings without question or be lost forever.

It was only after the Russian Revolution that Christians began to view Communism as the Antichrist system. Yet for 400 years before 1917, Catholicism was so identified by Protestants. All of the Reformers from Luther and Calvin to Knox and the rest of their contemporaries were convinced that the Roman Catholic Church was representative of the great apostasy prophesied in Scripture. Such was the view of most Protestant leaders from Wesley and Whitefield to Spurgeon and D. Martyn Lloyd-Jones.

We might well ask what persuaded Protestants to change this long-established and deep conviction—for indeed it has changed! Although Roman Catholicism remains the same, many of today's leading evangelicals suggest that Protestants can cooperate with Rome in "evangelizing" the world. In actual fact, the Roman Catholic Church is the most powerful and effective enemy of Christianity in history. Its teachings are masterpieces of deception.

In reading not what ex-members or anti-Catholics write, but the official publications of the Roman Catholic Church itself, one soon discovers that it is the largest and most dangerous religious cult that ever existed. Yet today's "cult experts" rarely if ever include the Roman Catholic Church on their lists because it is now unacceptably "negative" to criticize Catholicism. That attitude represents a complete repudiation of the Reformation and the multitudes of martyrs who gave their lives to break the total control which Rome wields over men's minds and souls. Partnership with Rome sets the stage for the rise of Antichrist. One writer points out:

> The 1973 edition of OMF leader J. Oswald Sanders' book *Cults and Isms* placed Catholicism "at the head of the list of heresies." But the Roman Catholic chapter was dropped in his 1981 edition.
>
> Josh McDowell and Don Stewart [in their book *Understanding The Cults*] list 11 characteristics of cults. Roman Catholicism has every one of the characteristics, yet is not listed. . . . Why?[3]

Jehovah's Witnesses, Sun Myung Moon's Unification Church, and other cults all share cultic features that have long been elements of Catholicism. The first point that Mormon missionaries make sounds familiar, with only a few names and dates changed: that theirs is the one true Church, outside of which there is no salvation, and that its current head is the true representative of Christ on earth through apostolic succession back to Joseph Smith, God's true prophet. Catholics claim the same for their church and Pope.

Cultic doctrines often include much that sounds biblical. Mormons, for example, affirm that Christ died for our sins and rose the third day. His sacrifice, however, was not enough. It is good deeds, obedience to the Mormon hierarchy, and participation in the Temple rituals that must *earn* the eternal life that Christ actually offers as a free gift. So it is in Roman Catholicism: The Church is the dispenser of salvation through the rituals performed by its priesthood, without which mankind would be lost in spite of all Christ has done. Like Mormonism and other cults, Catholicism denies to the individual assurance of salvation through a personal relationship with Christ. In place of the One who said, "Come unto *me*," Rome says, "Come unto *me*" and insists that salvation is not "by grace through faith" but must be earned through Church membership and obedience to her many rules and regulations.

Another primary mark of a cult is a perceived infallibility of the leadership, resulting in unquestioning submission to dogmatic authoritarianism. The head of the cult is never wrong. He sets the rules of life, defines terms, and literally thinks for his followers. No cult exercises such thought control more thoroughly or efficiently than the Roman Catholic Church through the alleged infallibility of its Pope and priestly hierarchy. While there has been superficial encouragement to read the Bible since the Second Vatican Council (held 1962–65 and known as Vatican II), Catholics cannot let Scripture speak for itself, but must see it *only* as the Church interprets it. In June 1990 the Vatican's watchdog of orthodoxy, German Cardinal Joseph Ratzinger, with papal approval, released in eight languages a 7500-word "Instruction" for theologians and bishops. As the *Los Angeles Times* reported:

> Asserting central authority...the Vatican on Tuesday bluntly told Roman Catholic theologians—and by extension questioning Catholics—that it will not tolerate public dissent from official church teachings....
> "Freedom of the act of faith cannot justify a right to dissent," the document asserts...neither can dissent be justified as a matter of following one's conscience....
> "To succumb to the temptation of dissent...is to allow the leaven of infidelity to the Holy Spirit to start to work," it insists.[4]

Catechisms distinctly declare that "man can obtain a knowledge of God's word [only] from the Catholic Church and through its duly constituted channels." Catholics *must* "accept whatever the Divine Church [outside of which there is no salvation] teaches on Faith, Morals and the Means of Grace."[5] Catholic apologist Karl Keating writes unapologetically: "The Catholic believes in inspiration [of the Bible] because the Church tells him so—that is putting it bluntly—and that same Church has the [sole] authority to interpret the inspired text."[6] That Church's teachings *must be obeyed unquestioningly by all members* or they are eternally damned.

The huge Church Council, Vatican II, made changes that should have revealed to Catholics that Rome was not infallible as she claimed. Catholics were suddenly allowed to eat meat on Friday, though previously those who did so went to hell if they failed to confess to a priest. Certain "saints" (such as St. Christopher) were demoted, and the requirement that the Mass must be recited in Latin was dropped. But this was really just so much window dressing. The heretical doctrines of salvation that provoked the Reformation were not changed and the cultic grip of the church was actually tightened, as the following excerpts from Vatican II indicate.

> But the task of giving an authentic interpretation of the Word of God, whether in its written form or in the form of Tradition [which is equal to the Bible], has been entrusted to the living teaching office of the church *alone*.[7]

> But by divine institution it is the *exclusive* task of these pastors *alone*, the successors of Peter and the other Apostles, to teach the faithful authentically, that is with the authority of Christ. . . .[8]

> We believe in the infallibility enjoyed by the Successor of Peter [i.e. the Pope] when he speaks ex cathedra as shepherd and teacher of all the faithful, an infallibility which the whole Episcopate [i.e. the bishops, cardinals et al] enjoys when it exercises with him the supreme magisterium [emphasis added].[9]

As the Reformation gathered momentum the Council of Trent met during 1545-63 to discuss the demands of the Reformers: that the Bible rather than the Church should be the final authority; that salvation is by grace through faith alone instead of through good deeds, suffering for one's sins, and the sacraments ministered by the Church; that prayers should not be made to the "saints" nor should their images be venerated; that instead of the elite class of supposedly celibate clergy, the Bible taught the "priesthood of all believers," etc. The outcome was inevitable.

Every heretical dogma was reaffirmed and *every* belief upon which Protestantism was founded and for which countless martyrs gave their lives was rejected by the Council of Trent. Its Canons and Decrees (as Vatican II once again reaffirmed) are considered to be a summation of Roman Catholicism valid for all time. Today's catechisms, more than 400 years later, continue to require all Roman Catholics to pledge absolute and unquestioning obedience to the dogmas reaffirmed at Trent. A standard oath begins:

> I accept, without hesitation, and profess all that has been handed down, defined and declared by the Sacred Canons and by the general Councils, especially by the Sacred Council of Trent and by the Vatican General Council [Vatican II], and in a special manner concerning the primacy and infallibility of the Roman Pontiff. . . .[10]

It is extremely difficult for Roman Catholics to escape the cultic grip in which they are held, because they have been convinced that their Church controls the gates of heaven. To disobey her is to be eternally damned. Thus even though many Catholics become disillusioned and no longer attend Mass or go to confession, at death they still want a Catholic funeral "just in case" and hope that their relatives will continue to have Masses performed to get them out of purgatory. The cultic oath which they have sworn continues to hold them in its grip:

> I recognize the Holy Roman, Catholic and Apostolic Church as the mother and teacher of all . . . and I promise and swear true obedience to the Roman Pontiff, successor of St. Peter, Prince of the Apostles, and Vicar of Christ. . . .
>
> This same Catholic Faith, outside of which nobody can be saved, which I now freely profess and to which I truly adhere, the same I promise and swear to maintain and profess . . . until the last breath of life. . . .[11]

It is not difficult to see how this absolute, unthinking submission to their Church hierarchy prepares Catholics for the total submission that will be required by the Antichrist. If the Pope identifies this impostor as the Christ, the obedience of Catholics is assured. Submission to the Pope is far broader than most people realize. It is generally believed that the Pope is "infallible" only when he speaks *ex cathedra*, but that is not the case. The following pronouncement of Vatican II is unequivocal:

> This loyal submission of the *will* and *intellect must be given*, in a special way, to the authentic teaching authority of the Roman Pontiff, *even when he does not speak ex cathedra*, in such wise, indeed, that his *supreme teaching authority* be acknowledged with respect, and that one sincerely *adhere to decisions made by him*, conformably with his manifest mind and intention . . . [emphasis added].[12]

The Roman Catholic Church, as the sole interpreter of Scripture, seduces its members into embracing a different God, a different Jesus Christ, and a different plan of salvation from that taught in the Bible. Confusion arises because Rome uses biblical terms such as "justification by grace," the "Virgin Birth," the "blood atonement of the cross," and the "Resurrection of Jesus." Yet what Rome means by such language is entirely different from what evangelicals believe and the Bible teaches.

It takes but a few minutes of reading its own publications, readily available to any interested party, to realize that Roman Catholicism has completely corrupted and firmly opposes the gospel which evangelicals preach. D. Martyn Lloyd-Jones explained the cause of confusion among so many Protestants:

> In one sense . . . you might well think that the Roman Catholic Church is the most orthodox Church in the world. . . . [It] believes that Jesus of Nazareth was the eternal Son of God; it believes in the Virgin Birth; it believes in the Incarnation; it believes in His miracles; it believes in His substitutionary work upon the cross and His resurrection [etc.]. . . .
>
> But at this point the subtlety comes in and the difficulty arises. To all that [orthodox truth] she "adds," with a damnable plus, things which are utterly unscriptural and which, indeed, become a denial of the Scripture. So she lands us eventually in a position in which, if we accept her teaching, we are believing a lie![13]

For example, to its confession that Christ died for our sins, Romanism adds dogmas whose effect is to deny that His death was sufficient. One's own good deeds, obedience to the Church, and participation in its sacraments must be added to what Christ has done. The Rosary, the Confession to a priest, baptism into the Church, and indulgences earned are also required. And in addition to Christ's suffering on the cross the individual must also suffer for his own sins in purgatory, where the soul, though cleansed by the blood of Christ, must be more thoroughly "purged." Then there is the endless list of alms, good deeds, and Masses that others must engage in after one is dead in order to obtain his or her release from purgatory and entrance into heaven at last.

In contrast, the apostle Peter declared that the resurrection of Christ had secured for believers "an inheritance incorruptible and undefiled and that fadeth not away, reserved in heaven for you, who are kept by the power of God through faith unto salvation.... For Christ also hath once suffered for sins, the just for the unjust, that he might bring us to God [i.e. to heaven]" (1 Peter 1:4,5; 3:18). Paul assured the believers that to die was "to be absent from the body and to be present with the Lord [in heaven, not in purgatory]" (2 Corinthians 5:8).

As for deviating from this truth, Paul was very explicit: "There be some that . . . would pervert the gospel of Christ. But though we or an angel from heaven preach any other gospel unto you than that which we have preached unto you, let him be accursed" (Galatians 1:7-9). The Roman Catholic Church, from the Pope down, preaches a far different gospel from that which the apostles preached. For leading untold millions astray with a false gospel they qualify for the curse that Paul solemnly pronounced. Yet Rome boldly pronounces its own eternal curse upon those who dare to preach Paul's gospel: that the death of Christ upon the cross paid the full debt for our sins and that salvation is not by works but a free gift of God's grace to all who believe. The Council of Trent declared (and Vatican II has confirmed):

> If anyone says that after the reception of the grace of justification the guilt is so remitted and the debt of eternal punishment so blotted out to every repentant sinner, that no debt of temporal punishment remains to be discharged [by the person's own suffering] either in this world or in purgatory before the gates of heaven can be opened, let him be anathema [eternally damned].[14]

> [We affirm] that there is a purgatory, and that the souls there detained are aided by the suffrages of the faithful and . . . [that] the bishops shall see to it that the suffrages of the living, that is, the sacrifice of the mass, prayers, alms and other works of piety which they have been accustomed to perform to the faithful departed, be piously and devoutly discharged in accordance with the laws of the Church. . . .[15]

The rejection of the biblical gospel could not be more clearly stated! In its place a lie is proclaimed which flagrantly denies Paul's declaration: "For by grace are ye saved through faith, and that not of yourselves: It is the gift of God—not of works, lest any man should boast" (Ephesians 2:8,9). To say that "every repentant sinner" for whom Christ suffered the full penalty demanded by God's justice must nevertheless suffer for his sins, even after receiving "the grace of justification," repudiates the cross and is a denial of the entire Bible. How then can Protestants propose to join Catholics in "evangelizing the world"? D. Martyn Lloyd-Jones protested:

> There are movements afoot . . . which are trying to bring a kind of rapprochement between Roman Catholicism and Protestantism. . . . This [Roman Catholic] system is altogether more dangerous than is Communism itself. . . .
> Roman Catholicism is the devil's greatest masterpiece! It is such a departure from the Christian faith and the New Testament teaching that . . . her dogma is a counterfeit; she is, as the Scripture puts it, "the whore." . . .
> Let me warn you very solemnly that if you rejoice in these [ecumenical] approaches to Rome you are denying the blood of the martyrs! . . . There are innocent people who are being deluded by this kind of falsity, and it is your business and mine to open their eyes. . . .[16]

144 ◆ Dave Hunt

Concerning the sufficiency of Christ's sacrifice upon the cross the Bible is abundantly clear: "Nor yet that he should offer himself often.... For then must he often have suffered [for sin]... but now once in the end of the world hath he appeared to put away sin by the sacrifice of himself" (Hebrews 9:25,26). Yet the false gospel preached by the Roman Catholic Church completely contradicts these and the many other similar Scriptures. Rome insists that, in order to be efficacious, Christ's death must be reenacted on Catholic altars around the world in mystery form and in an "unbloody manner" through endless repetitions of the "sacrifice of the Mass." This is made possible through the priests' alleged power to turn bread and wine into the literal body, blood, soul, spirit, and divinity of Jesus Christ. (See Appendix C.)

The horrible deception is made all the more persuasive and destructive by Protestant leaders suggesting that the Roman Catholic Church preaches the biblical gospel. For example, the host and hostess of a popular Christian TV show (who head the world's largest Christian television network) frequently give viewers the false impression that Roman Catholic doctrine is no different from that of evangelicals. On one program, while interviewing three Catholic leaders, the host declared that the difference between Protestant and Catholic doctrines was merely "a matter of semantics." As for Transubstantiation, a heresy so great that thousands died at the stake rather than accept it, he declared:

> Well, we [Protestants] believe the same thing.... We were really meaning the same thing but just saying it a little differently.... I [am] eradicating the word Protestant even out of my vocabulary....
>
> I'm not protesting anything... [it's] time for Catholics and non-Catholics to come together as one in the Spirit and one in the Lord.[17]

Such misinformation is deadly. It is misleading evangelicals into accepting Catholics as genuine Christians, when in fact they need to hear the biblical gospel and be delivered from the false hope offered by Rome. It is also leading astray many others who are sincerely seeking the truth but are being given the false impression that there is no difference between the New Testament gospel and the doctrines of Rome.

If Martin Luther were living today and opposed the many heresies of Roman Catholicism as he did in the 1500's, he would be accused of causing "division" not only by the Catholics, as he was then, but by his fellow Protestants as well. Protestant leaders who are encouraging cooperation with Rome are opposing the very Reformation that gave them the freedoms they now enjoy, and they are making a mockery of the hundreds of thousands of martyrs who gave themselves to the flames rather than make the compromise which these Christian leaders now promote. Crying out against the already growing trend among Protestants in his day to accept Catholicism, C. H. Spurgeon passionately declared:

> I dread much the spirit which would tamper with Truth for the sake of united action, or for any other object under heaven. ...Not so thought our fathers, when at the stake they gave themselves to death... for truths which men nowadays count unimportant, but which being truths were to them so vital that they would sooner die than suffer them to be dishonoured.
>
> O for the same uncompromising love of truth!...I pray God evermore to preserve us from unity in which the truth shall be considered valueless, in which principle gives place to policy.
>
> May there ever be found some men... who shall denounce again and again all league with error and all compromise with sin, and declare that these are the abhorrence of God....
>
> The destruction of every sort of union which is not based on truth is a preliminary to...the unity of the Spirit.

Were Spurgeon alive today he would be shocked to see that the situation, bad as it was in his time, has deteriorated rapidly in the past few years. It is now common for Christian leaders to justify their adulterous partnership with Catholics in "world evangelism" by saying, "I will not separate myself from anyone who 'names the name of Christ.' " Of course Mormons "name the name of Christ," as do Jehovah's Witnesses, Christian Scientists, and other cultists, occultists, and New Agers—and their "Christ" is a blasphemous counterfeit. So is the "Christ" of Roman Catholicism.

That even evangelicals who should be stemming the tide of delusion are becoming parties to preparing the world for the false Christ who will head the revived Roman Empire is the great tragedy of our day. And the demise of Communism in Eastern Europe has created a euphoria that encourages further carelessness with regard to sound doctrine and opens the door to a false gospel.

Whatever the future of Communism, the world is not destined to come under the dominion of a Marxist dictator, but of Antichrist. Atheism will not triumph, but a false religion. And the Roman Catholic Church will play a key role in bringing this about, and thus in determining mankind's destiny. Yet we need not helplessly wring our hands at the tragedy. There is great joy in standing true to God's Word and great opportunity to rescue many from eternal doom.

12 *Ecumenism and the Coming New World Order*

MOST OF THE WARS that have been fought down through history were *religious* wars. Then with World Wars One and Two religion was no longer a factor. The world seemed to have entered a new era where science, not religion, would mediate man's destiny. If peace were to be established it would be purely on the basis of political, economic, and military arrangements. Or so it seemed.

In recent years, however, the importance of religion in relation to global peace has become increasingly clear. The strong resurgence of Islamic fundamentalism has confronted the world once again with the specter of "Holy War" fueled by fanatical convictions that cannot be swayed by reason and are impervious to military, economic, or political pressures. It is now apparent that the need for peace among the world's religions is as great as the need for peace among the world's nations, and that the latter cannot be achieved without the former. Yet the prospects for bringing peace between warring religious factions in Ireland, Sri Lanka, India, and Pakistan, much less in the Middle East, seem dim at best. John Paul II believes that he is destined to bring this rapprochement about. Indeed, it will happen—but in a way that may surprise everyone.

Once again we can glean at least a partial understanding of things to come by turning to history. It was the religious unity achieved under Constantine and his aides, the popes, an office which he created, that ushered in a new era for the Roman

Empire. As we have already seen, a similar unity must be realized again if that Empire is to be revived as prophesied.

It was Constantine who called the Council of Nicaea, which is known as the first *ecumenical* council. Christians look back to it gratefully because it kept out of the church the serious heresy of Arianism, which denied the deity of Christ. Yet Constantine could not have cared less about the theological issues. His concern was getting the bishops to *agree*—never mind the substance. The following excerpt of a letter from Constantine shows that the whole purpose of his religious policy was to promote political unity:

> I had proposed to lead back to a single form the ideas which all people conceive of the Deity; for I feel strongly that if I could induce men to unite on that subject, the conduct of public affairs would be considerably eased. But alas! I hear that there are more disputes among you....
>
> The cause seems to be quite trifling... a question in itself entirely devoid of importance; and you, Arius, if you had such thoughts, should have kept silence.[1]

Though Constantine considered the question of Christ's deity meaningless, he realized that continued disagreement on that issue would have disastrous political consequences for the Empire. Such a dispute could not be allowed to continue. Will Durant explains Constantine's dilemma and the solution he imposed upon the church:

> ... if division were permitted on this question, chaos of belief might destroy the unity and authority of the Church, and therefore its value as an aide to the state.
>
> As the controversy spread, setting the Greek East aflame, Constantine resolved to end it by calling the first ecumenical— universal—council of the Church. He summoned all bishops to meet in 325 at Bithynian Nicaea, near his capital Nicomedia, and provided funds for all their expenses.... The Council... issued with the Emperor's approval the [Nicene] creed....
>
> An imperial edict ordered that all books by Arius should be burned, and made the concealment of such a book punishable with death.... The Middle Ages had begun.[2]

The new Emperor who will rule the revived Roman Empire, the Antichrist, is not yet in position to accomplish the essential Constantinian strategy. In his absence, and in preparation for him, an ecumenical union of all religions is being aggressively pursued by Pope John Paul II. Never before in history has there been anything to approach his tireless and persuasive diplomacy with the leaders of the world's religions over the past ten years. In Geneva, Switzerland, addressing the World Council of Churches (representing 400 million Protestants worldwide), John Paul II declared:

> From the beginning of my ministry as bishop of Rome, I have insisted that the engagement of the Catholic Church in the ecumenical movement is irreversible.[3]

Indeed, the "engagement of the Catholic Church in the ecumenical movement" was significant even before the present Pope took office. This fact may seem to be in conflict with its claims of being the only true and infallible church. However, while damning ex-Catholics and Protestants, Catholicism allows for those outside its fold to be saved if ignorant of its claims and sacraments and if they are sincere in their own faith. Thus Mother Teresa and those who work with her never attempt to convert to Christ the dying people for whom they care. Instead, Mother Teresa declares:

> If in coming face to face with God we accept Him in our lives, then we . . . become a better Hindu, a better Muslim, a better Catholic, a better whatever we are . . . . What God is in your mind you must accept.[4]

The fact that many people worship false gods, which the Bible condemns, never enters the equation. Mother Teresa proclaims the counterfeit "gospel" that Protestants endorse by joining Catholics in "evangelizing the world." She is accurately expressing the very nature of Roman Catholicism which, as the "whore of Babylon," must continue its spiritual fornication in order to fulfill Scripture and play its prophesied role in the revival of the Roman Empire. Examples of that harlotry among Catholic leaders are legion.

A month before his death, celebrated Catholic monk Thomas Merton told an ecumenical gathering of representatives from numerous religions in Calcutta: "My dear brothers, we are already one. But we imagine that we are not. And what we have to discover is our original unity." Merton was echoing not only Mother Teresa but what many other Catholics, including popes, have long been saying. For example, three Catholic priests state in their book, which bears the official Imprimatur:

> We should not hesitate to take the fruit of the age-old Wisdom of the East and "capture" it for Christ. . . .
> Many Christians who take their prayer life seriously have been greatly helped by Yoga, Zen, TM, and similar practices. . . .[5]

Does Rome really approve of mixing Hindu and Buddhist practices with Catholicism? As we have pointed out a number of times, Catholicism is already such a mixture, for it grew out of a merger between paganism and "Christianity." Responding to the growing involvement among Catholics in TM, Zen, and other forms of Yoga and Eastern mysticism,[6] Cardinal Ratzinger (Vatican guardian of Catholic orthodoxy) issued a 23-page letter in mid-December 1989 to 3000 Roman Catholic bishops expressing concern. The statement, however (approved by Pope John Paul II), did not condemn Eastern mysticism or New Age meditational/Yoga techniques, but in fact suggested "tak[ing] from them what is useful. . . ."[7]

John Paul II has publicly encouraged such a syncretistic attitude. At the Universities of Calcutta and New Delhi in his 1986 visit to India, for example, the Pope told huge Hindu audiences:

> India's mission . . . is crucial, because of her intuition of the *spiritual* nature of man. Indeed, *India's greatest contribution to the world can be to offer it a spiritual vision of man.*

And the world does well to attend willingly to this ancient
wisdom and in it to find enrichment for human living.[8]

What an incredible statement from the head of "the one true
Church" regarding an idolatrous, demon-worshiping religion
that has brought absolute horror to India! Try to imagine the
apostle Paul in Athens and, instead of arguing against its
idolatry, as he did, praising the "ancient wisdom" of Zeus
worship and suggesting that Greek paganism had a valuable
"spiritual vision of man" to offer to the world! Yet such is
Roman Catholicism today, as it has been since the days of
Constantine. And such it must be to play its last-days role in
helping to establish a new world order based upon the religious
tolerance advocated by Gorbachev.

Merton wrote that "Buddhism and Christianity are alike in
making use of ordinary everyday human existence as material
for a radical transformation of consciousness." He taught that
the transformation of consciousness which Zen Buddhism calls
"the Great Death" was identical to what Christians call
"dying and rising with Christ"—that both led to the "death of
self" and to a "new life" not found in some future paradise, but
in "living here and now."

Not so! The irreconcilable difference between Christianity
and every other religion is Christ Himself and His death,
burial, and resurrection on this planet for our sins. Christ's
purpose was to reconcile us to God so that we could live not just
"here and now" but forever with Him in heaven. Ecumenism
denies the essential uniqueness of Jesus Christ. The apostle
Paul didn't try to die to self through mystical techniques which
are popular today among Catholics/Buddhists/Hindus/New
Agers and increasingly even among professing evangelical
Christians. His death to self came about by faith in Christ's
death for his sins—a faith that is not only absent from but
specifically rejected and opposed by the basic tenets of Hinduism, Buddhism, and other religions. Paul declared victori-
ously and with deep gratitude:

> I am crucified with Christ, nevertheless I live; yet not I, but
> Christ liveth in me; and the life which I now live in the flesh I
> live by the faith of the Son of God, who loved me and gave
> himself for me (Galatians 2:20).

The Roman Catholic hierarchy has a long history of leadership in ecumenism. A book could be filled with examples, but a few must suffice. Popes John XXIII and Paul VI joined such notables as the Dalai Lama, Anwar el-Sadat (a Muslim), and U.N. Secretary General U. Thant (a Buddhist), to form The Temple of Understanding, known as the United Nations of World Religions. Its Director of International Programs is Luis M. Dolan, C.P., a Catholic priest. Catholic Archbishop Angelo Fernandes was for its first eight years the President of the Geneva-based World Conference on Religion and Peace, organized to bring together "a growing network involving all the major religions of the world." When Fernandes retired he was replaced by ten presidents representing six world religions.

"His Holiness" the Dalai Lama, who is "God" to most Tibetan Buddhists, has been well-received by Roman Catholic leaders around the world. He met twice with Pope Paul VI and has met five or more times with his good friend John Paul II. "Both of us have the same aim," says the Dalai Lama.[9] At the start of his first U.S. tour the "God-king-in-exile" was feted in 1979 at New York's St. Patrick's Cathedral at what *Time* magazine called "an extraordinary interreligious festival" hosted by Cardinal Cooke. Declaring that "all the world's major religions are basically the same," the Dalai Lama was given a standing ovation by the overflow crowd.[10] Said Cardinal Cooke:

> This is one of the dramatic movements of the Spirit in our
> time. We make each other welcome in our churches, [Buddhist] temples and synagogues.[11]

By "Spirit" the Cardinal meant the Holy Spirit, but ecumenism in fact involves an alien spirit. Jesus called the Holy Spirit not only the Comforter but "the Spirit of Truth, whom the world [i.e. non-Christians] cannot receive" (John 14:17). That "all the world's major religions are basically the same" is a lie aimed at the exclusive claims of Christ. The ecumenical movement is a denial of biblical truth and particularly of Christ's claim that He is the only Savior and that all must believe on Him or be lost forever.

Another Catholic leader who was a major promoter of global religious unity was Augustin Cardinal Bea, a Jesuit and for 19 years Rector of Rome's Pontifical Biblical College. Cardinal Bea annually hosted "Agapes of Brotherhood," which were attended by hundreds of international guests representing the world's major religions: Buddhists, Muslims, Shintoists, and everything in between. Typical of the Cardinal's speeches was one at the Seventh Agape in which he "stressed the brotherhood of man and the Fatherhood of God, which, he said, embraces all men. . . ."[12] Yet Jesus told even the religious Jews, "Ye are of your father the devil" (John 8:44) and warned Nicodemus that he must be "born again" by the Holy Spirit to become a child of God or he couldn't see God's kingdom.

Cardinal Bea, who was Pope Pius XII's personal confessor and a close advisor to several other popes, saw the blossoming Charismatic movement as a vehicle for Roman Catholicism's ecumenical goals. The Cardinal sought out David DuPlessis (known as "Mr. Pentecost"), whom he invited to the Second Vatican Council.[13] DuPlessis and other leading Pentecostals and Charismatics accepted gladly and became Rome's unwitting pawns. Thus began a growing acceptance of Catholicism by Protestant Charismatics. Today's Charismatic movement is a major bridge to Rome.

Another promoter of religious unity who used the Charismatic movement[14] to further Rome's ecumenical aims was Leon Joseph Cardinal Suenens. The Cardinal was influential in the General Council formed in the early 1970's by Shepherding/Charismatic leaders—a Council which secretly guided the Charismatic movement for years. The minutes for its May-June 1977 meeting reveal that Cardinal Suenens was an unknown directing hand behind the scenes:

> We, as a Council, are committing ourselves to work together with the Cardinal for the restoration and unity of Christian people and world evangelization in projects to be mutually agreed upon.
>
> In each project, headship, authority and method of functions will be mutually determined by the Cardinal and the Council in the light of the requirements of each situation.

"World evangelization" with Suenens, who promoted a false gospel? For example, the Cardinal had hosted and given the opening speech at the Second World Conference on Religion and Peace in Louvain, Belgium, in 1974. The Louvain conference, which received Pope Paul VI's blessing, particularly emphasized the important role that religious unity must play in establishing the coming world government. A continual call was sounded for "a new world order." Under Catholic leadership, the Louvain Declaration stated:

> Buddhists, Christians, Confucianists, Hindus, Jains, Jews, Muslims, Shintoists, Sikhs, Zoroastrians and still others, we have sought here to listen to the spirit within our varied and venerable religious traditions . . . we have grappled with the towering issues that our societies must resolve in order to bring about peace, justice, and ennobling quality of life for every person and every people. . . .
>
> We rejoice that . . . the long era of prideful, and even prejudiced isolation of the religions of humanity is, we hope, now gone forever.[15]
>
> We appeal to the religious communities of the world to inculcate the attitude of planetary citizenship. . . .[16]

While the Catholic hierarchy and especially the Pope fulfill the major directing role, ecumenism has a broad leadership, including even Korean Messiah Sun Myung Moon. This burgeoning movement has been laying the foundation for a "new world order" for years. Its main appeal for unity is the desperate need for global peace. Moon, founder of the Inter-Religious Federation for World Peace, declares: "All men and

women of religion should now tear down the walls of sectarian-
ism . . . for the greater goal of . . . world peace."[17] Walls have
indeed come down. Calling him "the most brilliant anticom-
munist and the number one enemy of the state," Moscow
News added happily that it was "time to reconcile" after
Gorbachev had "personally hosted Moon in the bowels of the
Kremlin." Moon responded that the Soviet Union, which he
formerly equated with Satan, was going to "play a major role
in the plan of God to construct a world of peace."[18] How
swiftly the pieces begin to fit into place!

Another facet of the ecumenical movement involves "Interfaith Councils" which are springing up around the world.
There are more than 70 of these now in the United States, and
the number is growing. The following description of the first
meeting of the Washington State Interfaith Council shows that
religious differences can indeed be set aside in the interest of
global peace and a new world order:

> Swami Bhaskarananda, a Hindu, chanted a prayer to God . . .
> Ismail Ahmed, a Moslem, recited a short prayer to God. . . .
> Trust, the members agreed, was their most important short-
> term goal.
>
> Meeting at the Vedanta Society on Capitol Hill, those who
> signed the council's charter expressed their hopes for the group
> as they stood in front of an altar adorned with pictures of Sri
> Ramakrishna, Jesus Christ and Buddha.
>
> "My support and heart is in this group," said Pasha Moha-
> jerjasby, a member of the Baha'i faith. "Baha'is believe that
> world peace is not only possible but inevitable. . . ."
>
> Bhaskarananda told the group that Hindus believe "in the
> harmony of all faiths". . . .[19]

Encouraging such ecumenism, the Pope has declared that
"Christians must work with [all] other religions to secure
peace." He has pledged that "the Catholic Church intends to
'share in and promote' such ecumenical and inter-religious
cooperation."[20] To that end the Catholic Church maintains
an ongoing dialogue with representatives of the four major

non-Christian religions. Writing in *The Tibetan Review* (and quoted enthusiastically in *Catholic World*), a Buddhist monk evaluated the goals of this dialogue:

> The unity of religion promoted by the Holy Father Pope John Paul II and approved by His Holiness the Dalai Lama is not a goal to be achieved immediately, but a day may come when the love and compassion which both Buddha and Christ preached so eloquently will unite the world in a common effort to save humanity from senseless destruction, by leading it toward the light in which we all believe.[21]

To Pope John Paul II must go much of the credit for the fact that the huge and globally-interconnected ecumenical movement is now exploding. Just as Gorbachev has changed the political world, so the Pope has changed the religious world. Using his immense prestige and the emotional appeal of global peace, the Pope was able in 1986 to gather the leading figures of 12 world religions together in Assisi, Italy, to pray to whatever "God" each believed in, beseeching these deities to bring peace to the world. To justify honoring the prayers of even witch doctors and fire worshipers, John Paul II told participants that "the challenge of peace . . . transcends religious differences."[22]

The Pope's unprecedented ecumenical accomplishments have inspired many world leaders and have resulted in new ecumenical movements for world peace. One of the most significant of these, the Global Forum of Spiritual and Parliamentary Leaders on Human Survival, began almost unnoticed in October 1985 when "spiritual leaders" from the world's five major religions and elected officials from five continents met to explore ideas for ecological salvation and world peace. Out of this meeting grew a working partnership between the world's religious and political leaders—an alliance that had been unthinkable since the days of ancient Rome:

> We have explored the nature of the relationship between political and religious life, and . . . have agreed that we both

[political and religious leaders] need and desire to work together... and shall promote at regional, national and local levels all possible collaboration between spiritual leaders and parliamentarians.

We are entering an era of global citizenship.... This new consciousness transcends all barriers of race and religion, ideology and nationality....

We hold up the vision of a new community, where the long and tragic history of human violence gives way to an age of mutually assured welfare and peace.[23]

That pact led to a five-day Global Forum conference at Oxford, England, in April 1988 in which spiritual and legislative leaders from 52 countries met to "join all faiths with all political attitudes." Participants included U.S. senators and leading scientists, members of the Supreme Soviet and the Soviet Academy of Sciences, the U.N. Secretary General and the Archbishop of Canterbury, Mother Teresa and the Dalai Lama, cabinet members, cardinals, swamis, bishops, rabbis, imams, and monks.[24] Conferees issued a joint "Final Statement of the Conference" which declared:

We have [been]... brought together by a common concern for global survival, and have... derived from our meeting a vivid awareness of the essential oneness of humanity... the realization that each human person has both a spiritual and a political dimension....[25]

Each one of us has been changed by our Oxford experience... and [we] have undertaken commitments that are irrevocable.[26]

The latest Global Forum met January 15-19, 1990, in Moscow. It was cohosted by what the conveners called a "unique alliance": "the Supreme Soviet, the country's first freely elected parliament; all faith communities of the USSR, coordinated by the Russian Orthodox Church; the USSR Academy of Sciences; and the International Foundation for the Survival and Development of Humanity." The Moscow Forum saw more than 1000 participants from 83 countries call for a "new planetary perspective" involving a "new spiritual and ethical basis for human activities on earth."

Such an ecumenical partnership between religious and political leaders is essential to the rise of Antichrist. "Christian psychology" has played a vital and unrecognized role in setting the stage for such unity. It represents the ultimate ecumenism in which Christians join not merely with other religions but with atheists and humanists as well. Christ becomes the partner of Freud, Jung, Rogers, Maslow, and a host of other anti-Christians whose theories supply that part of "God's truth" which was apparently left out of the Bible through Holy Spirit oversight. Psychology provides the common language for a "spiritual dialogue" between Christians and humanists that leads to a new ecumenical mutual "understanding."

Psychology's false idea that we must always be "positive" and never criticize anyone subtly encourages the delusion that all religions are equally valid. That belief is slipping into mainstream denominations and even presumed evangelical circles. Justifying such heresy, one of today's most influential church leaders, a Southern California televangelist whom we have already quoted, declares: "... what sets me apart from fundamentalists [is that they] are trying to convert everybody to believe how they believe. ... We know the things the major faiths [religions] can agree on. We try to focus on those [common beliefs] without offending those with different viewpoints. ..."[27] Such false "Christianity" no longer holds truth to be important and thus can be embraced by the followers of all religions without changing their own beliefs. It lays the perfect foundation for the rise of Antichrist.

A well-known organization which promotes that same gospel must be mentioned because of its importance. Freemasonry secretly fosters ecumenism and quietly prepares its members to accept and be part of the coming new world order. What makes Masonry so influential is the fact that so many of its millions of members occupy leadership positions around the world. In our own country there is nearly always a significant percentage of Masons on the White House staff and in the Cabinet, Senate, Congress, Supreme Court, and Pentagon, as well as in top business management.

Masonic authority Carl H. Claudy boasts of Masonry's tolerance of all religions: "Masonry does not specify any God of any creed; she requires merely that you believe in some Deity, give him what name you will . . . any god will do. . . ."[28] Albert Pike, former Supreme Pontiff of Universal Freemasonry, likewise exults:

> Masonry [is that religion] around whose altars the Christian, the Hebrew, the Moslem, the Brahman [Hindu], the followers of Confucius and Zoroaster, can assemble as brethren and unite in prayer. . . .[29]

So the Pope's ecumenical prayer gathering at Assisi was only repeating publicly what Masonry has been practicing privately for centuries. That fact is extremely significant if we have indeed (as the evidence seems to indicate) arrived at that time in history when the Roman Empire is about to be revived, setting the stage for a new world order with its accompanying new world religion acceptable to all faiths. Clearly Masonry has prepared many of those who are presently world leaders to play a key role in these events because they have already been practicing in secret what the world one day must embrace openly. Consider the following prayer given in the opening ceremonies for the 31st degree of the Scottish rite:

> Hear us with indulgence, O infinite Deity. . . . Let the great flood of Masonic light flow in a perpetual current over the whole world and make Masonry the creed of all mankind.[30]

In spite of the fact that it is an undeniably anti-Christian religious cult, Masonry has among its members many who call themselves Christians. Their influence as church leaders contributes to the fact that in mainstream denominations the uniqueness of Christ is increasingly being denied. Early in 1990 at its annual convention the Michigan Episcopal Diocese refused to vote upon the resolution that "Jesus is the Christ, 'the only name given under heaven by which we may be saved.'" The resolution, which simply quoted the Bible, was called "divisive and demeaning to people whose faith in God is as strong as ours though it is differently defined." A substitute resolution was voted upon and passed which committed Episcopalians to proclaim a "Good News" that could be affirmed by every religion and thus had no saving value.

Behold the emergence of the ecumenical apostate church, the bride of Antichrist! "Positive Christianity" is the enemy of the cross. The truth offends those who don't want to hear it. Yet to speak anything less is to trifle with the eternal destiny of souls. Ecumenism's promise of "unity" is tempting, but it denies Christ and paves the way for the Antichrist and his new world religion. It is a unification that will ultimately lead to destruction.

There is now no stopping the exploding ecumenical movement with its embrace of all religions. America's most highly respected Christian psychologist refers enthusiastically to the "great camaraderie among the top leaders of virtually all religious groups in the United States."[31] A group of Christian theologians has called for "a move away from the insistence on the superiority or finality of Christ and Christianity toward a recognition of the independent validity of other ways." They justify such heresy by saying that "economic, political, and especially nuclear liberation is too big a job for any one nation, or culture, or religion...."[32]

Is it mere coincidence that both religious and political unity are coming together at this moment? The time is ripe. Even Iraq's naked aggression in taking over Kuwait in August 1990 became the basis for giving the world new hope for an end to military conflict. As Marlin Fitzwater, White House spokes-man, declared: "The process of war is forging a new blueprint for world peace."[33]

Saddam Hussein's call for a Holy War (*Jihad*) not only weakened Arab solidarity but raised questions about the very concept of *Jihad*. Such questions when pondered in the days ahead could lead Muslims to begin to see themselves not as a separate world at odds with everyone else but as part of a religiously pluralistic international community that is learning to live and respect and cooperate together.

The unprecedented solidarity of the members of the United Nations (including many Arab states) standing together against Hussein's aggression has given rise to the optimistic hope that at last the U.N. is fulfilling its purpose. Keeping the peace worldwide suddenly seems to be a viable possibility, causing political leaders to join the religious world's call for a "new world order."

After being discussed privately between President George Bush and his aides, the theme of a "new world order" began to come out openly for the first time. Just before leaving for Helsinki, Finland, early in September 1990 to discuss the Persian Gulf crisis at his summit meeting with Soviet President Gorbachev, Bush expressed the hope that "the foundation for the new world order would be laid in Helsinki" and that it would be established under the United Nations. At the news conference with Gorbachev following their historic meeting, President Bush declared optimistically:

> If the nations of the world, acting together, continue as they
> have been we will set in place the cornerstone of an interna-
> tional order more peaceful than any that we have known.[34]

Pushing that same theme following the summit, Secretary of State James Baker declared on the nationally televised program *Face The Nation* on September 10, 1990, "We're on the verge of forming a new world order." In the past such talk would have been dismissed as Utopian nonsense, but now the media was taking it seriously. *Time* magazine reported that "the Bush administration would like to make the U.N. a cornerstone of its plan to construct a new world order."[35] *Newsweek* magazine said, "As George Bush fished, golfed and pondered the post-cold-war world in Maine last month, his aides say that he began to imagine a new order."[36] Newspapers across the country carried headlines such as "President to hail 'new world order' "[37] and quoted a senior White House official who (referring to the Bush/Gorbachev meeting) declared: "I think it's . . . a very hopeful sign that we're entering a new world order where the East–West, US–Soviet competition is not going to be the dominant event."[38]

Addressing the United Nations on September 25, 1990, Soviet Foreign Minister Eduard Shevardnadze denounced Saddam Hussein's actions as a "threat to a new world order." Interestingly, Mikhail Gorbachev was the first world leader to come out publicly with talk of a "new world order," and he did so nearly two years before George Bush caught the vision. In his historic address to the United Nations on December 7, 1988, the Soviet President made this dogmatic and even prophetic statement:

> Further global progress is now possible only through a quest for universal consensus in the movement towards a new world order.[39]

The credibility of this idea no longer seems in question. That new world order, however, will be ruled by the Antichrist. The religious preparation for his rise to power is as essential as the political. Both are well underway. To consummate the process one vital ingredient is missing, which God Himself will supply.

13 | *Ecological Concern and Global Peace*

W HO HAS NOT REVELED in the breathtaking beauty of a sunset, or the myriad stars sparkling on a cold, clear night, or the almost-magical shades and shadows playing on the silhouettes of distant mountains at dusk, or the delicate pastels that paint the desert at sunrise, or the sun sparkling on rivers and lakes? And who has not stood motionless to watch in fascination and wonder some of the endless variety of creatures that this planet boasts? Words fail to describe the attractive loveliness of this earth! Yet its ungrateful inhabitants have been systematically abusing it and are only now awakening to the fact that they are destroying the environment upon which their very life and survival depends. And even after that realization has taken hold there has been a reluctance to face the gravity of the situation and to engage in the necessary action. Consequently, ecological collapse is a far greater threat than most people realize—and time could be running out.

In contrast to mankind's belated ecological awareness, biblical prophecy anticipated this problem thousands of years ago and indicated that God's judgment would fall as a result. A major purpose of the judgment to be poured out upon the earth, as John saw it in the vision recorded in Revelation, would be to "destroy them which destroy the earth" (11:18). A number of God's judgments are ecological in nature, devastating the grass and trees and polluting the oceans and rivers. The implication is that man has brought the dire consequences upon himself.

With the opening of closed borders, it is only now coming to light that the pollution in some areas of Eastern Europe is beyond any short-term remedy. Forests have died; rivers and lakes have become chemical cesspools, crops hopelessly contaminated, farm animals diseased; and thousands of children face premature death. Air pollution in Southern Poland has reached such deadly levels that the government is considering issuing gas masks to the citizenry. Widespread emergency measures must be taken immediately, but Eastern Europe lacks both the funds and the technology to address the problem. Pollution knows no borders, so the West must step in to help both with expertise and huge expenditures.

Of course the West has its own severe environmental problems. Autopsies on young children who die in auto accidents in the Los Angeles area reveal that their lungs are blackened and their arteries clogged. And so it goes throughout the industrialized world. Each year another thousand species are exterminated in what biologists have termed "nothing less than a holocaust of nature."

We need not cite further details. It is sufficient for our purposes to recognize that the global ecological crisis we face has the potential to unite mankind in a common international cause. Thus the environmental movement could play a significant role in bringing the unity essential to the rise of Antichrist.

Global peace is the key. A genuine peace would not only remove the threat of a nuclear holocaust and further contamination of nuclear testing, but it would be the only means of cleaning up the environment. With closed borders, the extent of pollution could not be known and there could never be the international cooperation that is required for a sound ecology. Furthermore, with the untold billions of dollars and so much manpower still committed to war preparedness, the wherewithal would be lacking to rescue the environment in time.

Global unity is thus essential to human survival—and it will be adopted on that basis.

The world desperately needs assurance of lasting peace so that it can take the resources until now committed to the manufacture of instruments of destruction and instead use them to rescue planet Earth and to give her inhabitants a better life. Fortunately, the realization that the weapons we now have could bring an end to civilization as we know it acts as a tremendous deterrent to war and provides a powerful motivation to settle our differences. Still, there is the lust for power on the part of leaders, and the fear of enemy attack. Yet at least we are moving in the right direction—but will it prove to be too little too late?

Dwight D. Eisenhower reportedly said, "Indeed, I think that people want peace so much that one of these days governments had better get out of their way and let them have it." We have just seen oppressive Communist regimes in Eastern Europe forced to "get out of the way" of millions of ordinary citizens who marched in the streets and otherwise let it be known that they would settle for nothing less than freedom and democracy. There is now a growing ground swell of a similar grassroots movement of hundreds of millions of determined people around the world demanding an immediate solution to these two interrelated issues of ecology and peace. Perhaps the time of which Eisenhower spoke has come at last—and not a moment too soon.

As we have seen, after ignoring the ecumenical movement for years, political leaders have recently begun to realize the importance of religious unity if the desired new world order is to be achieved. The result has been a significant new partnership between government and religion very much like Constantine established—an important step in preparing the world for the revival of the Roman Empire and its coming political/religious leader. The motivation is good: peace and environmental protection, common concerns of great importance around which all religions can ecumenically unite. The

World Council of Churches has now decided that the major test of orthodoxy is one's position on the environment.

Unfortunately, Jesus Christ, without whom there can be no real peace or ecological healing, is left out of the deliberations. Why? Has He been proved a fraud? No. It is simply that the issue of truth is now considered irrelevant. It would not be in keeping with the tolerant ecumenism of the new world order to acknowledge Christ's unique claims. Nor do "Christians" who join the peace and environmental movements present Christ in the context of such issues. Thus the door is opened for the Antichrist to bring his solution.

Laying the foundation for the coming world religion, ecological concerns are being expressed increasingly even by atheists in *spiritual* pantheistic/New Age terms, as though the universe were a living and even conscious entity (the Gaia hypothesis) with whom we must make peace and live in harmony. At the January 1990 Moscow Global Forum already referred to, physicist Fritjof Capra said that *spirituality* is "common to all humanity." He then defined spirituality as "the experience of being connected to the cosmos as a whole . . . that gives meaning to life." Yet, if one denies the intelligent, purposeful Creator God of the Bible and opts for vague, impersonal "creative forces," as one must in the new world order, then the cosmos has no purpose and life no meaning.

In his plenary address at the same Moscow conference, U.S. Senator Al Gore declared: "I do not see how the environmental problem can be solved without reference to spiritual values found in every faith." He was *not* referring to biblical Christianity, which is *unique*, but to an ecumenical "spirituality" based upon what he called "a new faith in the future of life on earth . . . [providing] higher values in the conduct of human affairs." Confirming the direction in which we are heading, the final "Moscow Declaration" called for "a global council of spiritual leaders" and the "creation of an inter-faith prayer . . . a new spiritual and ethical basis for human activities

on Earth: Humankind must enter into a new communion with
Nature. . . .''

On the contrary, humankind must get back in touch not with
nature itself but with nature's *Creator*. Planetary pollution is
the result of the pollution of sin in the human soul. There is
only one solution: the blood of Jesus Christ the Lamb of God
poured out upon the cross in payment of the penalty for sin
demanded by God's justice. All the talk about "spiritual
values" is like a salve to the conscience, mere tokenism,
tipping one's hat to whatever "God" there may be, a delusion
of Satan to blind mankind to the real problem.

"Spiritual values" is a vague term that no one defines, yet
everyone seems pleased with themselves for using it, as though
common ground for uniting science and religion has been
found and something meaningful has been communicated. In
fact, neither is true. "Spiritual values" is another form of "the
Emperor's new clothes." No one knows what the term means.
Yet it has become an integral part of suggested solutions to the
world's problems. To put it bluntly, "spiritual values" is the
new shibboleth of the environmental and peace movements.

Even some evangelical leaders seem pleased with all the talk
about "spiritual values." They react as though it indicates that
those who use the term are somehow kindred spirits, when in
fact they could be atheists and/or occultists totally opposed to
Christianity—and generally are.

England's Prince Philip, cofounder of the World Wildlife
Fund (WWF), is one of the world's leading environmentalists.
WWF funded the start of the Washington D.C.-based North
American Conference on Religion and Ecology (NACRE),
which is determined to recruit the local churches for the
environmental movement. It even provided pastors with an
"Easter Day 1990" sermon that robbed Christ's death and
resurrection of its real meaning and turned it into a symbol of
the earth's ecological agony and the "resurrection" that our
efforts can effect. NACRE, which was one of the key sponsors
of Earth Day 1990, calls for "a spiritual rebirth of Western
man" (*Eastern* man through Yoga, etc., is already tuned in) as

the secret to solving the ecological crisis. Its president, Donald Conroy, declares: "If the religious communities around the globe awaken to the ethical and spiritual dimensions of the environmental threat, there is hope for the Planet."

In a recent speech at Washington D.C.'s National Press Club, Prince Philip let it be known that the "spiritual values" of the environmental movement are not those of biblical Christianity. After declaring, "We need a religious and spiritual motive to encourage respect and care for nature," he went on to argue against Christianity's view of saving souls for eternity:

> After all, there can be little advantage in attempting to save souls or in seeking enlightenment or salvation if humanity's very existence on this earth is threatened by its own activities. [1]

The militant and growing Greenpeace movement addresses valid concerns. It is, however, an attempt to bring peace on earth without the Prince of Peace. God put rebellious Adam and Eve out of the Garden of Eden and guarded the tree of life with the flaming sword of His holy judgment upon sin. Christ took that sword in His heart for us and became "the way" to the life which He alone *is* and which He alone can give. Environmentalist movements, for all the good they represent, are attempts to restore mankind to an earthly paradise without reconciliation to God through Christ's redemptive work upon the cross.

Prince Philip is representative of the growing numbers of nominal "Christians" who are turning back to paganism as a result of their ecological concerns. Though his wife, Queen Elizabeth II, is the head of the Church of England, in that same speech at the National Press Club the Prince said:

> It is now apparent that the ecological pragmatism of the so-called pagan religions such as that of the American Indians, Polynesians, Australian Aborigines, was a great deal more realistic in terms of conservation ethics than the more intellectual monotheistic philosophies of the revealed religions. [2]

Thus ecological concern subtly fosters rejection of the Bible and Christianity. To speak of "spirituality" and "freedom of religion" is popular. To suggest that Jesus Christ as the Savior of sinners is mankind's only hope is not tolerated by those who preach tolerance. All religions must join together in a generic, pagan "spirituality" to rescue the planet. Environmental Protection Agency chief William K. Reilly, who calls himself a "pure Irish Catholic," proposes a "spiritual vision" of conservation.[3] "Spiritual" could mean Hinduism, Buddhism, witchcraft, or Islam—or it could have nothing to do with religion. One could have a "spiritual" experience at a rock concert or an opera, or on an LSD trip. The door is open—to anything except evangelical Christianity.

In his address to the Moscow Global Forum of Spiritual and Parliamentary Leaders on Human Survival, Mikhail Gorbachev called the conference "a major step in the ecological consciousness of humanity." He drew cheers from delegates when he pledged "to ban nuclear tests completely, for all times, and at any moment, if the U.S. does the same . . . [and] to open our territory for inspection. . . ."[4] He went on to call for "a new contemporary attitude to Nature . . . returning to Man a sense of being a part of Nature."

Again it is a pitiful attempt to escape the real issue. Man's problem is not that he is out of touch with *nature*, but that he is out of touch with *God*—in fact he is in rebellion against his Creator. If the "God" that formed us is nature itself—if we are simply the result of natural forces that have made us what we are—then no matter what we did it would be natural and could not be considered pollution or exploitation of nature. Nature does not pollute or exploit itself. *Whatever* nature and her creatures do is a "natural act" and cannot be faulted.

If an earthquake and tidal wave cause a beautiful Pacific island to disappear, there is nothing *wrong* with that, for there are no morals in nature. It is not *wrong* for a lion to kill an antelope for lunch, or for beetles or parasites to destroy acres of forest. Then why is it *wrong* for man to destroy a rain forest or to dump mercury into the ocean, if he is truly the natural product of evolutionary forces? Would not any act by any man be just as natural as the acts of all other natural creatures? It would no more be *wrong* for our factories to create pollution than for a volcano to spew its ash and poison gases into the air.

Yet we know that we do act against nature. Moreover, we have a conscience about it. That would only be possible if nature is not all there is but was itself created by a God who is separate and distinct from the universe and who made man in His image and to whom man is accountable for how he uses or abuses the rest of God's creation. There is no other explanation for our sense of harming nature and of feeling guilty for doing so.

The videotape promoting Global Forum includes clips of speeches by Mother Teresa, Mikhail Gorbachev, and other admired leaders. In showing excerpts of talks given by various world leaders at Moscow, the narrator introduces Cornell University Professor of Astronomy and Space Sciences, Carl Sagan, with these auspicious words: "Carl Sagan sounded a *spiritual* note." Really? That would be quite remarkable for a man who is an avowed *materialist*! Here is what Sagan said that evoked this comment and so impressed the Moscow audience:

> As scientists, many of us have had profound experiences of awe and reverence before the universe. We understand that what is regarded as sacred is more likely to be treated with care and respect. Our planetary home should be so regarded.

It is astonishing that Christians seem quite pleased when a Carl Sagan sounds a *spiritual* note—as though they now hold a belief in common that unites them, when in fact they are as far apart as heaven and hell. Sagan is an atheist. His use of "sacred" is dishonest. In every sense a pagan, this "high priest of cosmos worship" has said, "If we must worship a power greater than ourselves, does it not make sense to revere the Sun and stars?"[5] Of course it doesn't! Sagan is expressing the neopantheism of academia called *ecotheology*. Another of its advocates, Georgetown University professor Victor Ferkiss, says it "starts with the premise that the Universe *is* God." Like Sagan, he seems convinced that this belief will "prevent the environmental exploitation of the Universe."[6] Even if it did, that would not make it *true*—but who cares about *truth* anymore? In comparison with the ecological crisis we face, the question of truth seems abstract and impractical.

Moreover, to believe that the universe is God would not prevent environmental exploitation. On the contrary, it would encourage it. If the universe is "God," then each of us is part of "God" and can do no wrong. Thus the very term "exploitation of the Universe" would be meaningless. Sagan and Ferkiss and others who espouse their beliefs are simply restating the old paganism in new terms. It is astounding that so many evangelicals involved in the environmental movement seemed pleased with talk of "reverencing the cosmos," as though this had something in common with belief in the God of the Bible. They ought to know that Sagan's cosmos worship stands in total opposition to God and is the sworn enemy of the gospel.

In Romans 1, Paul deals specifically with this age-old perversion of the truth about God which is revealed in His creation. And He indicts with rebellion all those who worship the creation instead of its Creator. There is no essential difference between an animist bowing before a stick or stone which he credits with some "spirit power," a witch worshiping "Nature, O mighty Mother of us all," and university professors worshiping the atom or the cosmos as "God." All are condemned as pagans, whether ancient or modern, ignorant or academically respected. Paul wrote:

> For the invisible things of him [God] from the creation of the world are clearly seen, being understood by the things that are made, even his eternal power and Godhead, so that they are without excuse; because that, when they knew God [from His creation], they glorified him not as God, neither were thankful, but became vain in their imaginations, and their foolish heart was darkened.

> Professing themselves to be wise, they became fools...
> who changed the truth of God into a lie, and worshipped and
> served the creature [creation] more than [instead of] the Cre-
> ator... (Romans 1:20-25).

What we are seeing is a repudiation of the Reformation and
a return to a pagan orientation in relation to nature. It may at
times be clothed in the weak "Christian" terms of Roman
Catholicism to satisfy those who consider themselves to be
Christians but who do not follow the Bible. It is part of the
remarkable return to the religion of Rome, currently underway, along with the revival of that Empire in preparation for
the rise of Antichrist. This process is encouraged by the Pope's
overt approval of paganism, and by Christians who join the
environmental movement and work to save the planet without
clearly declaring that the only hope for mankind is to be
reconciled to God through Jesus Christ.

The concerns of the environmentalists are genuine. Yet
their humanistic solutions and the homage they pay to "Nature" are attempts to escape accountability to the personal
God who created them. In the place of God's moral absolutes
one can then boast of the "tolerance" which Gorbachev says is
the cornerstone of the new world order. If we are not accountable to a personal God, but to "Nature," which knows no
morals, then we can broad-mindedly condone homosexuality,
abortion, and all manner of immorality while at the same time
priding ourselves that we are acting "responsibly toward the
environment." Paul goes on in Romans 1 to say rather bluntly:

> And even as they did not like to retain God in their knowledge,
> God gave them over to a reprobate mind... [to] unrighteous-
> ness, fornication, wickedness, covetousness, maliciousness;
> full of envy, murder, debate, deceit, malignity; whisperers,
> backbiters, haters of God, despiteful, proud, boasters, inven-
> tors of evil things, disobedient to parents, without under-
> standing... (Romans 1:28-31).

What an accurate description of today's world! Yes, we are
guilty of polluting our environment and ought to correct that

evil. Yet many of those in the forefront of the crusade against environmental pollution are at the same time demanding greater "freedom" to pollute our souls and minds and those of our children. And to ease the conscience, they make periodic use of the new shibboleth, "spiritual values," to show that they are not against "religion" and do have standards.

Global Forum's newsletter, *Shared Vision*, declares that "we need to remember our natural origins and re-learn how to love and respect nature. The love of our eternal parents, Earth Mother and Sky Father, is all embracing. . . ." The rejection of God the Father and His Son Jesus Christ could not be stated more plainly. Yet many who call themselves Christians are joining the move "back to nature" in order to show their ecumenical solidarity with all who are concerned about the well-being of our planet.

In October 1988, a typical gathering of environmentalists from all over North America met in the Santa Cruz, California, redwoods. It "opened with a prayer by Native Americans, thanking Grandfather God 'for all the good things you have put on Mother Earth.' " Speakers included a "Baptist minister— an ecumenical peace activist." The meeting "closed with a community-building, earth-celebrating 'spiral dance' ritual led by well-known writer, activist, and feminist 'witch', Starhawk," long associated with Catholic Priest Matthew Fox at his Holy Names College in Oakland, California.[7]

Using similar pantheistic/New Age language, John Paul II has promoted a kindred concept in numerous speeches. In his 1990 World Peace Day message on the "Feast of the Holy Mother of God," the Pope said, "A harmonious universe is a cosmos endowed with its own integrity, its own internal, dynamic balance."[8] The Archbishop of Canterbury, Robert Runcie, has hosted in Canterbury Cathedral the "Canterbury Festival of Faith and the Environment" featuring "joint prayer and worship . . . with Buddhists, Muslims, Baha'is, Jews, Sikhs, and Hindus." The same mixture of paganism and "Christianity" that Constantine achieved is now being revived in preparation for the new Constantine, the Antichrist.

Ecology and peace are the two great concerns that are sparking the new unity of all religions. Nothing else matters. Doctrinal beliefs are irrelevant. Such was the conclusion of the World Conference: Religious Workers for Lasting Peace, Disarmament and Just Relations among Nations held in 1977 in Moscow. Delegates came from more than 100 countries and included "Buddhists and Christians, Hindus, Judaists and Muslims, Sikhs and Shintoists, clergy and laity, teachers and high priests. . . ." The final statement signed by the conferees included the following:

> Our religious beliefs did not keep us apart, for we found our ethical concerns similar, and in our concern for the welfare of the whole humanity we have found our common ground.
>
> We did not discuss our differences in doctrines . . . [but how] to find ways of striving together for peace with justice. . . .
>
> May peace with justice triumph! May mankind be enabled to move towards the development of its full potential! May humanity be united in our common striving for peace![9]

It is astonishing not only what ungodly but what bizarre "spirituality" the world is willing to embrace in its search for peace and ecological salvation. Maharishi Mahesh Yogi claims that the practice by the many followers worldwide of his brand of Hindu Yoga, which he calls Transcendental Meditation (TM), is bringing peace to the world. "Ideal communities" of perfect peace are being established by the TM movement around the world. Maharishi's followers now credit their master and TM with bringing about the dramatic transformations sweeping Eastern Europe and the end of the Cold War. Who is to say that they are wrong? Indeed, scientific verification of Maharishi's claims has allegedly been made by numerous reputable university professors and scientists.

If millions of people, many of them highly intelligent and well-educated, can be persuaded to believe the incredible claims of Maharishi, then it is not difficult to imagine the world worshiping the Antichrist. Satan's Messiah, with his seemingly unlimited psychic power, will be light-years ahead of any of today's gurus.

The Dalai Lama makes claims that are no less extravagant than Maharishi's. He too promises global peace through the practice of his own brand of Yoga, which is similar to TM but, according to him, far more powerful. It goes by the imposing title "Tibetan Tantric Buddhist Deity Yoga." He promises to usher in global peace by turning mankind into little gods capable of creating the "illusion" of peace. That's all life is, he says, an illusion, and it's just a matter of creating a different one from the illusion of evil that we've all been captive to for so long.

Does anyone take him seriously? The media does and is kinder to him than it is to George Bush or Margaret Thatcher. And his efforts are also supposedly behind the recent turn of events in Eastern Europe. Admirers of the Dalai Lama credit the Kalachakra rituals he has been leading around the world with helping to create a spiritual atmosphere which made possible the recent shredding of the Iron Curtain. So seriously are the Dalai Lama's global peace mission and Deity Yoga taken, and so highly is he regarded, that he was awarded the Nobel Peace Prize on October 5, 1989.

Pope John Paul II has his own theory about how global peace will come—a theory that gives no more credit to Jesus Christ and is every bit as bizarre as the peace plans of Maharishi or the Dalai Lama, yet is taken seriously by hundreds of millions of Roman Catholics. As we have earlier noted, the head of the Roman Catholic Church is fully convinced that global peace, when it comes, will be through daily recital of the Rosary and the triumph of the "Immaculate heart" of the apparition of "Mary" known as "Our Lady of Fatima." At the same time the Pope does not condemn other beliefs, but to serve his own agenda credits the prayers and efforts of all religions as playing a part in the healing of planet Earth.

Since it is a key factor in establishing world peace, ecumenism will be unstoppable. Those who criticize it on the basis of biblical truth will seem to be small-minded. After all, as Prince Philip suggests, it hardly seems practical, when the survival of our species on earth hangs in the balance, to worry about heaven or hell. Environmental concerns and the need for peace at any price clearly take priority. And who will be concerned that the angels' message of "peace on earth" at the birth of Jesus Christ has lost its true meaning and that what is being offered is a delusion that will ultimately lead to destruction?

How amazing it is that for so many who talk about "spiritual values" there is a total disregard of the fact that man is a spiritual being who continues to exist even after his material body is dead. The focus is upon *time*, while eternity is neglected; upon *this* life, while the life to come, whether in heaven or hell, is forgotten. We might well ask, paraphrasing Christ's solemn words, "What shall it profit modern man if he gains an ecologically sound and peaceful world and loses his own soul!"

We can take comfort in God's promise that even earth's deserts will "blossom like a rose" when His Messiah rules from Jerusalem for 1000 years. Even the millennium, however, will end in war as multitudes who have enjoyed God's blessings rebel and seek to overthrow His kingdom. Our ultimate hope is the completely new and sinless universe of pure bliss for those who allow God to fit them for it by making them "new creations in Christ Jesus."

Satan's plan is intellectually more acceptable and far more appealing to human pride. In the days ahead we will all be called upon to work together in promising alliances to forge an Edenlike new world of equality and sufficiency for all. Let us beware that we are not duped into joining the wrong side in a seemingly good cause.

14 | *Was Jesus of Nazareth Really the Christ?*

W HEN ASKED WHY HE doesn't believe that Jesus was the Messiah, the average Jewish person will most likely reply, "Because He didn't bring peace." On the surface, the logic of such a position seems irrefutable. After all, the Hebrew prophets promised that the Messiah would establish over the entire earth a kingdom of perfect and perpetual peace, and Jesus failed to do so. Case closed. Take, for example, the prophecy of Isaiah that Christians quote so often, especially at Christmas:

> Of the increase of his government and peace there shall be no end, upon the throne of David and upon his kingdom, to order it and to establish it with judgment and with justice from henceforth even for ever. The zeal of the Lord of hosts will perform this (Isaiah 9:7).

God had promised David through Nathan the prophet, "I will set up thy seed after thee . . . and I will establish his kingdom forever . . ." (2 Samuel 7:10-17). Micah had added his testimony: "The Lord shall reign over them in mount Zion . . . forever" (Micah 4:7). The angel Gabriel had confirmed these prophecies to the virgin Mary: "He shall reign over the house of Jacob forever, and of his kingdom there shall be no end" (Luke 1:33). Here is a further sample of what the prophets declared with one voice concerning the coming kingdom of the Messiah:

> The wolf and the lamb shall feed together, and the lion shall eat straw like the bullock. . . . They shall not hurt nor destroy in all my holy mountain, saith the Lord.
>
> Rejoice ye with Jerusalem. . . . For thus saith the Lord, Behold, I will extend peace to her like a river, and the glory of the Gentiles [shall come to her] like a flowing stream . . . (Isaiah 65:25; 66:10-12).

> I will bring again the captivity of my people Israel . . . they shall serve the Lord their God, and David their king [Messiah], whom I will raise up unto them. . . . I will punish all that oppress them. . . .
>
> He that scattered Israel will gather him and keep him, as a shepherd doth his flock. . . . They shall not sorrow any more at all (Jeremiah 30:3,9,20; 31:10,12).

Obviously these prophecies have not been fulfilled. Skeptics justify their unbelief by arguing, "Christianity has been around for nearly 2000 years and we still don't have peace and the world is in a mess—so why should I believe the 'Peace on earth' message that Christians trot out every Christmas?" Of course, education has been around much longer than that, and still the majority of people are not well-educated in spite of libraries filled with hundreds of thousands of books. Christ's salvation is not automatically imposed upon the world: It must be believed and received by individuals for it to be effective.

The coming of the Messiah to reestablish Israel as the head of the nations and to inaugurate worldwide peace was the great hope of the Jewish people. Messianic prophecies, however, contained some strange contradictions that Israel's religious leaders found incomprehensible and that most Jewish people today are not willing to face. For example, Isaiah also prophesied concerning the Messiah: "He is despised and rejected . . . we hid as it were our faces from him. . . . He was taken from prison and from judgment . . . he was cut off out of the land of the living; for the transgression of my people was he stricken [killed]" (Isaiah 53:3,8). The Jews unwittingly fulfilled such Scriptures in having Jesus crucified.

God chose Abraham, Isaac, and Jacob and intended that He Himself would rule their descendants. Israel was to be a theocracy in the fullest sense, a living demonstration of the relationship that men and nations should have with God. Thus when Israel wanted a king like the nations around her, God said to Samuel, "They have rejected *me* that *I* should not reign over them . . ." (1 Samuel 8:7).

So the Messiah, if He was to establish the true kingdom, would have to be God Himself come as a man to rule over Israel. Indeed, the prophets clearly stated that the Messiah would be God come down to earth through a virgin birth to live as a man among His creatures: "A virgin shall conceive, and bear a son. . . . And his name shall be called Wonderful, Counsellor, the mighty God, the everlasting Father . . ." (Isaiah 7:14; 9:6).

The rabbis would not believe that God had to become a man in order to effect our salvation—so they crucified Jesus for claiming to be God. And certainly God couldn't die, so that proved Jesus was a fraud! Nor could a dead man rule on David's throne, so the rabbis also claimed that He couldn't have been the Messiah because He didn't establish the kingdom. When He rose from the dead, they bribed the guards to explain the empty tomb by saying that His disciples had stolen the body while they slept. Today we understand what His contemporaries did not but which the prophets clearly foretold: that the Messiah would establish His 1000-year millennial kingdom at His *second coming.*

Israel expected the Messiah to ride with flashing sword at the head of an army and to conquer her Roman oppressors. There was no comprehension that the worst enemy was sin and self within, and that the mission of the Messiah was to deliver mankind from moral and spiritual bondage. That all of the animal sacrifices were but picturing the fact that the Messiah would have to die for their sins was a concept totally incomprehensible to all of Israel.

Some sincere people have doubts because they have heard "scholars" declare that the New Testament wasn't written by the apostles but by zealous church leaders hundreds of years later, so its testimony concerning Jesus of Nazareth is mostly fabricated and certainly unreliable. However, not only are the facts to the contrary, but such a suggestion is self-contradictory. That someone evil enough to perpetrate such a fraud could produce a fictional Jesus whose words and deeds have been acknowledged even by critics to be the most perfect example of goodness is preposterous.

Historically we know that the New Testament documents were widely circulated in the early church before the end of the first century. Furthermore, they contain detailed data that could only have been known by someone who was alive writing at the time. For example, Luke wrote:

> Now in the fifteenth year of the reign of Tiberius Caesar, Pontius Pilate being governor of Judea, and Herod being tetrarch of Galilee, and his brother Philip tetrarch of Iturea and of the region of Trachonitis, and Lysanias the tetrarch of Abilene, Annas and Caiaphas being the high priests . . . (Luke 3:1,2).

No one pretending to be Luke and writing decades (let alone hundreds of years) later could have known such details concerning the names and locations of rulers and priests. It has only been through modern archaeological discoveries that all of these data have been verified to be 100 percent accurate. The very existence of Pontius Pilate was denied by skeptics until recently, when the first archaeological proof that he lived was uncovered. No, contrary to what the critics would have us believe, we have far better evidence that Jesus of Nazareth lived, died, and rose again, just as the New Testament recounts it, than we have for what we know about other historic characters such as Julius Caesar or Alexander the Great.

Consider the contrast between the overwhelming numbers of ancient biblical manuscripts available for study—and the paucity of manuscripts for anything else dating back to the same period. For the Book of Mormon there are *no ancient records*—only the one copy in Joseph Smith's own hand allegedly "translated" from "gold plates" that have vanished. For Caesar's *Gallic War* (58-50 B.C.) we have nine or ten manuscripts of any value, the earliest of which is dated about *900 years* after Caesar. Of the original 142 books of the *Roman History of Livy* (59 B.C. to 17 A.D.), only 35 have survived, contained in about 20 manuscripts. Of the 14 books of the *Histories of Tacitus* (100 A.D.), only 4½ survive, while of the 16 books of his *Annals*, ten survive in full and two in part, contained in only two manuscripts, one of the ninth century and one of the eleventh. As for *The History of Thucydides* and *The History of Herodotus* (fifth-century B.C.), we have about eight manuscripts of each.

By contrast, scholars have in excess of *15,000* manuscripts of the Bible for study! And their accuracy? The critics were certain that the copy of Isaiah contained in the Dead Sea Scrolls (dating to about 125 B.C.) would be far different from the earliest manuscript of Isaiah previously available, which dated to about 900 A.D. But the famous Isaiah scroll housed in its own museum in Israel today proved to be nearly identical to what we already had.

The question of whether Jesus of Nazareth was the Christ does not arise because of any deficiency in the Bible, but because He apparently failed to fulfill everything the prophets foretold. Actually, *all* of the numerous prophecies concerning the coming Messiah detailed in the Old Testament were fulfilled by Jesus of Nazareth to the letter—all *except* for re-establishing the kingdom of Israel and bringing global peace. That apparent failure gave seeming biblical justification to those who had Him crucified. It also caused great confusion and disillusionment among His followers.

Even John the Baptist, who had been sent by God to prepare Israel for her Messiah, began to doubt that Jesus could be the promised One. Disenchanted and distraught, he sent two of his disciples to ask Him, "Art thou he that should come? Or look we for another?" (Luke 7:20). The question was astonishing when one considers who John was, and the overwhelming proof he had already received that Jesus was without doubt Israel's promised Messiah.

"There was a man sent from God whose name was John" is the way the Fourth Gospel introduces the one whom Isaiah described as the Messiah's forerunner: "The voice of him that crieth in the wilderness, Prepare ye the way of the Lord . . ." (Isaiah 40:3). Chosen by God for this honor, John the Baptist (so the angel Gabriel promised) would be "filled with the Holy Ghost even from his mother's womb" (Luke 1:15). Sure enough, as a six-month-old fetus he had leaped in Elisabeth's womb (Luke 1:41) at the sound of the voice of the Virgin Mary, who had come to tell her cousin that she was "with child of the Holy Ghost" (Matthew 1:18).

Knowing fully who he was and what he was to do, John the Baptist had begun to prepare Israel for her Messiah by preaching repentance and baptizing in the River Jordan all who heeded his message. No mystic, John had received specific revelations from God that had been fulfilled in vivid, concrete experience:

> He that sent me to baptize with water, the same said unto me, Upon whom thou shalt see the Spirit descending, and remaining on him, the same is he which baptizeth with the Holy Ghost.
> And I saw and bare record that this is the Son of God (John 1:33,34).

After baptizing Jesus, John had seen the Spirit descending like a heavenly dove and abiding upon Christ in fulfillment of God's word. John had lost some of his own disciples when he had faithfully pointed them to Jesus and declared by divine revelation, "Behold the Lamb of God, which taketh away the sin of the world" (John 1:29). And when some informed him that the number of his disciples was diminishing while Christ's were increasing, John had replied, "He must increase, but I must decrease" (John 3:30).

Yet this chosen prophet had come to the point where it no longer seemed to make sense that Jesus was the Messiah. John had been arrested by King Herod, was languishing in the palace dungeon, and was about to lose his head. How could this possibly be happening to *him*, God's special messenger, who had introduced the Messiah to Israel? Had he somehow been duped? If Jesus were really the Christ, empowered by God to set up His kingdom and reign upon David's throne, then surely he, John, would not be in prison!

We do not know how long John had wrestled to avoid that agonizing conclusion. The truth was shattering—but what further proof was needed that his cousin Jesus was a well-meaning but self-deceived impostor? In one last attempt to salvage his faith John sent two of his shrinking cadre of disciples to observe and question Jesus. In their presence Jesus did many miracles and sent them back to tell John what they had witnessed. We are not told John's reaction, but must assume that God sustained him in his hour of trial.

John the Baptist's question required a very specific response: "Art thou *he that should come*?" It would do no good for Jesus to solemnly swear that He was the Christ. Whether or not He was the Messiah *that should come* depended solely upon whether He fulfilled the Messianic prophecies. That was why Jesus warned His disciples "that they should tell no man that he was Jesus the Christ" until He had fulfilled the prophecies and risen from the dead (Matthew 16:20,21; 17:9).

Unfortunately, John, though a man of God, no more understood the messianic prophecies than did Christ's disciples or Israel's religious leaders. And that same confusion regarding what the prophets foretold remains the issue today in relation to Christ's second coming, which is why we need to give it close attention.

There are more than 300 prophecies foretelling the coming of the Jewish Messiah in the Old Testament. Around 200 are duplicates, leaving about 100 specific criteria to be fulfilled. Here are a few representative examples: that He would come at a particular time (see the next chapter); that He would be born in Bethlehem (Micah 5:2) of a virgin (Isaiah 7:14) and of the lineage of David (Psalm 89:3,4,28-36); that He would ride into

Jerusalem on a donkey and be hailed at that time as the Messiah (Zechariah 9:9); that His own people would finally reject Him (Isaiah 53:3); that one of His own disciples would betray Him (Psalm 41:9; Zechariah 13:7) for 30 pieces of silver (Zechariah 11:12); that He would be crucified by Gentiles and Jews working together (Psalm 22:16); and that He would be resurrected (Psalm 16:10).

Christ had repeatedly explained to the twelve that He must be crucified and rise from the dead the third day. That concept, however, was so contrary to their understanding of a Messiah who would conquer Israel's enemies that they couldn't accept the plain meaning of His words. Nor could they comprehend the apparently contradictory prophecies. Isaiah's statement that the Messiah "was cut off out of the land of the living" (53:8) seemed irreconcilable with his statement two verses later, "he shall see his seed, he shall prolong his days" (53:10). There had to be some secret interpretation—but they had been afraid to ask Jesus.

One thought obsessed the disciples: that when Christ established His kingdom they would reign with Him in great glory and power. So absorbed were they with the prospect of reigning on thrones in Jerusalem that at the Last Supper they showed only a brief flurry of concern when He sorrowfully said that one of them would betray Him, then quickly returned to arguing among themselves "which of them should be accounted the greatest" (Luke 22:24).

Imagine, then, the terrible shock to these would-be princes when Jesus, apparently helpless, was bound by the mob that Judas brought to the Garden of Gethsemane and led away to judgment and certain death! This was the One who, when a storm had threatened to swamp their small boat, had with a word subdued the raging wind and waves into immediate calm. With that same supreme authority He had commanded health to the sick, sight to the blind, and food to the hungry—and the dead had even come forth from the grave at His command. They had witnessed His miraculous power many times. What possible explanation could there be for His helplessness now?

There seemed to be only one answer to that question: They had somehow been deceived by this Nazarene. How that was possible, they couldn't imagine—yet the fact of His arrest and pending execution as a criminal spoke for itself. It was galling to think that the rabbis had been right all along in accusing Him of being an impostor. That was the last thing the disciples wanted to believe, yet if He were the Messiah no one could have taken Him.

When they heard Him say, sadly and with apparent resignation, to the mob that came to arrest Him, ". . . this is your hour, and the power of darkness" (Luke 22:53), their whole world fell apart. Those who only a short while before at the Last Supper had sworn that they would die rather than deny Him fled for their lives and left Him to His fate. Little did they realize that they all—Judas, the soldiers, the rabble, themselves, and the Roman and Jewish authorities—were fulfilling what the prophets had said. So it had to be; and like the powers of darkness, His own disciples would not realize that on the cross Satan would be defeated.

Jesus's statement, *"This is your hour, and the power of darkness,"* marked a complete change in how the battle against Satan was to be fought. Until then no one could lay a violent hand upon Christ or His disciples. The Pharisees had often tried to take Him captive, but He had always been beyond their power: "Then they sought to take him; but no man laid hands on him because his hour was not yet come" (John 7:30; cf. Luke 4:30; John 8:20; etc.).

Now at last that hour had come, and He submitted Himself to their abuse. Thereafter Satan and his minions would be allowed to do their worst. The same would also be true from that moment on for every person who would become a Christian. The hatred, shame, rejection, persecution, and martyrdom that their Lord had suffered would be theirs to bear as well—but His followers didn't understand.

So it was that the two disciples on the road to Emmaus blurted out their disillusionment "concerning Jesus of Nazareth" to the "stranger" who came alongside and began to walk with them: "We trusted that it had been he which should have redeemed Israel" (Luke 24:21). The complete shattering of that hope had come so swiftly and unexpectedly: "The chief priests and our rulers delivered him to be condemned to death, and have crucified him" (Luke 24:20).

So blinded were they by sorrow and misunderstanding that they did not recognize their resurrected Lord walking beside them. Even though "certain women" claimed to have seen a "vision of angels, which said that he was alive" (Luke 24:23), that was small consolation. "Visions" should not be trusted without some solid evidence to support them. Peter and John had investigated and had found the tomb empty. That seemed to be the final blow. With the body missing, they couldn't even build a shrine over His remains.

So, for lack of understanding, the whole wonderful dream of the One they had thought was the Messiah taking the throne of David and setting up His kingdom, with them ruling on thrones beside Him, had turned into a nightmare. All of the disciples were now in terror of suffering His horrible fate. They had no conception of what the Hebrew prophets had declared: that He would be "wounded for our transgressions . . . bruised for our iniquities" (Isaiah 53:5), that He was dying for the sins of the world.

How ironic that the very death which their own prophets had foretold and which we now understand was necessary for our salvation was "proof" to Christ's contemporaries that He was not the Savior! "If thou be Christ, save thyself and us" (Luke 23:39) was the challenge thrown at Him by the thieves who were being crucified at His side. Had He "saved Himself," no one else could have been saved—but they did not understand. "If he be the King of Israel, let him now come down from the cross, and we will believe him" (Matthew 27:42) was the mocking taunt of the religious leaders gloating beneath His uplifted and pain-racked body.

The absence of divine intervention was convincing. The chief priests and scribes had reminded all who came to watch Him expire in agony, "He trusted in God; let him deliver him

now, if he will have him: for he said, I am the Son of God"
(Matthew 27:43). Was not His desolate cry just before He
expired, "My God, my God, why hast thou forsaken me?"
(Mark 15:34) an admission at last that He was no servant of
God at all, much less His Son? That the heavens remained like
brass after that pitiful plea seemed more than sufficient proof
that this Galilean ex-carpenter had been an impostor.

Was not the logic irrefutable and solidly based in Scripture?
After all, the prophecies made it quite clear that the Messiah
would restore the throne of David and Israel's greatness,
ushering in a golden age of peace for the entire world. Jesus of
Nazareth had failed completely. He had not brought peace at
all. In fact, His own words, as the disillusioned disciples
thought back upon them, should have warned them at the time
that He wasn't the Messiah: "Think not that I am come to send
peace on earth: I came not to send peace, but a sword. For I am
come to set a man at variance against his father, and the
daughter against her mother, and the daughter-in-law against
her mother-in-law" (Matthew 10:34,35). Out of His own
mouth He seemed condemned.

Far from bringing peace, He had brought strife and division
among friends and even within families. And instead of raising
an army to free Israel from the Roman yoke, as the Messiah
surely would have done, this meek and mild impostor had led a
ragtag band of former fishermen, tax-gatherers, and pros-
titutes about the country preaching nonviolence. By pretending to be the King of Israel He had aroused the wrath of
Rome and only made matters worse.

At last the rabbis were rid of Him. Consciences once pricked
by His troublesome preaching of righteousness could now rest
at ease. Jesus of Nazareth was dead, His disenchanted and
cowardly followers scattered and in hiding. That was the
end—so everyone thought—though in fact it was only the
beginning. Yet His own disciples did not understand the truth
until He showed Himself alive to them "by many infallible
proofs" (Acts 1:3) after His resurrection.

At the root of John the Baptist's doubts and the disillusionment of Christ's disciples were issues that remain with us today and are the cause of growing confusion and controversy in the church: the *kingdom* and the *cross*. They were mistaken about *how* and *when* Christ would establish His kingdom. As for the cross, they did not understand that at all. It didn't fit the picture of a mighty conqueror who would destroy his enemies and rule with a rod of iron (Psalm 2, etc.). The fact that Jesus had displayed such power, working all manner of miracles, even raising the dead, made it very confusing that He should then be crucified in apparent weakness.

There are many in the church today who are still confused over *how* and *when* Christ will establish His kingdom. Nor do they accept that the *cross* should characterize the Christian life. Instead, they believe that Christians should rule the earth. After all, when Christ commissioned His disciples after His resurrection to "go ye into all the world, and preach the gospel" (Mark 16:15) He declared that "All power is given unto me in heaven and in earth" (Matthew 28:18). As His representatives, then, surely Christians are no longer to turn the other cheek but to conquer the world in His name. It is now widely taught that the church's task is to take over everything from public education and the media to the reins of government in setting up Christ's kingdom as He watches approvingly from heaven. That such is not the case can be easily established from Scripture.

As Christ showed Himself alive to the disciples for 40 days after His resurrection they asked Him, "Lord, wilt *thou* at *this time* restore the kingdom *to Israel*?" Their question revealed their basic understanding: 1) that it would not be the church but *Christ* (wilt *thou*) who would *personally* establish the kingdom; 2) that He had not yet undertaken that task but would do so at some *future* time; and 3) that the kingdom pertained to *Israel*, not to the church. Had they been mistaken on any of these points, surely Christ would have corrected them. The fact that He did not is reason enough for us to adopt the same three basic beliefs with regard to the kingdom. Christ simply told them that it was not for them to know *when* He would return to take David's throne and restore the kingdom to *Israel*—but He certainly left intact their belief that *He* would do exactly that.

After Christ's resurrection His disciples were able at last to understand that there was *one way* to reconcile the prophetic contradictions of One who would come in weakness, yet in strength, who would be rejected and killed, yet who would reign forever. Clearly there had to be *two comings*! Christ had to come *once* to die for our sins and thereby establish His kingdom within the hearts of His followers—and then, after ascending into heaven, He would *come again* to rule the world from Jerusalem. How else could *all* of the prophecies be fulfilled, including those that foretold His rejection, death, and resurrection?

When the Messiah was "cut off [i.e. killed], but not for himself [He died for us]" as Daniel prophesied (9:26), it was not the defeat that His opponents perceived it to be. Instead, it was God's decisive move in this cosmic struggle for the throne of the universe. The battle was actually fought and won—with Satan defeated—on that cross outside the gates of Jerusalem 1900 years ago. What remains is to implement that victory in Christ's followers through their faith in Him.

Why the cross? Was it really necessary? In fact, it was the *only way* whereby mankind could be rescued from the judgment it deserved, and the *only way* Satan could be defeated. While we will come back to this issue in more depth later, it is essential at this point to understand that, in Christ, God Himself came to this earth to pay the penalty that His own justice demanded for sin.

Every sin, no matter how small in our eyes, is an offense against God's infinite justice and as such requires an infinite penalty. We as finite beings could never pay it in full. We would be separated from God forever, sharing Satan's eternal doom. God, being infinite, could pay such a penalty, but it wouldn't be just for Him to do so because He is not a member of our race.

190 + *Dave Hunt*

So in love and mercy God became a man through the virgin birth. He, of course, did not cease to be God, for that would be impossible; nor will He ever cease to be man. Jesus Christ is now and will always be the one and only God-man; and because of who He is, He was able to pay the penalty demanded by His own justice—a penalty that we could never pay. Having paid that debt in full, He offers pardon for sins and eternal life as a free gift of His grace to whoever will repent of his sin and believe in Him.

Had the battle ensuing from Satan's rebellion been fought on the basis of sheer power, God would instantly have destroyed Satan. But that would not have served His purpose, since Satan had to be allowed to tempt mankind. Because God loves us and seeks to win our love, it was necessary that we be given full opportunity to choose whichever we believed was most attractive, whether God and the blessings He offers or the entice-ments presented by Satan. That Satan has the power to present the ultimate alternative to God plays an essential role in God's plan for mankind.

Suppose a king seeks a bride among the women of his realm. He faces several problems. He doesn't want the woman he chooses to marry him for position, wealth, or power—for the *gifts* he may give her—but because she loves *him*. Therefore he must not command her to marry him even though he has the authority to do so. Moreover, she must be free to choose anyone else whom she might desire. If she truly loves another, then the king would not want to coerce her, for if forced to be his wife she would always be resentful and unhappy. For the same reason God will not force anyone to spend eternity with Him. That would turn heaven into hell and fill it with unhappy, resentful people. Our hearts must be won.

What if the king tells the woman he desires to marry that she can choose whomever she will instead of him—but then he banishes from his realm all other men who might possibly be his rivals for her affection? That would be unfair and it would make the contest for her love a sham. Satan, as the ultimate rival suitor for the affection of mankind, will not be banished by God until the end of history. In serving God's purposes to win a bride for His Son, Satan will seduce the ecumenical world church into becoming the bride of the Antichrist.

Though his show of love is a pretense, lust thinly disguised, Satan has power, wealth, success, and seemingly the ultimate pleasure to offer those who will worship him. God is saying to mankind: "If Satan's way is really best, if he has more genuine love, joy, pleasure, and satisfaction to offer than I have, then by all means follow him." David as psalmist, having weighed the alternatives and having seen the truth, declared:

> Thou wilt show me the path of life: In thy presence *is* fullness of joy; at thy right hand there are pleasures for evermore (Psalm 16:11).

What about that second coming? Christians have often made the mistake of setting a date for Christ's return. We do not believe that is possible. On the other hand, biblical prophecies do give us many clues concerning the timing of the second coming in relation to other events, some of which are already casting their shadows out of the future across today's world scene.

15 | *A Question of Timing*

I T IS EXCITING TO REMEMBER that through Daniel God gave the exact date of the triumphal entry of the Messiah into Jerusalem which is now celebrated as Palm Sunday, a fact to which we have already referred. While no date was given for the birth of the Messiah, there were definite criteria laid out in the prophecies that would enable Israel to know when (and when not) to look for Him. The same is true of the second coming. We have already given a number of reasons that our generation has for expecting its soon occurrence—reasons which no past generation had. Now we wish to become more specific about the timing of that imminent fabulous event.

As we have already noted, it is essential to distinguish between the rapture and the second coming. At the rapture Christ does not come to earth itself, but catches His bride, the church, up from the earth to meet Him in the air and then takes her to heaven. The second coming occurs about seven years later, when Christ comes to earth to confront the Antichrist and his armies at Armageddon and to rescue Israel. He then remains here to rule over the nations of the earth from David's throne in Jerusalem for 1000 years.

There are no special events that must precede the rapture and thus no signs to tell us when it is near, because the church is to expect Christ at any moment. The signs are for *Israel* to tell her when the second coming is about to occur. Of course, as the signs for the second coming accumulate, as they are doing today, eventually the rapture *must* take place. It is certainly legitimate to attempt to understand how near we may be to our Lord's second coming by examining current events for the "last-days signs" which the Bible offers.

It is helpful first of all to see how the *timing* of Christ's first advent was related to other key events. We then have some insights in looking for similar events-related *timing* with regard to His second coming. Paul wrote, "When the fullness of time was come, God sent forth his Son . . ." (Galatians 4:4). He could only come *at that time* to a particular place and special people at a propitious point in their history and in the history of the world.

We have already seen the part played by the Roman Empire in affecting the location of Jesus' birth and in determining the manner of His death in fulfillment of prophecy. And we have noted that just as the Roman Empire had to be in existence at the first advent, so it must be present in revived form for the second coming. What else determined the specific timing of Christ's first coming?

Isaiah declared that a forerunner would precede the Messiah to cry "Prepare ye the way of the Lord" (Isaiah 40:3). Consequently, it was useless for Israel to look for her Messiah until this special messenger sent by God had come upon the scene to set the stage for Him. Malachi reconfirmed this prophecy (Malachi 3:1), then put a further limitation upon the timing of the Messiah's appearance: "The Lord, whom ye seek, shall suddenly come to his temple . . ." (3:1). The word *Lord*, which was used by Isaiah also, was a puzzle to the rabbis. How could the Messiah be the Lord Himself, i.e. *Jehovah*?

That the Messiah indeed had to be God come to earth as a man was made very clear by the prophets. Speaking through Malachi, God said, "He shall prepare the way before *me*"— and that it was *His temple* to which He would suddenly come. Other prophecies were equally clear, but we must defer that subject until later.

From the above, we discover two conditions that had to prevail for Israel to expect her Messiah to appear. It would have been foolish to look for Him at any other time—and still is.

One factor was the presence of the *messenger* who was to set the stage for His coming, and the other was the presence of the *temple*.

Malachi's conclusive statement that the Messiah would suddenly "come to his temple" meant that it was futile to look for Him during Israel's Babylonian captivity. The temple did not exist at that time, having been destroyed by Nebuchadnezzar's army. Therefore those who hoped that the Messiah would come and rescue Israel in those days hoped in vain. The temple had to be rebuilt first, and that would not occur until the days of Ezra.

Just as obviously, the Messiah could not come after the rebuilt temple was destroyed by Titus in 70 A.D. If He hadn't come by then, it was too late and still is today. Yet devout Jewish families often leave an empty place at the table when they eat, particularly at Passover time, in case Elijah should suddenly appear. That seems to make sense according to one of Malachi's prophecies—"Behold, I will send you Elijah the prophet before the coming of the great and dreadful day of the Lord" (Malachi 4:5)—but it ignores what Malachi said about the temple. Leaving an empty chair for Elijah has been, and still is, a foolish and vain gesture, for there has been no temple for the Messiah to "suddenly come to" for the last 1900 years.

Christians, who believe that John the Baptist was "Elijah" the forerunner (Matthew 17:10-13) and that Jesus of Nazareth was the Messiah, are convinced that Malachi 3:1 was fulfilled when Christ "suddenly came to" Herod's temple in Jerusalem just before His crucifixion. In abruptly throwing out those who had desecrated God's house with their unlawful money-changing and commerce, He fulfilled yet another prophecy: "The zeal of thine house hath eaten me up" (Psalm 69:9), a Scripture which occurred to the disciples immediately (John 2:17).

Many biblical prophecies have a double application. If Malachi 3:1 and Psalm 69:9 are in this category, then the temple will have to be rebuilt yet again before the second coming—and it will need to be cleansed by the Messiah once more. This will, in fact, happen. The question is not *whether* Israel will rebuild the temple, but only *when*. In spite of the numerous preparations already underway, however, any discussion of that subject is largely speculative at this time. There are other circumstances of which we can be more certain in establishing the timing of Christ's second coming, and to those we turn our attention.

We must first of all consider other factors involved in the timing of the Messiah's *first coming*. In blessing his sons before he died, Jacob (Israel) made this amazing prophecy: "The scepter shall not depart from Judah, nor a lawgiver from between his feet, until Shiloh come; and unto him [Shiloh, the Messiah] shall the gathering of the people be" (Genesis 49:10). In about 7 A.D. the Romans took from the Jewish leadership the right to pronounce the death penalty, resulting in Christ's death by crucifixion instead of by stoning, the Jewish means of execution. This deprivation of legal authority was the final act of removing the scepter and power of lawgiving from Judah. It had not previously happened, not even during the Babylonian captivity. Thus the Messiah had to be *born before* 7 A.D. *and killed after*, which of course was true of Jesus.

It is clear from these few prophecies (and others could be mentioned) that the Messiah must already have come. Yet Israel is still waiting for Him in apparent ignorance of the Scriptures. For those religious Jews who know that it must be in place for the Messiah it is easy to see the importance of rebuilding the temple. However, they refuse to admit that He has *already* come and are not aware that their rebuilding of the temple will help to set the stage for His *second coming*—and also for the rise of the Antichrist, for whom the temple must also be in place (2 Thessalonians 2:4).

We have already referred to some of Daniel's remarkable prophecies. He made it clear that the Messiah's kingdom would be established at a time that could not be reconciled with the political situation prevailing during Christ's first advent: "In the days of these kings shall the God of heaven set up a kingdom which shall never be destroyed . . ." (Daniel 2:44). As we know, Daniel was referring to the kings represented by the ten toes of the "fourth [world] kingdom" (2:40) depicted by the image in Nebuchadnezzar's dream, which historians recognize as the Roman Empire.

The "days of these kings" had not yet come during Christ's first advent. The empire was ruled not by *ten kings* but by Caesar from his palace in Rome. Thus Israel's Davidic kingdom could not have been reestablished at the time when Israel rejected Jesus for not doing so. The rabbis should have known this but did not. However, those ten kings will be represented upon earth when Christ comes back to set up that "kingdom which shall never be destroyed." There must be a *second coming*.

That Christ *must* come again to reign personally and visibly over this earth from Jerusalem is as basic as the Christmas story. We have already noted that in announcing to her that she would give birth to the Messiah, the angel Gabriel told the virgin Mary:

> He shall be great, and shall be called the Son of the Highest; and the Lord God shall give unto him the throne of his father David; and he shall reign over the house of Jacob forever, and of his kingdom there shall be no end (Luke 1:32,33).

We are reminded annually of this promise by the thousands of choirs singing around the world at that special season of the year such soul-stirring choruses as Handel's: "And He shall reign for ever and ever and ever and ever. . . !" Quite obviously, this reign was not established on earth the first time Christ came. That fact, as we have noted, was a major reason why many refused then, and still refuse, to believe that Jesus of Nazareth was the Messiah.

It is therefore clear that if Christ really is the Messiah of Israel, as Christians believe Him to be, then He *must return to earth* to fulfill these unmistakable prophecies. Only then will the Messiah's coming have fulfilled the angels' promise:

198 ◆ *Dave Hunt*

"Peace on earth!" Yet many who call themselves Christians no longer believe what they sing in carols at Christmas. For a large part of the church today the promise that Christ will literally return to this earth to reign on the throne of David has joined the realm of pleasant and melodious myth.

Since Christ and Antichrist must meet face-to-face upon earth in final conflict, the coming of each must be timed to bring them together at that climactic event. So we cannot consider the question of the timing of Christ's second coming without giving careful attention to the Antichrist's appearing. The coming *revelation of Jesus Christ* to His bride, to Israel, and to the world, and the concurrent *revelation of the Antichrist*, are so interrelated that neither can take place without the other. Nor can either come to pass except "in the fullness of time" when the world stage upon which this incredible drama will be played out is fully set with the props and the supporting actors and actresses all in place.

Paul wrote, ". . . and then shall that wicked [one] be revealed, whom the Lord . . . shall destroy with the brightness of his coming" (2 Thessalonians 2:8). Obviously, if one effect of Christ's second coming will be to destroy the Antichrist, then Christ cannot return to earth again in power and glory to reign on David's throne until the Antichrist has first established his own counterfeit worldwide kingdom. But the Antichrist cannot be revealed until the true church, the bride of Christ, has been removed from the earth. That fact will become clear as we proceed. Thus we see once again that the rapture and the second coming are two separate events.

What about the teaching among Christians that Nero was the Antichrist and that the events prophesied by the apostle John in the Book of Revelation have already occurred? That idea can be dismissed very easily. There is no record that Christ visibly descended from heaven to destroy Nero, yet Scripture is very clear in stating that He will do so to destroy the Antichrist. No historian has yet claimed that events such as those described in the following Scriptures pertaining to the second coming of Christ have already occurred either at 70 A.D. or at any other time in the past:

> For as the lightning cometh out of the east and shineth even unto the west, so shall also the coming of the Son of man be (Matthew 24:27).

> And they shall look upon me whom they have pierced [to death on the cross], and they shall mourn for him . . . (Zechariah 12:10).

> Behold, he cometh with clouds; and every eye shall see him, and they also which pierced him; and all kindreds of the earth shall wail because of him. Even so, Amen (Revelation 1:7).

Numerous Scriptures, such as Revelation 13, make it clear that Antichrist will be in control of the world when Christ returns. It takes the "brightness of his [Christ's] coming" to unseat this evil world ruler. Consequently, those who teach that we are now in the millennium, at the end of which Christ will return, or that Christians must take over the world before Christ can return, are leading people astray.

When will the Antichrist rise to power? In view of the *timing* that was involved in Christ's first advent, it is not surprising to discover that Christ's great adversary can also only be revealed *at a particular time in relation to other conditions and events.* Paul wrote, "Now ye know what withholdeth [prevents] that he [Antichrist] might be revealed *in his time* . . ." (2 Thessalonians 2:6).

Obviously something specific must occur first in order for the revelation of Antichrist to take place. Indeed, it cannot happen until *then.* This fact is very clear. Paul had apparently already explained in oral teaching what was preventing Antichrist's rise to power before he wrote his second epistle to the Thessalonians, for he reminds them, "And now *ye know* what withholdeth. . . ."

Clearly, from Paul's day until now, something specific has been preventing the Antichrist from being revealed. Could the fact that the revival of the Roman Empire has not yet occurred, which we have seen must occur before the Antichrist can rise to power, be the hindrance to which Paul refers? No, for he goes on to say, "*He* who now letteth will let, until *he* be taken out of the way" (2 Thessalonians 2:7). Thus it is both *something* (an event) and *someone* that prevents the Antichrist from being revealed. Moreover, this one who "hinders" must be "taken out of the way" or the Antichrist cannot come forward and do his evil work. Until that occurs, there is no point in looking for the Antichrist or for the second coming of Christ.

Who could be preventing the Antichrist from being revealed? He must be stronger than Satan, for the Antichrist comes "after the working of Satan with all power" (2 Thessalonians 2:9). Certainly only God is stronger than Satan. Therefore He is the One who hinders. God could not be acting alone, however, but through another agency, because He cannot be "taken out of the way." He is ever present everywhere. Nor could Paul have had Christ in mind. He had already left this earth, and the second coming does not occur until after the Antichrist has been revealed.

Could Paul be referring to the power of God operating through some specially chosen man or woman? No, because Satan has been prevented from establishing the Antichrist for more than 1900 years—a period of time far exceeding the lifespan of any individual. We are forced to conclude that "he who now letteth" refers to God operating through a continuing corporate body of believers, the church, which has been in existence since Pentecost. It is *the church* which must be "taken out of the way" (to heaven) for Antichrist to be revealed "in his time."

Paul seemed to be referring to the rapture, that incredible event unique to Christianity, when Christ would instantly take His bride, the church, to be with Him in heaven. That assumption would fit with the phrase *ye know*, for Paul had explained the rapture to the Thessalonian believers in great detail:

> For the Lord himself shall descend from heaven with a shout, with the voice of the archangel and with the trump of

> God; and the dead in Christ shall rise first; then we which are
> alive and remain shall be caught up together with them in the
> clouds, to meet the Lord in the air; and so shall we ever be with
> the Lord (1 Thessalonians 4:16,17).

Christ had promised His disciples: "In my Father's house
are many mansions . . . I go to prepare a place for you . . . [and]
I will come again, and receive you unto myself; that where I
am, there ye may be also" (John 14:2,3). This was the great
hope of the early Christians. To the Philippians Paul wrote:
"Our conversation is in [of] heaven; from whence also we look
for the Savior, the Lord Jesus Christ" (Philippians 3:20). And
to Titus: "Looking for that blessed hope . . ." (Titus 2:13).
Hebrews 9:28 says, "Unto them that look for him shall he
appear the second time without sin unto salvation." A posttribulation rapture would have the church looking for the
Antichrist, who would have to appear first, not for Christ.

One does not "look" for someone unless that one is expected momentarily. The hope of the *imminent* return of
Christ pervades the New Testament. That this was the expec-
tation of the early church cannot be denied, regardless of how
one wishes to interpret the Bible today. When Paul listed the
reasons why he was confident that the Thessalonians had
become true Christians, he included, along with the recognition that they had "turned to God from idols to serve the living
and true God," the fact that they "wait[ed] for his Son from
heaven" (1 Thessalonians 1:9,10). That expectancy was considered one of the marks of a genuine believer in Paul's day.

Whether the church would be raptured before or after the
great tribulation—or not until the end of the millennium—has
long been a point of sharp controversy among Christians.
There are many perspectives from which this question could
be addressed. We have no time to deal with most of the
arguments, nor is that necessary. Why the church must be
removed from earth before the Antichrist can be revealed will
be presented in the next chapter.

As world events hasten history to its climax, the importance

of understanding and heeding prophecy becomes clear. Had
John the Baptist, Christ's disciples, and the rabbis heeded *all*
of the prophecies, they would not have expected Christ to
establish His kingdom in their day. The *timing* was wrong.
Christ chided the two disciples on the road to Emmaus:

> O fools, and slow of heart to believe all that the prophets
> have spoken; ought not Christ to have suffered these things,
> and to enter into his glory?
> And beginning at Moses and all the prophets, he expounded
> unto them in all the Scriptures the things concerning himself
> (Luke 24:25-27).

The reprimand that Christ gave these two disciples seems
harsh, but it tells us how He views those who fail to heed "*all*
that the prophets have spoken.*" He would say the same thing
to us today. Very few Christians have spent the time and effort
necessary to understand, much less do they believe, *all* of the
prophecy given to us in Scripture. No wonder so many church
leaders in our day still overlook the criteria that so unequivo-
cally determine the *timing* of Christ's return.

To summarize, the data we have considered thus far seem to
indicate that the second coming cannot occur until five related
events have taken place first: 1) unprecedented spiritual deception in the world and the great apostasy in the church;
2) the rapture of true believers; 3) the revival of the Roman
Empire; 4) the joining of all religions under a pseudo-Chris-
tianity and the leadership of the Pope; and 5) the revelation of the
Antichrist and establishment of his worldwide rule. There can be
no doubt that as never before in history points 1), 3), and 4) are
well on their way to fulfillment. The rapture must be very near.

One vital and difficult question remains: What could possibly cause rival nations to unite in a new world government
and rival faiths to join together in a new world religion? What
extraordinary event could cause all of earth's inhabitants to
submit to the Antichrist as world dictator—and even to worship him? There is one surprising, yet obvious, answer.

16 | *A Tale of Two Comings*

M ANY CHRISTIANS BELIEVE THAT a devastating war of global proportions will be the means whereby a desperate world will submit to the leadership of the Antichrist. Some writers even suggest that the rapture will take place simultaneously with a nuclear holocaust so that the world will assume that the missing Christians are among the victims and thus not suspect that they have been taken bodily to heaven. That scenario, however, would rob the rapture of its most powerful effect, as we shall see.

Moreover, to suggest that World War III will usher in the great tribulation conflicts with Paul's statement that the day of the Lord will begin suddenly, when the world thinks it has at last achieved peace and safety. That view also makes little sense. Two appalling wars of global proportions that cost tens of millions of lives have not produced the Antichrist; nor would a third. It would be more likely to increase tensions and jealousies and leave the world more divided than ever before, with wounds and bitterness that might require years or even generations to heal. No, preparing the world to embrace the Antichrist will require something truly extraordinary. Let us consider what that could be.

The unprecedented events which shook Eastern Europe in 1989 demonstrated that, in spite of the swift and miraculous changes which occurred, the general public still had its own mind and could be very difficult to control. Gorbachev still faces many challenges to his program of *perestroika*. In spite of

204 ◆ Dave Hunt

his great popularity as the one who made new freedoms possible, the ultimate outcome still hangs in the balance as this book goes to press.

In some of the satellite countries such as East Germany and Czechoslovakia the euphoria of newfound freedom quickly turned to disappointment. Enraged mobs went back to the streets making fresh demands upon the new regimes that they had welcomed with such fervor only a few days before. In Romania the people were, within a week, marching in the streets again protesting what they perceived as a betrayal of their trust by the new leaders. That country could have another bloody revolution if current trends continue. These recent experiences provide fresh evidence that it will take something far more remarkable than we can fully imagine to cause the world to unite under the Antichrist, let alone to worship him.

Whatever it is that effects this transformation, it must impact simultaneously the entire human race, not merely a particular country or region. The Antichrist will control the whole earth: "Power was given him over all kindreds and tongues and nations. And all that dwell upon the earth shall worship him..." (Revelation 13:7,8). What could possibly bring mankind—even the Muslims, Jews, Hindus, and Chinese—to this point?

The ideal event for effecting such a dramatic alchemy—and doing it swiftly in one stroke—is the *rapture*. In fact, *the rapture is the only conceivable event that could cause the entire world to unite in a new world government and a new world religion and to submit suddenly to the leadership of the Antichrist as the world dictator.* Here we have another compelling reason why the rapture must precede the revelation of the Antichrist and the great tribulation. Let us try to envision that incredible event.

Imagine the moral and spiritual vacuum that would result if all those who proclaimed the truth of the gospel and who lived it and were thus "salt and light" to the world were instantly removed from this earth. Families, neighborhoods, schools, businesses, and churches would be left without any influence for Christ and God. The Spirit of God would cease convicting the consciences of those who had already rejected Christ. The snowball effect of such an instantaneous worldwide removal of all moral restraint would be beyond comprehension. Humanism would at last be unhindered to prove its sufficiency to create the ideal life.

Equally staggering would be the social and political impact of scores of millions of people suddenly vanishing from this earth. The event itself would be so sudden, so universal, and so eerie that its shattering effect upon the emotional stability of survivors is impossible even to imagine. Hundreds of millions would have witnessed personally the terrifying, instantaneous disappearance of one or more persons and would have found it beyond belief. The effect of seeing with their own eyes what their minds knew was impossible could drive millions mad.

Driverless cars and pilotless aircraft alone would account not only for worldwide devastation but for inconceivable panic. Interrupted surgeries, empty lecterns, unmanned rescue vehicles, decimated communications systems, the disruption of goods and services—life as we know it would descend into an abyss of chaos and human carnage. The shock, bewilderment, and stark horror of this historic global event would paralyze the world. Any explanation would initially be completely beyond the comprehension and even the imagination of the most brilliant minds.

An unreasoning terror of not knowing what had happened and when it might be repeated would grip the world. Was it a mass abduction? What galactic force was toying with mankind? What else might this incredible and apparently merciless power do? What was the fate of those who had vanished? Had they been abducted to some distant planet as slaves? Or had they simply been disconnected from the physical universe and had ceased to exist? *Who would be taken next?*

Governing bodies, from local school boards to universities and the corporate giants of business and industry, from city councils to state and national congresses, from senates and parliaments to the President's cabinet, the Pentagon, and the

Kremlin would be meeting in emergency sessions—with missing members in many cases. The United Nations would be at a loss to explain what had happened or to plan a course of action to prevent a recurrence.

It would take months to restore order out of the incalculable chaos. The credit card, banking, and insurance confusion would be almost impossible to untangle. In many cases large segments of business and industry would be paralyzed by the disappearance of the operators of sophisticated computers and key pieces of equipment. Engineers and scientists with specialized skills would be missing, with no one to unravel the puzzles left behind.

The disruption on a global scale would be beyond calculation. Hardest hit would be the United States. If there are only a quarter of the born-again Christians that polls indicate, the rapture would decimate this country, a possible reason why the United States is not mentioned in prophecy. Professing Christians hold key positions everywhere. Their disappearance would cause the United States to teeter on the brink of collapse, to be possibly taken under the wing of Western Europe, where the church is largely dead and a far smaller segment of society would be missing.

In China or Africa there may well be far more missing, but those who have vanished will be mostly common laborers whose ranks can quickly be filled by the unemployed and, if need be, by students and army rank and file. In Russia it will be the same, with millions missing, but few who held positions of importance. A surprising number will have vanished from Israel, while in Muslim, Hindu, and Buddhist countries the number will be minimal. The global sense, however, of irrecoverable loss and of bewilderment and consternation will be shared by all mankind.

The rapture is clearly the only conceivable event that could create the worldwide panic and stark terror, the utter hopelessness and desperation that could cause mankind to welcome a world dictator. In fact that would seem to be the logical outcome. The sudden mass disappearance of scores of millions of persons from all over the world would almost certainly give those who remained in every nation a new sense of belonging to one another, of needing one another, of having together survived a cataclysmic disaster with cosmic implications. A close unity would be spontaneously created as the world faced the sheer magnitude of the catastrophe.

At first there would be no rational, scientific explanation. The one possibility that no one would even consider—not even those who once were taught it and believed it—would be that the rapture of the church had occurred. God will not allow the truth to be known. Then out of the chaos the Antichrist will arise, a man with all of the power of Satan, who will perform signs and wonders, present a "scientific" and assuring explanation for what happened, and offer a sensible and hopeful course of action.

The entire world would suddenly have come under an overpowering delusion sent from God Himself. There would be no conscience any longer to pull people back from the brink of doom. Not that mankind would immediately go morally berserk. No, just as Satan seduced Eve to raise her self-image, to become a better person, even to become like God, so he will seduce the entire world:

> And then shall that wicked [one] be revealed... whose coming is after the working of Satan with all power and signs and lying wonders, and with all deceivableness of unrighteousness in them that perish, because they received not the love of the truth, that they might be saved.
> And for this cause God shall send them strong delusion, that they should believe a lie, that they all might be damned who believed not the truth, but had pleasure in unrightousness (2 Thessalonians 2:8-12).

One can only speculate as to what convincing hypothesis the Antichrist will provide to account for the mass disappearance. There are several explanations already in circulation, any one of which might be accepted when the rapture occurs. Many New Agers, for example, are expecting the sudden disappearance of tens of millions of people around the world. It will take place when a large enough segment of mankind is ready to make a quantum leap to a higher dimension of consciousness, thereby creating a new species: *Homonoeticus*. At that time all those who are not spiritually tuned in and are thus not ready to participate in this historic evolutionary leap will be instantly removed to a nonphysical dimension where their karma will have to catch up with them before they will be allowed back on the physical plane. So goes one popular theory.

Some UFO cult members have also received "revelations" concerning an impending mass disappearance. The day is soon coming, according to various "transmissions," when the extraterrestrials who allegedly put mankind on this planet in the first place will take over to prevent ecological collapse or a nuclear holocaust. At that time, when the "new world order" is imposed, all those who are not willing to submit to it will be instantly beamed aboard a fleet of UFO's. These rebels will be taken to a slave planet where their minds will be reprogrammed before they will be allowed back on earth. To such flights of fantasy have man's follies led him!

The leaders behind the "World Instant of Cooperation" (a time when hundreds of millions of people in every country simultaneously pray, chant, and meditate annually for peace), also believe that a significant proportion of mankind will have to be removed in order to "cleanse" the planet. While their "revelation" calls for a gradual removal of millions over an extended period, an instantaneous disappearance would, of course, accomplish the same objective. A leader in that movement writes:

> Many changes will soon take place in the world . . . through the force of nature as she seeks, by law, to reclaim her planet. . . .
> To do this she must eliminate the force of negative energy emanating from the race consciousness of man that is causing the imbalance. . . . had more people risen to a higher level of consciousness before this time, the spiritual energy would have corrected the imbalance and nature would not have to take matters into her hands. . . .

> Nature will soon enter into her cleansing cycle. Those who
> reject the earth changes... will be removed during the next
> two decades.[1]

There are professing Christians, actively engaged in "world
evangelism" and who believe that the church is supposed to
take over the world for Christ, who also expect a sudden mass
exodus. It is not the rapture, however, which they anticipate.
(Of course, true Christians will be taken at the rapture whether
they believe in it or not.) They take the words of Jesus, "Then
shall two be in the field; the one shall be taken and the other
left" (Matthew 24:40) not to mean the rapture but the instant
removal to judgment of the "carnal Christians" who are not
part of the "last-days great move of God." These are the ones
who are holding back blessing for the church, the "gloom-and-
doomers" who believe in the rapture and Armageddon, whom
the Lord will suddenly remove so that His work can go forward
in great revival, unhindered by their "negativism."

For those left behind, these are four different theories for
explaining the sudden mass disappearance of millions. Signifi-
cantly, though held by different groups, they all have one factor
in common: It is the *unworthy* who are taken away! Certainly
those who remain will consider themselves fortunate to still be
on earth no matter what explanation is accepted. Each will be
only too happy to have the Antichrist's special number (probably a microchip implant) placed on hand or forehead as his
guarantee of protection from any future disappearance.

Gradually, with the reestablishment of order and the continual unfolding of Antichrist's incredible powers, a new sense of
pride and destiny will take hold. There will be unanimous
agreement that what seemed to be a universal calamity was
actually a favorable event of great significance for the evolu-
tion of the human species. The unfit have been eliminated and
those remaining will experience a growing awareness that
within each of them a mysterious inner transformation has
taken place. A new and superior species fitted for a higher
destiny is emerging on planet Earth!

There will be a growing excitement as the realization deepens that a New Age has dawned—a golden era of unprecedented opportunity, of peace and worldwide cooperation bringing unlimited prosperity for the human race. Mankind will no longer be divided into competitive nation-states and quarreling religious factions, but will realize its long-forgotten universal brotherhood and be united once and for all in the single (and at last seemingly attainable) goal of turning this world into a paradise. The dream of the Carl Sagans of earth being welcomed into an intergalactic community will have been given new substance.[2]

Churches will be filled to overflowing. There will be a great revival of the false "Christianity" that will hail the Antichrist as "Christ" and under which all faiths will join in the new world religion of Antichrist worship. The apostasy, which Paul said must precede the revelation of the Antichrist (2 Thessalonians 2:3), and which is already in progress, will have done its work. The sudden removal by the rapture of all those who had attempted to stand for sound doctrine will have left an apostate "Christian" church which, under the Pope's leadership, becomes a haven for all religions.

Again the necessity of the *pretrib* rapture is seen. Genuine Christians would expose and oppose the Antichrist, so they must be "taken out of the way" to allow him and his followers full freedom to create their humanistic Utopia. God intends to demonstrate fully the truth of the gospel: that there is no hope for mankind except through the salvation that is freely offered to all in Christ Jesus. To prove this fact, Satan and his earthly followers must be given the fullest opportunity to turn the world into a paradise if they can. "The god of this world" must rule the world for a time through Antichrist—and the removal of all genuine Christians is essential to that purpose.

True Christians would be compelled by the Holy Spirit within them—if they were present in the world after the Antichrist came to power—to refuse to take the mark of the beast or to worship his image. As a result, they would all be killed. There is no indication that God protects believers during the great tribulation. On the contrary, we are clearly told:

> And it was given unto him [Antichrist] to make war with the saints and to overcome them . . . and he [the false prophet] had power to . . . cause that as many as would not worship the image of the beast should be killed . . . and that no man might buy or sell, save [except] he that had the mark . . . of the beast . . . (Revelation 13:7,15-18).

Surely the church, Christ's bride, must have been removed, for the Antichrist could not make war with and overcome her against whom our Lord said, "The gates of hell shall not prevail" (Matthew 16:18). Then who are these "saints"? They can only be those who have not come under the strong delusion to believe the lie because they previously never heard and rejected the gospel. Millions will believe in Christ during the great tribulation and will pay for their newfound faith with their lives. John tells us:

> After this I beheld . . . [in heaven] a great multitude, which no man could number, of all nations, and kindreds, and people, and tongues . . . before the throne and before the Lamb, clothed with white robes. . . .
> These are they which *came out of great tribulation*, and have washed their robes, and made them white in the blood of the Lamb (Revelation 7:9,14).

A posttribulation rapture would hardly be a "blessed hope." In fact, it would be a nonevent, for there would be few if any Christians left alive to rapture at that time. Could any Christian take Antichrist's mark and thus survive to be raptured at the end of the great tribulation? Indeed not! The Bible warns:

> If any man worship the beast and his image, and receive his mark in his forehead, or in his hand, the same shall drink of the wine of the wrath of God, which is poured out without mixture into the cup of his indignation; and he shall be tormented with fire and brimstone in [hell] . . . (Revelation 14:9,10).

So the pretribulation rapture of the church removes the restraining influence of God operating through millions of Christians, which makes it possible for the Antichrist to be revealed and to pursue his program of world dominion unhindered. It also removes the church from this earth, in fulfillment of God's promise to keep her from the wrath that will be poured out upon the ungodly (1 Thessalonians 1:10; 5:9; Revelation 3:10). In his vision, John saw indescribable supernatural worldwide destruction moving "every mountain and island . . . out of their places." He heard God's voice commanding seven angels to "pour out the vials of the wrath of God upon the earth" (Revelation 16:1). The bride of the Lamb (2 Corinthians 11:2; Ephesians 5:31-33) will not be present to experience that wrath.

Just as Noah was taken off the earth and placed in the ark of safety before the flood, and Lot was removed from Sodom to make way for its destruction, so the church will be taken from earth before God's judgment falls upon it in unprecedented and worldwide devastation. Paul reminded the believers in Thessalonica:

> For when *they* [the ungodly] shall say, Peace and safety, then sudden destruction cometh upon *them* [not upon *us*]. . . .
>
> But *ye, brethren* [in contrast to *they/them*], are not in darkness, that that day should overtake *you* as a thief. . . .
>
> For God hath not appointed *us* [in contrast again to *they/them*] to wrath, but to obtain salvation by our Lord Jesus Christ. . . .
>
> [So] rest with *us*, when the Lord Jesus shall be revealed from heaven with his mighty angels, in flaming fire taking vengeance on *them that know not God*, and that obey not the gospel of our Lord Jesus Christ . . . (1 Thessalonians 5:3,4,9; 2 Thessalonians 1:7,8, emphasis added).

Many Christians, of course, object to the pretribulation rapture, the effects of which we have just described. They do so on the grounds that it would require Christ to return *twice* to earth: once *before* the great tribulation to rapture His church, and then again *afterward* to annihilate the Antichrist and his forces surrounding Jerusalem and to rescue Israel. "Where in the New Testament does it state that there will be *two* second comings or even *two phases* to the second coming?" is the seemingly logical question asked by those who reject the idea of a "secret rapture."

The obvious response is to ask in turn: "Where in the Old Testament does it declare that there will be *two* comings of the Messiah?" Nowhere does it say so. None of the prophets stated it in so many words—but the implication was clearly there. As we have already seen, it was impossible to put into one event and into a single time frame what the Hebrew prophets said about the Messiah: that He would be killed, and yet that He would establish and govern an everlasting kingdom; that He would be rejected by Israel, and yet that He would reign forever on David's throne. *There had to be two comings.* There was no other way to reconcile what otherwise would have been hopelessly contradictory prophecies.

It is not surprising, then, that the New Testament prophecies concerning the second coming present a similar problem and require a similar solution. One simply cannot fit into one event and one time frame what the New Testament says about the return of Christ. We know, for example, that He must return to accomplish two purposes: 1) to catch the church up to meet Him in the air and take her home to His Father's house of "many mansions"; and 2) to come visibly to earth itself in power and glory to destroy the Antichrist, stop the destruction at Armageddon, rescue Israel's surviving remnant, and set up the millennial kingdom. The two accomplishments are so diverse that logistically they would not fit into one event.

Moreover, several Scriptures refer to these great happenings as though they were *not* part of the same occurrence. Paul writes: "Now we beseech you, brethren, by the coming of our Lord Jesus Christ, *and* by our gathering together unto him" (2 Thessalonians 2:1). It sounds as though the *coming* is distinct from *our gathering together unto Him.* Surely Christ's coming in power and glory to earth to punish the ungodly is not the same event as His gathering Christians in the air to take them home to a heavenly reward.

One coming is for Israel, the other for the church. These two events have nothing in common and could hardly take place at the same time. Paul refers to one as "the glorious appearing" and the other as "that blessed hope" (Titus 2:13). One is the visible display of His power and glory in judgment upon the world, and the other is the catching away of His bride to a heavenly marriage and honeymoon in a secret rapture purposely hidden from unbelievers.

Christ's coming to earth to "stand in that day upon the mount of Olives" (Zechariah 14:4) is hardly compatible with the promise that we will "meet the Lord in the air: and so shall we ever be with the Lord" (1 Thessalonians 4:17). His coming "with ten thousands of his saints to execute judgment upon all [the ungodly]" (Jude 1:14,15) could hardly be the same happening as "the dead shall be raised incorruptible, and we shall be changed" (1 Corinthians 15:52). His visible coming in power and great glory like lightning streaking across the sky (Matthew 24:27) when "every eye shall see him" (Revelation 1:7) hardly seems to be describing the same thing as "I will come again and receive you unto myself, that where I am, there ye may be also" (John 14:3).

Christ brings with Him to Armageddon the "armies which were in heaven...clothed in fine linen, white and clean" (Revelation 19:14). Since the heavenly marriage occurs earlier in this same chapter the implication is clear that His bride "arrayed in fine linen, clean and white" (verse 8), who will never thereafter be separated from Him (*and so shall we ever be with the Lord*), is by His side in resurrected bodies returning with Him in triumph to earth to reign.

There are further reasons why there must yet be *two comings*. Not only are the two tasks which Christ returns to accomplish so diverse that they do not fit well into one event, but the conditions prevailing upon earth when He returns clearly describe *two different time periods*. Christ stated, for example, that His coming would be during a time of peace, prosperity, business, and pleasure—a time when the last thing the world expects is judgment:

> But as the days of Noah were, so shall also the coming of the Son of man be.
>
> For as in the days that were before the flood they were eating and drinking, marrying and giving in marriage, until the day that Noah entered into the ark, and knew not until the flood came, and took them all away, so shall also the coming of the Son of man be (Matthew 24:37-39).

Jesus could hardly be describing His second coming at the end of the great tribulation after God's wrath has brought destruction and the world's armies are in the midst of the battle of Armageddon. At that time there would not be the usual "working in the field" and "grinding at the mill" of normal life, much less the feasting and pleasure characteristic of the world just before the flood. He seems to be describing the period that Paul had in mind when he wrote, "When they shall say, Peace and safety."

The last thing the preflood world expected was judgment from God. Yet by the time of the second coming at Armageddon the world of that day will already have been conscious that God's judgment is being poured out upon her and will have cried out "to the mountains and rocks, Fall on us, and hide us from...the wrath of the Lamb" (Revelation 6:16). Clearly there yet *must* be *two comings*. Nor have we exhausted the reasons for this view by any means.

Christ comes at a time when even Christians are sound asleep (Matthew 25:5); yet He comes when the terror and destruction will be so great that no one could sleep: "For then shall be great tribulation, such as was not since the beginning of the world to this time, no, nor ever shall be. . . . Immediately after the tribulation . . . they shall see the Son of man coming in the clouds of heaven with power and great glory" (Matthew 24:21,29,30).

He warns that He will come when conditions in the world would cause us not to expect Him: "For in such an hour as ye think not the Son of man cometh" (Matthew 24:44). Yet He comes when the Antichrist has been in control and all life on this planet is about to be destroyed. Surely any Christians on earth who had any idea of prophecy would know that Christ *must* intervene at that point.

Christ warned: "Except [the destruction during] those days should be shortened, there should no flesh be saved . . ." (Matthew 24:22). Then He promised that "for the elect's [Israel's] sake those days shall be shortened" (verse 22). How? Surely only by His coming to this earth visibly in power and glory as described a few verses later—which is definitely *not* the rapture.

Just as it was impossible to put together into one event what the Old Testament said about the Messiah's coming, so it is equally impossible to put together into one event what the New Testament says about His coming again. In the same manner that His disciples should have reasoned that there had to be more than one coming of the Messiah, we too are driven to conclude that two comings of Christ must *yet* occur.

Some suggest that Christ catches up the church to meet Him in the air, then brings her immediately back to earth with Him to rescue Israel and destroy her enemies. That hardly seems a fulfillment of His promise to take His own to His father's house—nor is it the way a bridegroom would treat his bride. Why would Christ leave His bride on this earth during the great tribulation to be wiped out by the Antichrist? Why not take her to heaven, as Revelation 19:7-10 indicates, for some intimate time together before bringing her back to earth to reign with Him for 1000 years?

The pretribulation rapture allows time in heaven for Christ to deal with His own as Scripture declares He will: "We must all appear before the judgment seat of Christ, that every one may receive the things done in his body, according to that he hath done, whether it be good or bad" (2 Corinthians 5:10). Being caught up to meet Him momentarily in the air and then to come right back to earth with Him for Armageddon does not qualify.

While entire books have been written against the pretrib rapture, no argument can nullify the major reasons we have given for its necessity: 1) The *pretribulation rapture* is the *only* event that could conceivably cause the world to unite under and to worship the Antichrist—and it is the *ideal* event to cause such a transformation; 2) the *pretrib rapture* is *essential* to remove the restraining influence of the Holy Spirit operating in Christians and thereby give the Antichrist the free hand he must have; and 3) the *pretrib rapture* is *necessary* because, as we have shown, only by the removal of the church can two prophecies both be fulfilled that would otherwise be in hopeless conflict: a) that the Antichrist will have complete power over all of earth's inhabitants, including "saints," and will kill all who refuse to worship him, and b) that the gates of hell will not prevail against the church.

The mass disappearance of millions of people will have frightened the world into the arms of the universal "Christ" of the new world religion, who will calm their fears and bring order out of chaos. This new faith will not appear to be without reason, for the Antichrist will seemingly prove that he is the Christ by bringing global peace. Reassured, pacified, and fiercely loyal, the world will enthusiastically welcome its "Savior."

17 | *The Arab-Islamic-Israeli Question*

THAT THE SUDDEN MASS disappearance of multiplied millions of people around the world, together with the display of Godlike powers by the Antichrist, could cause mankind to worship him and to adopt the new world religion may make sense for atheists or Hindus or Buddhists and especially for pseudo-Christians. Muslims, however, could be a different story. Like Hindus and Buddhists, the Arab world would have very little firsthand experience of the trauma caused by the rapture. Unlike syncretistic religions, Islam allows no compromise and a large percentage of its followers are extremely fanatical in their faith.

Further doubts are raised about Arab loyalty to the Antichrist (let alone worshiping him) if Daniel 9:27 and Ezekiel 38:11 teach, as many students of prophecy believe, that the Antichrist makes a pact with Israel guaranteeing her safety (a pact which he later breaks to lead an all-out attack upon Israel). Such an arrangement, while it lasts, would make the Antichrist the enemy of Arabs. How then could the nearly 1 billion Muslims be expected to become a part of the Antichrist's worldwide revived Roman Empire?

Here again we see some remarkable developments in the Arab world taking place at this strategic time in history along with the incredible developments in Eastern Europe. The similarities are striking. Much attention has been given to the Iron and Bamboo Curtains of Communism. Worldwide knowledge of the errors and terrors of that system has contributed to its downfall. At the same time little notice has been given to the no less extreme and cruel wall that Islam has erected around Arab countries. Recent developments in the Middle East, however, particularly since Iraq's invasion of Kuwait, are bringing significant changes.

Recent events are causing the world to take notice at last of the Islamic Curtain. Behind that wall of prejudice any religion except Islam is forbidden. Converts to Christianity have not only been imprisoned for abandoning Islam but have been killed in large numbers in Turkey, Afghanistan, Pakistan, and many other Islamic countries, often by their own family members. Freedom of the press and of speech and of assembly along with freedom of religion and the import of Bibles and Christian literature have been denied behind the Islamic Curtain just as behind the Iron Curtain.

The pressure of world opinion applied year after year and the knowledge of the outside world gained through international radio and television networks played an important part in the fall of Communism in Eastern Europe. It was no longer possible to deceive citizens into believing the lie that their economy was better than that of Western countries, once a visible comparison could be made through the knowledge of the West that came via television.

Most important, however, was the fact that the system simply didn't produce the paradise that it had been claimed would result from the practice of Communism. It was the harsh reality of daily experience that could no longer be denied that eventually broke the back of the regimes in Eastern Europe— and must do the same elsewhere, wherever that system is in control. It is inevitable that the same disillusionment will develop in Islamic countries. There is growing evidence that it is happening already.

Islam, which has allied itself with Communist nations against Israel, has produced conditions similar to those behind the Iron Curtain in every Arab country where it has been able to remain in control politically as well as religiously. Like Marxism, Islam has failed to produce the ideal society it promised. Thus many Arab countries today, in spite of their billions of dollars in annual revenues from oil, remain among the most primitive nations in the world, outside of the few large modernized cities. No one can deny that Islam has perpetuated an autocratic feudalism and held back democracy, which is still unknown in Islamic countries. The rights of individual citizens, particularly those of women and minorities, are systematically suppressed, often cruelly and in the name of Allah.

As with Communism, the oppressive totalitarianism of Islam has also brought some moral blessings. Like the Iron and Bamboo Curtains, the Islamic Curtain, while apparently tolerating a great deal of homosexuality, has kept out much of the Western world's decadence—abortion, youthful rebellion, organized crime, drugs, pornography, and other forms of immorality so rampant in nominally "Christian" countries such as the United States. One important fact, however, must be borne in mind: The immorality in the West is recognized as contrary to the teachings of the Bible and is pursued in defiance of Christ rather than in His name, while in Islamic countries much evil is due to the Koran itself and is practiced in the name of Allah and in obedience to his prophet, Muhammad.

No one calls for a Holy War in the name of Christ as is done in the name of Allah. Terrorism and the taking of hostages is not done in the name of Christ, but is done in the name of Allah with good conscience. The IRA do not claim to be Christians but Catholics—and certainly they cannot justify terrorist tactics from the teachings of Jesus. Christ taught us to love our enemies, to turn the other cheek, and He sought to win men's hearts with His love. In contrast, Muhammad taught that Islam should be spread by force, and that those refusing to submit should be killed.

Many of the most important verses throughout the Koran advocate the killing of apostates and non-Muslims. Muhammad himself led 27 invasions, claiming that God had ordered him to spread Islam at the point of the sword. Not only

Muhammad's own kinsmen, the Quraish tribe, but almost all
of Persia and Turkey, for example, originally became Muslims
in this way. The Bani Qareza tribe surrendered to Muhammad
in good faith, laying down their arms, and Muhammad then
killed hundreds of the men and divided the women and money
between himself and Saad Ibn Muaaz as war booty.

While the Koran does not explicitly say so, the teaching in
Islam today is that those who die fighting in its defense go
immediately to paradise. That belief made the Arab armies
virtually invincible. After Muhammad's death they conquered
Persia, Turkey, and all of North Africa, then crossed the
Mediterranean to conquer Spain and were well on their way to
taking all of Europe when they were defeated in A.D. 732 at the
Battle of Tours in France. Thus was the "faith" of Islam taken
to the world. It was either submit to Allah and to the teachings
of his prophet, Muhammad, or die. Such is the shameful
heritage of Islam in those countries which it presently controls.
It is still quite in keeping with their religion for Muslims to
consider it their honorable duty to kill Christians and Jews.

Yes, there were the crusaders, who struck back against the
Arab invaders, but they did so in disobedience to the Bible.
Inspired by Pope Urban II, the members of the First Crusade
went to recover "for the Church" the land that belonged to
Israel. Plundering, raping, and murdering along the way, they
slaughtered all the Muslims and Jews in Jerusalem when they
took that "holy city" in the name of the Roman Catholic
Church. They were acting in direct violation of the teachings
of Jesus, whose cross they claimed to be carrying. Not to be
outdone by Islam's promise of instant paradise for those who
died in *Jihad*, the Pope motivated his troops by offering a
"plenary indulgence remitting all punishments due to sin...
to those who should fall in the war."[1]

The call by various popes for holy wars ranks among the
worst contradictions of true Christianity from the Dark Ages,
and would never be repeated today. The shrill cry of *Jihad*,
however, is still heard and heeded today, for it is in perfect harmony with Islam and with the deeds of its prophet,

Muhammad. It is impossible to understand the current situation in the Middle East, much less anticipate probable future developments there, except in the context of the religion that grips and motivates the Arab world.

We don't have time to deal with Islam thoroughly, but a brief understanding of it is essential, particularly in view of the fact that it is the fastest-growing religion in the world today. It is spreading everywhere and is likely to be encountered no matter where one lives or travels. In an article titled "What Part Will Religion Play in Emerging Global Struggles?" one syndicated columnist reminds us:

> In Chicago, which was once considered the heart of Midwestern America, there are now more Moslems than Methodists, more Buddhists than Presbyterians, more Hindus than Congregationalists. . . .
>
> It's not particularly chic to mix talk about religion and politics, but there is a connection.[2]

Indeed there is a connection, and nowhere is that more apparent than in the Middle East, where Islam is the driving force behind the passion to obliterate the very presence of Israel. Islam means surrender to Allah, the God whose revelations were allegedly dictated to the prophet Muhammad and written down in the Islamic scriptures, the Koran. We can't possibly enumerate the many reasons why the Koran reflects Muhammad's own narrow ideas rather than being the eternal revelation of God. One major contradiction, however, requires mention. In its early chapters the Koran endorses the Old Testament and the Gospels of the New Testament as inspired by God, appeals to their authority to authenticate Muhammad's own revelations, and urges obedience to their precepts. For example, Allah says:

> It was we who revealed the Law. Therein was guidance and light. By its standards have been judged the Jews by the prophets who bowed to God's will . . . for to them was entrusted the protection of God's Book. . . .

And in their footsteps we sent Jesus the son of Mary, confirming the Torah that had come before him. We sent him the gospel. Therein was guidance and light and confirmation of the law that had come before him as a guidance and admonition to those who fear God. . . .

Let the people of the gospel judge by what God has revealed therein. . . . To thee [Muhammad] we sent the scripture in truth [Koran] confirming the scripture [Bible] that came before it . . . (Sura 5:47-51).

Yet the Koran, after endorsing the Bible, contradicts it by declaring: that God is a single personage rather than one God existing eternally in the three Persons of Father, Son, and Holy Spirit; that Jesus did not die upon the cross for our sins and rise again; that salvation is by one's own good works rather than by grace through what God has done for us; etc., etc. The only way Muslims can reconcile the obvious contradictions between the Koran and the Bible which it affirms is to declare that the Bible has been corrupted since the days of Muhammad, which Muslims insist is the case. That this is a blatantly false charge, however, is demonstrated by the many manuscripts in existence from the time of Muhammad and before, which are identical to the Bible we have today.

Of course the Bible must be discredited in order to maintain the claim that the Arabs, as descendants of Ishmael, are the true heirs of God's promises to Abraham. The Koran declares that it was Ishmael, not Isaac, whom Abraham was told to offer to God and to whose descendants the land of Canaan was given. The Bible says the opposite, but Muhammad was apparently ignorant of that fact at the time he wrote that part of the Koran which endorses the Bible. Some Arabs did settle in the Promised Land, though most of them were scattered throughout the oil-rich nations of the Middle East.

In 1948 both Jews and Arabs were living in Palestine. Under the Zionist movement Jews had been trying to return to the land of their ancestors for decades but most were being denied entrance. Horrified by the murder of 6 million Jews in Nazi extermination camps, the United Nations voted to partition Palestine in order to create a small Jewish state as a place for resettlement of the survivors of Hitler's Holocaust. The Palestinian Arabs were given the remainder of Palestine as a state of their own. The Arabs, however, insisted that Allah had promised it all to them and were not willing to allow a Jewish state even to exist.

Confident of victory, since Allah had also promised that the armies of Islam would always conquer, the Arabs attacked the Jews with the intention of driving them into the Mediterranean. Thus began the war of 1948. The Jews were forced to fight for their very survival against a far superior force in numbers and equipment. Israel had been allotted such a narrow strip of land along the sea that it was indefensible. Consequently, knowing that the Arabs would likely attack again, as part of her victory Israel pushed her boundaries outward to a more defensible position.

Jordan subsequently annexed the remainder of Palestine that had been given by the United Nations to the Palestinian Arabs. Since then in Jordan, Lebanon, and Syria, rather than being integrated into society the Palestinian Arab refugees have been put in camps, where many of them remain to this day. Thus the "Palestinian" problem has been kept alive before the world. The demand is always for Israel to give the Palestinians their own state, never for Jordan to return the land it took.

Since the overwhelming forces of seven Arab nations were defeated by tiny, newborn Israel in 1948, the relentless cry of the Arabs has been to destroy Israel, to drive their half-brothers the Jews into the sea. Our family can never forget being in Egypt in May 1967, just before the Six-Day War broke out. We were in Cairo when Egyptian President Abdul Nasser returned from Moscow, where he had been awarded the Soviet Peace Prize. As he landed at the airport this "man of peace" announced that war was imminent and that the Israelis would be annihilated. That goal still obsesses the Arabs, although recently even terrorists such as Palestine Liberation Organization's chief Yasser Arafat have given lip service to allowing a smaller Israel, with indefensible borders, to exist. The Israelis recognize such talk as public-relations window dressing. They live under the constant threat of all-out destruction if the surrounding Arab nations are ever able to accomplish it.

Had Israel been left in peace she would never have enlarged her borders. The Arabs have reaped the results of their own greed and hatred, which frustrates and angers them all the more. The extension of Israel's boundaries has *only* taken place as a result of wars she has been forced to fight in order to defend her very existence. Growing ever more apprehensive at being surrounded by Arabs who continually call for *Jihad* to annihilate her and who still outnumbered her by about 50 to 1 (it was even worse in the early days), tiny Israel, victorious only by God's grace, has extended her boundaries in each conflict to more defensible positions.

The Golan Heights, for example, were long used by the Syrians for unprovoked sniper and rocket attacks upon the Israeli farm settlements below. In the Yom Kippur war of 1973, while the Egyptians simultaneously attacked across the Sinai, the Syrians poured over the Golan and down into Israel with thousands of tanks. The Israelis, caught by surprise and with only a small fraction of the tanks and men, at great cost of life drove the Syrians back over the top of the Golan and the Egyptians back to the Suez Canal. Israel has since relinquished the territory it took from Egypt under a peace treaty with that country. On the other hand, in view of the continued threats of extermination from Syria, which like other Islamic nations refuses even to acknowledge its existence, Israel prudently retains the Golan Heights in order to prevent its use once again as in former days as a point of harassment and attack.

When Iraq's forces overwhelmed tiny and defenseless but oil-rich Kuwait it was only the swift action of the United States responding to Saudi Arabia's urgent appeal for help that prevented Saddam Hussein from moving right on and taking over that country as well. This brought about something that had previously been unthinkable: the presence of "infidels" upon the soil of the holiest Islamic nation within whose borders both Mecca and Medina, Islam's two most sacred shrines, are located. For the first time in its history, the United Nations responded almost unanimously to oppose with practical and severe steps an aggressor nation, raising hopes of a "new world order." Even more amazing, the majority of the Arab states sided with the U.N. against a fellow Islamic country.

There was one demand by Hussein, however, that appealed to most Arabs: that any withdrawal of his forces from Kuwait should be linked to a similar withdrawal of Israel from "occupied" Palestine. In their joint press conference in Helsinki, Bush and Gorbachev disagreed on this point. Bush, quite correctly, "saw no link between the Arab-Israeli dispute and the Gulf Crisis." Hussein's takeover of Kuwait was an act of unprovoked aggression, whereas Israel occupies territory that it was forced to take in self-defense. Nevertheless, Gorbachev, who had strongly expressed the USSR's "solidarity with the Palestine Liberation Organization" in his 1988 U.N. speech,[3] gave notice of things to come by insisting:

> It seems to me there is a link here because the failure to find a solution in the Middle East [Arab-Israeli question] at large also has a bearing on the acuteness of the particular conflict [Iraq-Kuwait] we've been talking about here.[4]

Muslims who protested the presence of "filthy foreigners" upon Islam's holy soil insisted that the Arabs would work out a solution if left to themselves. That rhetoric motivated the Arab masses to stage huge demonstrations in favor of "Holy War" against the United States. In actual fact, had the United States not stepped in immediately Iraq would have taken over Saudi Arabia and a few other countries as well. Its power would have grown to the point that it would have been a threat to every Arab state. The pleas of the entire Islamic world to give up the territories it was swallowing would have been scorned by Iraq.

Suddenly, thinking Arabs were forced to reevaluate their religion in face of the fact that the territory containing the holiest Islamic shrines had to be defended by infidels against Muslims! Those who had shrugged off the eight-year war

228 ◆ *Dave Hunt*

between two Islamic nations, Iraq and Iran, that had claimed more than 1 million lives and during which atrocities, including the use of poison gas, had been perpetrated in the name of Allah, were now faced with some serious questions. How could an Arab leader such as Saddam Hussein call upon all Arabs to join him in Holy War and at the same time ruthlessly trample other Islamic nations into the ground? Why were fanatical followers of Islam responsible for most of the terrorism and hostage-taking in the world and seemed prone to outdo infidels in all manner of atrocities? And if Allah was all-powerful, why did infidels have to defend Mecca—and *against Muslims*?

The Emir of Kuwait received a standing ovation and the promise of full U.N. backing when he appeared September 27, 1990, before that body's General Assembly to plead for its help against Iraq. Here again was a strange and embarrassing spectacle paraded before the world that contradicted the claims of Islam and tarnished the image of this religion which claims to be superior to all others. An Islamic nation was appealing to a world of infidels to help rescue it from another Islamic nation, which was at that moment plundering, destroying, raping, and torturing while calling for Muslims to join it in a "Holy War" in defense of its evil deeds!

Other embarrassing facts also had to be faced which could have as far-reaching effects in the Arab world as the recent move from Communism to democracy in Eastern Europe. The Emir of Kuwait was a feudal monarch who, prior to Iraq's invasion, had muzzled the press and jailed human-rights activists. It was unlikely that the U.N. was interested in reinstating a feudal lord, but rather in freeing his country from Iraq's unlawful takeover. As this book goes to press, the issues remain in doubt. When Kuwait is liberated, however, it would seem that the Emir will have to yield to pressures for democratic rule—as will other Arab rulers as well.

Much of the reason for the swift and near-unanimous action of the United Nations against Iraq was due to its concern that Saddam Hussein, who had proved to be virtually an Arab

Hitler, would take over and control so much of the world's oil reserves that he would have the industrialized nations at his mercy. The well-known fact, accepted in the past, that six ruling Arab families sitting on feudal thrones controlled 44 percent of the world's oil reserves suddenly became a concern. There are grassroots movements in those countries for greater freedom and rights for citizens. Inevitable political changes must come, weakening Islam's hold as well.

It would be surprising if we did not see as great changes in the Arab world as in the Communist world as the stage is set for the rise of Antichrist. The world grows smaller and more interdependent. Barriers are coming down. It is no longer possible to remain isolated behind either an Iron Curtain or an Islamic Curtain. Even the Bamboo Curtain around China must yield as well to worldwide pressures. It is only a matter of time.

As the collapse of Communism is providing great opportunity for the gospel to be made known, and many are coming to Christ in Eastern Europe, so the upheavals in the Arab world are bringing similar opportunities. After centuries of almost no response to the gospel, thousands of Muslims are now coming to Christ as a result of facing some of the serious shortcomings and contradictions in Islam. It promises heaven, but offers no assurance of getting there except by death in Holy War. As in Catholicism, where enough is never enough to keep one out of purgatory, so in Islam one never knows whether enough prayers have been said, enough alms given, and enough good deeds done to bring one to paradise.

Confronted at last by some of the embarrassing questions about Islam, the faith of many Muslims is being shaken. Why did Muhammad with his "new revelation" give his God the same name, Allah, as the chief idol in the *kaaba*, the ancient pagan temple at Mecca? And why, although he destroyed the idols which it housed, did Muhammad retain the *kaaba* itself as a sacred shrine? And why did he keep and continue to revere the Black Stone that had long been worshiped along with the idols in the ancient religious ceremonies of Mecca? And why do Muslims consider the *kaaba* holy and kiss its Black Stone as an important part of their pilgrimage to Mecca?

Such questions are causing many Muslims to receive the free pardon of sin and assurance of heaven that is offered in Christ. In contrast to Muhammad, Jesus, who as God could have destroyed His enemies with a word, let them crucify Him and died in our place to pay for our sins. For those who nailed Him to the cross and tortured and taunted Him, He prayed, "Father, forgive them, for they know not what they do." What a contrast to the famous Apostasy Wars, where Muslim forces fought against those who had turned away from Islam in order to bring them back to "faith" or kill them! And that primitive attitude still prevails in Islam.

Painful though the admission may be, intelligent, thinking Arabs can no longer deny that Islam has been responsible for perpetuating a barbaric medieval mentality. Surely they must recognize that the continued taking of hostages and the frequent spectacle on television of crazed mobs screaming "*Jihad! Jihad! Jihad!*"—"Death to Bush!" and "Death to the United States!" does not encourage Western viewers to put much confidence in a "peaceful Arab solution" to problems in the Middle East. And when a Salman Rushdie, because he writes something offensive to Muslims, has a price put on his head by Islam's foremost leader and must go into hiding to save his life from Muslim assassins—are Arabs proud of such barbarism and do they feel that it commends Islam to the world? As for the treatment of women, to be able to beat one's four wives and unlimited concubines and to divorce merely by pronouncing it done as the Koran decrees is criminal! Surely the time for change has come!

Unfortunately, the pressure for change is bringing a growing openness to ecumenism that is preparing the Muslim world to embrace the Antichrist. The new attitude was expressed by M.A. Zaki Badawi, principal of the Moslem College of London, while in attendance at the August 1990 San Francisco Assembly of the World Religions. In response to Sun Myung Moon's announcement that he was the new world Messiah,

Badawi made this interesting comment: "We don't accept Rev. Moon as Messiah, but we respect his vision of bringing the world's religions together." The next step is easy.

Satan's Messiah will have incredible powers that neither Moon nor any of the other lightweight antichrists can display. We have already noted that Jesus specifically declared that Israel would accept the Antichrist. It is no longer so difficult to imagine that with a little more preparation Muslims too will be able to embrace and even worship the counterfeit "Christ"—while still professing allegiance to Islam. For Islam's Allah, after all, is not the God of the Bible that Muhammad claimed him to be.

18 | *That Mysterious Trinity*

I F WE ARE TO UNDERSTAND the final conflict between Christ and Antichrist, we must know the nature of the God whom Satan opposes, and the false views of God which Satan has inspired in his cosmic and lengthy struggle with the Creator. In view of Christ's statement that eternal life is "to know the only true God, and Jesus Christ" (John 17:3), it is easy to see why a major part of Satan's strategy is to promote false concepts of God and to present to mankind a counterfeit Christ. Those whom Satan can keep from knowing the true God and Jesus Christ will share his eternal doom.

Throughout the world and in all ages there have been two general concepts of God: 1) pantheism/naturalism—that the universe itself is God; and 2) supernaturalism—that the Creator is distinct from His creation. Related to these are two more opposing views: 1) polytheism—that there are many gods (Mormons, for example, are polytheists); and 2) monotheism—that there is only one God.

Antichrist's claims are built upon a pantheistic/polytheistic worldview. If everything is God and there are thus many gods, it then follows that every person is a god whether he realizes it or not. It was on this basis that Satan became convinced that he could be "like the Most High." He apparently still labors under that delusion. The Antichrist, having apparently "realized" this inner potential, is in a position to help others to achieve their godhood also. Such is the great lie of the Serpent.

Supernaturalism/monotheism is divided into two rival beliefs: 1) that God is a single being; and 2) that God has always existed in three Persons who are separate and distinct, yet one. Only Christians hold the latter view—and even some who call themselves Christians reject it. Yet it is the only biblical, logical, and philosophically coherent view of God possible. It is also the only real opposition to the Antichrist's ecumenical world religion. All other views of God can be accommodated by the Antichrist—but not the biblical doctrine of the Trinity.

Pantheism is really a form of atheism and shares the same fatal flaws. If *everything* is God, then there is really no God. God over what, or in charge of what, or the Creator of what? Of Himself? Pantheism leads to numerous other contradictions. God would be the emptiness of a vacuum as well as the substance of matter; He would be sickness as well as health, death as well as life, evil as well as good. The very concept of God would be self-contradictory.

If the universe is God and thus all there is, then no outside reference point exists from which the universe can be evaluated and given purpose and significance. Nothing has meaning or value in itself, but only as some personal being has use for it and values it. The universe, and mankind as part of it, could have no meaning unless created for His purposes by Another, who must be separate and distinct from His creation. Pantheism can offer only meaninglessness, hopelessness, and ultimate despair.

As for polytheism, if there is more than one God, then who is in charge? If one God is stronger or has more authority than the others, then how could all of them be "God"? The many gods of polytheism fight wars and steal one another's wives, with no one to set the standards and call the universe to account. There is no basis for morals, truth, or peace in heaven or earth. Polytheism's basic problem is *diversity without unity*.

At the other extreme is the belief that God is a single Personage. It is held by both Muslims and Jews, who insist that Allah, or Jehovah, is "one." The same belief is also held by pseudo-Christian cults such as the Jehovah's Witnesses. Some aberrant Christian groups also claim that God is a single Personage and that Father, Son, and Holy Spirit are God's three "titles" or "offices." Here we have *unity without diversity*.

That God must have *both unity and diversity* is clear. The Allah of Islam, or the Jehovah of Jehovah's Witnesses and Jews, or the God of unitarian "Christian" groups would be incomplete in Himself. He would be unable to love or communicate before creating other beings capable of interacting with Him in these ways. (For God to be just, true, holy, and pure would not require the existence of other beings in order for these qualities to be expressed, as would be the case for God to experience love.)

The quality of love and the capacities for fellowship and communion, by their very nature, require another personal being with which to share them. And God could not fully share Himself except with another Being equal to Him. Yet the Bible says that "God *is* love" in Himself alone. This could only be true if within the Godhead itself there is a plurality of Personages, or divine Persons, who could express and experience love in relation to one another. Although the actual word "trinity" does not occur in the Bible, the concept is clearly expressed there, providing the unity and diversity that makes possible the love, fellowship, and communion within the Godhead.

The Bible presents a God who did not need to create any beings to experience love, communion, and fellowship. This God is complete in Himself, existing eternally in three Persons: Father, Son, and Holy Spirit, individually distinct from each other yet at the same time eternally one God. These three loved, communed, and fellowshiped with each other and took counsel together before the universe, angels, or man were brought into existence. Truly the biblical triune God "*is* love" (1 John 4:8,16)—and He alone.

In contrast, the God of Islam and contemporary Judaism could not *be* love in and of Himself, for whom could He love in the solitude predating His creation of other personal beings?

Such a deficiency in God would affect man at every level of his being. As one astute author, who tried Eastern mysticism and found it wanting, has said:

> The inconceivably complete identity of God is the paradigm of all personhood, as its very plurality is the foundation of all relatedness. Such is the "image of God" in which we are made. In that light, the doctrine of the Trinity is not some facile mystification, but a straightforward statement of the multiple personhood of God. . . .
>
> If God is a person, that . . . translates into moral absolutes for us. . . . humanity's alienation from God has occurred at precisely that level of character and relationship.[1]

Love is God's principal weapon in His battle with Satan for the souls and destiny of mankind. For the battle rages not only for man's *mind* but above all for his *love*. Every sin, therefore, has its root (as the Decalogue declares) in man's failure to respond to God's love in the fullness of the capacity for love which He has given us. As the first and greatest commandment declares:

> Thou shalt love the Lord thy God with all thy heart, and with all thy soul, and with all thy mind, and with all thy strength: this is the first commandment (Mark 12:30; Deuteronomy 6:5; etc.).

We don't have the ability within ourselves to keep this commandment, for "love is of God, and every one that loveth is born of God and knoweth God" (1 John 4:7). It is *God's love to us* that woos and wins our hearts and awakens in us a love for Him: "We love him because he first loved us" (verse 19). The great act (and thus the proof) of God's love is that God became a man in order to personally pay the penalty demanded by His justice against our sin. He could only do this because He is a personal and triune Being.

The heresy that God is a single Personage (Unitarianism) and not three Persons existing eternally in one God (Trinitarianism) invaded the church around 220 A.D. through a Libyan theologian named Sabellius. He attempted to retain biblical language concerning Father, Son, and Holy Spirit without acknowledging the triune nature of God. Sabellius claimed that God existed as a single Personage who manifested Himself in three activities, modes, or aspects: as father in the creation, as Son in redemption, and as Holy Spirit in prophecy and sanctification. Though condemned by the vast majority of Christians, this heresy survives to this day in such "Jesus only" groups as the United Pentecostal Church.

Jesus said, "The Father loveth the Son and hath given all things into his hand" (John 3:35). God's love is not just toward mankind but first of all among the three Persons of the Godhead. Father, Son, and Holy Spirit can't be mere offices, titles, or modes in which God manifests Himself, for such cannot love, consult, and fellowship together. Not only is the Son presented as a Person, but the Father and the Holy Spirit are as well. The Bible presents each as having His own personality: each wills, acts, loves, and cares, and can also be grieved or become angry. Unitarianism robs the Godhead of the essential qualities of self-existent and self-sufficient deity.

Godhead? Is that a biblical term? Yes, indeed. It occurs three times in the King James New Testament: in Acts 17:29, Romans 1:20, and Colossians 2:9. In contrast to *theos*, which is used consistently throughout the New Testament for God, three different but related Greek words occur in these verses (*theios, theiotes, theotes*), which the King James Bible, in contrast to other versions, carefully designates by the special word *Godhead*. That very term indicates a plurality of being.

Paul wrote, "In him dwelleth all the fulness of the Godhead bodily" (Colossians 2:9). This statement makes no sense if, as the "Jesus only" advocates teach, Christ is the only God, and the Father and Holy Spirit are merely "offices" or "titles." Paul would then be making the meaningless statement that in Christ dwelt all the fullness of Christ.

Did Paul mean that in Christ dwells all the fullness of *deity*, as non-King-James translations render it? That would detract from the deity of Christ. For if Christ is intrinsically God, then what is the point of saying that "in Him dwells all the fullness of deity"? But if Christ is the *Son* and there are two other *Persons* in the Godhead, then it does mean something: that when the Son became man He brought that fullness of the *Godhead* with Him into flesh.

The Antichrist comes in the place of the true Christ. Lacking the marks of crucifixion, as we have noted, he must therefore promote another view of Christ that denies that Jesus is the one and only Messiah. ("Christ" is simply the Greek equivalent of the Hebrew word "Messiah.") He must therefore deny that God has literally become a man and that this union between God and man continues eternally in the Person of Jesus of Nazareth, who died for our sins and is now resurrected. This common "antichrist" doctrine takes many forms and is found in many religions. Such delusions have all been part of a centuries-long preparation for the time when Antichrist will be accepted by the world as its true Savior.

Like Jews, Muslims find the trinity particularly objectionable. One of Islam's most important teachings concerns the "absolute oneness of Allah." Yet the Koran repeats the Genesis statement: "Let *us* make man in *our* image." Islam has no explanation for this contradiction.

The very first verse in the Bible presents God as a *plural* being. It declares: "In the beginning God created the heaven and the earth." Yet instead of the singular *Eloah* for God in the Hebrew, the plural, *Elohim*, is used. It literally means "In the beginning, *Gods* created. . . ." It is also Elohim [*Gods*] who say later in the chapter, "Let *us* make man in *our* image. . . ."

This *plural noun* (Elohim) is found over 2500 times in the Old Testament. Yet a *singular verb*, *bara*, is used in Genesis 1:1 and in almost every other place that Elohim is found. So we have both singularity (in the verb) and plurality (in the noun). The same is true all through the Torah and entire Old Testament. If God was a single Personage, then the single form, Eloah, would have been used, not Elohim. That fact is inescapable.

At the burning bush incident we read: "And God [Elohim] said unto Moses, I am that I am . . ." (Exodus 3:14). Here *Gods* speak, but they don't say "*We are*" but "*I am.*" Again that peculiar singularity and plurality at the same time in the same Being! So it is in Exodus 20:2—"*I am* the Lord thy God [Elohim]. . . ." And Leviticus 11:44—"*I am* the Lord your God [Elohim]. . . ."

Each time God uses Elohim (*Gods*) of Himself (90 percent of the time) instead of Eloah (*God*) (10 percent), He reveals to us the plurality in His Being. And when He uses a singular verb and pronoun along with Elohim, He is clearly telling us that He is a unity.

Nor is the word *Elohim* the only way in which God's plurality is presented. Consider, for example, Psalm 149:2 (NKJV): "Let Israel rejoice in their Maker" (literally "makers"); Ecclesiastes 12:1: "Remember now thy Creator" (literally "creators"); and Isaiah 54:5: "For thy Maker is thine husband" (literally "makers, husbands"). Unitarianism has no explanation for this consistent presentation of God's plurality all through the Old Testament.

Most Jewish people are not aware that the plural noun *Gods* is found in the very center of Israel's famous confession of the *oneness* of God. It reads in Hebrew: "*Shema yisroel adonai elohenu adonai echad*" (Deuteronomy 6:4). From this Scripture, Rabbi Moses Maimonides taught Jews to recite daily, "I believe with a perfect faith that the Creator, blessed be His name, is ONE."

Maimonides, however, perverted the Scripture, apparently deliberately. To express "ONE" he used the Hebrew word *yachid*, which means a single and *absolute one*. Yet Moses used *echad*, which could mean a *unity* of several into one. For example, it is used in Genesis 2:24, where man and woman become "*one* flesh"; in Exodus 36:13, when the various parts "became *one* tabernacle"; in 2 Samuel 2:25, when many soldiers "became *one* troop"; and elsewhere.

God is telling us something important about Himself by His choice of Hebrew words. Had God wanted to show that He is an *absolute one*, He would have chosen *yachid*, but instead He chose *echad*. Maimonides made a serious mistake in changing God's Word. As a result, millions of Jews have been led astray and still are to this day. Islam perpetuates the same error. God is not an *absolute one*; He is a *unity*, as Moses taught in the Torah.

We have already referred several times to some of Isaiah's remarkable prophecies, such as: "The Lord himself shall give you a sign: Behold, a virgin shall conceive, and bear a son, and shall call his name Immanuel" (Isaiah 7:14). The literal translation of the Hebrew word *Immanuel* is *with us is God*—not *spiritually* but *literally* present in this babe named Immanuel. And again Isaiah 9:6: "For unto us a child is born, unto us a son is given; and the government shall be upon his shoulder; and his name shall be called Wonderful, Counselor, *the mighty God, the everlasting Father....*"

The concept presented by the Hebrew prophets is found nowhere else in the world's religious literature, but is unique to the Bible: A Son would be born into this world who, though a man, would be the Mighty God. And though a Son, He would be the Everlasting Father. Isaiah presents the *deity* of Christ, the Fatherhood of God, and the oneness of the Father and the Son.

When Jesus asked the rabbis, "What think ye of Christ [Messiah]? Whose son is he?" they replied immediately, "The son of David" (Matthew 22:42). Christ then quoted, "The Lord said unto my Lord, Sit thou at my right hand until I make thine enemies thy footstool" (Psalm 110:1), and asked them, "If David then call him Lord, how is he his son?" (Matthew 22:45). The Pharisees were speechless. Only the trinity provides an explanation for these two "Lords," one of whom is God the Father and the other God the Son.

The rabbis surely knew that Jehovah had repeatedly declared, "I am the Lord thy God, the Holy One of Israel, thy Savior . . . and beside me there is no savior."[2] Then who else, if He was to save His people, could the Messiah be except the Lord God of Israel come down as a man? The full wonder of this staggering fact, so essential to our salvation, shattered the skepticism of doubting Thomas and caused him to exclaim, when confronted by the resurrected Christ, "My Lord and my God" (John 20:28).

Yet the rabbis accused Jesus of blasphemy because He said "that God was his Father, making himself equal with God" (John 5:18). They knew that He was claiming to be "the God of Abraham, Isaac, and Jacob," even though many today deny that Jesus ever made such a claim. This "blasphemy" became the charge with which the Sanhedrin condemned Him to death: "For a good work we stone thee not, but for blasphemy . . . thou being a man, makest thyself God" (John 10:33; Mark 14:64). They were blind to the prophecy of Zechariah that Israel would pierce *Jehovah*—and they fulfilled that prophecy, for Jesus was God, a conclusion one cannot escape.

When Christ returns visibly in power and glory at His second coming, the surviving Jews (whom He rescues from the Antichrist at Armageddon) will recognize Him by the marks of Calvary: "They shall look upon me whom they have *pierced*, and they shall mourn for him" (Zechariah 12:10). Jehovah, the God of Israel, is speaking. When was He *pierced*? The Hebrew word means the piercing to *death*, as when King Saul begged his armorbearer, "Draw thy sword, and *thrust* me through" (1 Samuel 31:4).

Zechariah's prophecy is both remarkable and clear: God Himself will come as a man to rescue Israel when, in the last days, they will be surrounded by the armies of the world and will stand on the brink of destruction. Nor does He come as an ordinary man, but as One who was thrust through to death and has come back to life. When Israel sees Him, they will know He is Jehovah by His power, and they will recognize Him as Jesus by the marks of crucifixion that His resurrected body still bears. In that moment all Israel will be convinced at last that Jesus of Nazareth, whom they crucified and have rejected for so long, is the Messiah long promised by their own prophets. They will repent and believe in Him (Zechariah 12:10–14:9).

Zechariah's prophecy should have made it clear to Israel all along that the Messiah would be Jehovah Himself: the *me* whom they will "look upon" and the *him* "whom they have pierced" are clearly one and the same. Jesus no doubt had this Scripture, among others, in mind when He declared, "I and my Father are one" (John 10:30). Here we confront a teaching that distinguishes the God of the Bible from every other concept of God known in the world's religions.

No wonder Paul wrote that if the "princes of this world" (the rabbis, Pilate, Herod, etc.) had only known the truth about Christ they would not have dared to crucify Him! (1 Corinthians 2:8). It was in reference to such blindness that Isaiah asked the solemn question: "Who hath believed our [the prophets'] report?" (Isaiah 53:1). That same query is appropriate today. Just as Israel's misunderstanding of God's triune nature caused her to reject her Messiah, so that same misunderstanding will allow her to be deceived into accepting the Antichrist. He comes, as we have seen, not as a member of the Trinity—in the name of the Father and under the anointing of the Holy Spirit—but "in his own name."

The New Testament presents three Persons who are distinct, yet each is God. At the same time we repeatedly have the clear statement that there is only one true God. Christ prays to the Father. Is He praying to Himself? "The Father sent the Son to be the Savior of the world" (1 John 4:14). Did He send Himself? Worse yet, did one "office" pray to and send a "title"? Christ said, "The words that I speak unto you I speak not of myself [on my own initiative], but the Father that dwelleth in me, he doeth the works" (John 14:10); "I will pray the Father, and he shall give you another Comforter... even the Spirit of truth" (John 14:16,17). Throughout the New Testament, Father, Son, and Holy Spirit are each separately honored and act as God, yet only in concert with one another.

The Old Testament also presents three Persons in the Godhead interacting with each other. Take for example the following:

> Hearken unto me, O Jacob and Israel, my called; I am he; I am the first, I also am the last. Mine hand also hath laid the foundation of the earth, and my right hand hath spanned the heavens ... from the time that it was, there am I; and now the Lord God, and his Spirit, hath sent me (Isaiah 48:12,13,16).

The one speaking refers to Himself as "the first and the last" and the Creator of all, so He must be God. But he speaks of two others in the same passage who must also be God: "the Lord God, and his Spirit, hath sent me." By whom could God be "sent" on some mission—and where? This can be none other than the Father and the Holy Spirit sending the Son into the world to be our Savior.

God is also called "the first and the last" in the New Testament—and so is Jesus. In Revelation 1:8 we read: "I am Alpha and Omega, the beginning and the ending, saith the Lord ... the Almighty." God, the Lord Almighty, is speaking. Yet John tells us he was being addressed by Jesus Christ. In the last chapter Jesus says, "Behold, I come quickly" (22:7), referring to His second coming. Then He adds: "I am Alpha and Omega, the beginning and the end, the first and the last" (22:13). Again Jesus is presented as God.

Isaiah gives further insight into past counseling among the Godhead when Father and Holy Spirit sent the Son into the world:

> Also I heard the voice of the Lord, saying, Whom shall *I* send, and who will go for *us*? Then said *I*, Here am *I*; send *me* (Isaiah 6:8).

"The voice of the Lord" said *all* of the above. "The Lord" God not only says, "Who will go for *us*?" but He also replies, "Here am *I*; send *me*." Here we see the essential unity and diversity in the Godhead at work. There are three Persons communing with each other and working together, yet they are not *three* Gods but *one* God.

The Bible reveals other decisions coming from the counseling together of the Godhead: "God said, Let *us* make man in

244 ◆ *Dave Hunt*

our image, after *our* likeness"; and again, "Let *us* go down, and there confound their language" (Genesis 1:26; 11:7). Why does God say, "The man is become as one of *us*" (Genesis 3:22), and "Who will go for *us*" (Isaiah 6:8)? Who is this *us* and to whom does *our* refer if God is a single Personage? It could not be some angelic beings, as Unitarians suggest. God would not say to them, "Let *us* make man," for no created being could cocreate with God. And that the Son was one of those included in *us* and *our* is quite clear, for we are told that "without him was not any thing made that was made" (John 1:3).

Even if angels were made in the image of God, they would not intrinsically possess the likeness of God. If God were speaking to created beings He wouldn't say "in *our* image" but rather "In *my* image as I made you." Whoever is referred to by *us* and *our* must be equal with God. We are told that the Son existed eternally "in the form [Greek *morphe*—of the very nature] of God" (Philippians 2:6). He *is* "the brightness of his [God's] glory, and the express image of his person" (Hebrews 1:3).

One cannot escape the fact that all through the Bible God is presented as a *plurality* and yet as *one*, as having *both diversity and unity*. This concept of God is unique among all the world's religions. To reject the triune nature of God is to reject the God of the Bible—and to come, ultimately, under the delusion that will cause the world to obey and worship the Antichrist when he comes.

It is a mystery that God can exist in three Persons yet be one God, but both Scripture and logic demand this fact. It is also a mystery how God could have no beginning and create everything out of nothing, yet it must be so. There is much else that we cannot explain—love, beauty, truth, or what a human soul or spirit is—but we don't reject it on that basis. God has revealed His triune nature to us so that we can believe in and know Him. We dare not reject what He says or lower Him to the level of our finite minds.

God is not some "force" inherent within the universe that we can tap into and use to our own advantage—nor is the universe an extension of Him. The First Law of Thermodynamics declares that energy can neither be created nor destroyed, yet we know that the universe could not have been here forever. Were that the case, our own sun would have burned out by now. The secret to its existence in time is not to be found within the universe itself but in its Creator, who must exist outside of and separate from it.

The Second Law of Thermodynamics declares that the amount of usable energy in the universe is steadily decreasing, causing the universe to run down like a clock. Eventually all the planets will have fallen out of orbit and all the stars will have burned out—and death will reign throughout. All the schemes and dreams of mankind, the corporate plans, the political strategies, the heroic deeds, the triumphs and tragedies, the agonies and ecstasies will be like sand castles washed into a cosmic ocean of nothingness. If God is merely the universe or part of it or a force within it, He too will be extinguished.

The God of the Bible, however, is the Creator of the universe, separate and distinct from it and not subject to the laws He made to govern it. And therein lies the only hope for mankind, for the God of the Bible can in fact reach into the dying universe and re-create it to be totally new. Reincarnation can only recycle that which is steadily sinking into oblivion. Resurrection, on the other hand, represents an influx of God's power from outside bringing immortality to that which otherwise would be eternally dead.

Such is the God whom we must know personally in order to be saved. And such is the God whom the Antichrist denies. It is this triune God who made man in His image and who alone could come as a man and still remain God. He alone could rescue mankind from sin and self and from eternal separation from His love and presence.

When God said, "Behold, I will send my messenger, and he shall prepare the way before *me*" (Malachi 3:1), He was saying that He Himself would come to this earth as the Messiah. All through the Old Testament God repeatedly said: "I, even I, am the Lord; and beside me there is no savior" (Isaiah 43:11, etc.). And how does He save us? By giving us a law to keep? No, the law can only condemn lawbreakers.

Suppose a person is arrested for some crime. He pleads with the judge, "If you let me off this time, I promise I will never break the law again." But the judge replies, "If you never break the law again you are only doing what the law demands. You get no extra credit for that. You can't make up for breaking the law in the past by keeping it in the future. The penalty required for disobeying the law in the past must be paid."

God loves even the vilest sinner, but it would be unjust to forgive him unless the penalty that His justice demands has been paid. It was in order to pay the penalty we owed for our sins that God became a man. In so doing He did not cease to be God, and He will never cease to be man. If Jesus Christ were not the one and only God-man, perfect and without sin, He would have had to die for His own sins. But because of who He is, He was able to die in our place and pay the infinite penalty that we deserved.

Jesus Christ now offers eternal life as a free gift of God's grace to all who will believe that He died in their place and will open their hearts to receive Him as their Savior and Lord. Such a plan of salvation is unknown in the world's religions and is anathema to New Age teachings. It is possible only because of the unique triune nature of the God of the Bible, who stands in complete contrast to all rival gods.

God's love toward mankind is not some impersonal cosmic force that operates inexorably by a universal law. It is intensely personal. God loves each of us with a passion. We find that incredible fact extremely difficult to believe, much less to understand. We look within ourselves to find the *reason* for His love. Yet it would not be comforting if God loved us because we somehow deserved or had aroused His love, because we could change and lose that appeal and thus lose His affection. It is, instead, assuring to know that He loves us *because of who He is in Himself*—and *in spite of* who and what we are. Since God *is* love and since He never changes, we are secure for eternity and need never fear that we could lose His love by anything we might do or neglect to do.

How can we be certain that God loves us? Paul wrote that God demonstrated His love "in that, while we were yet sinners, Christ died for us" (Romans 5:8). God has so fully proved His love through the cross of Christ, as only the personal, triune God could do, that no reasonable person could ever doubt it. John reminds us:

> For God so loved the world that he gave his only begotten Son, that whosoever believeth in him should not perish but have everlasting life (John 3:16).
>
> In this was manifested the love of God toward us, because that God sent his only begotten Son into the world that we might live through him.
>
> Herein is love, not that we loved God, but that he loved us and sent his Son to be the propitiation [the basis of forgiveness] for our sins (1 John 4:9,10).

If God loves us so much, then why will many people be separated from Him for eternity? There are three reasons: 1) God is holy and just. His love cannot nullify these aspects of His character. Love wants to forgive, but justice must be satisfied and dictates the terms of our forgiveness. 2) While God in love has fully paid the penalty demanded by His justice, man must respond. The payment of this penalty cannot be credited to those who deny the obligation. 3) Moreover, love will not force itself upon anyone. Those who would be forgiven and reconciled to God must be willing to accept the remedy He offers. Those who refuse consign themselves to eternal separation in spite of God's provision.

True biblical love is no mere emotion that sweeps over a person, as Hollywood depicts it—a "falling in love." Instead, it involves a moral choice and total commitment, from which love never turns back but faithfully pursues the loved one's good, even to its own loss, and patiently endures all until it has triumphed. Such is God's commitment to those who respond to His love—He will never leave or forsake us (Hebrews 13:5). A lack of such commitment on our part to God and to one another destroys marriages and families and produces the full range of chaos in human relationships that characterizes today's world. What a tragic testimony to man's separation from his loving Creator!

19 | *Christ and Antichrist in Final Conflict*

The collapse of Communism in Eastern Europe and the introduction of "freedom of religion" is not a setback for Satan. The "tolerance" that Gorbachev now promotes plays into the Serpent's hands. Atheism is not the ultimate triumph that Satan seeks, but to persuade mankind to believe in *false* gods, and eventually in the "God-power" within. Those who think they have been liberated to fulfill their own desires are blind to the fact that they have subtly become the slaves of the Enemy of their souls and are doing his will.

Satan transforms himself "into an angel of light" and inspires his emissaries to masquerade as "the ministers of righteousness" (2 Corinthians 11:14,15). He is the father of "positive thinking," and is a master at "how to win friends and influence people." He prevents his false theology from being unmasked by accusing those who attempt to expose it of being "negative" and "divisive."

The Serpent did not urge Eve to shake her fist at God and denounce Him, nor did he inspire her to practice overtly evil acts. On the contrary, he enticed her with promises of a better "self-image," of being a wiser and better person—of even becoming "like God." What could be wrong with that high ambition? Evil is far more seductive and effective when it is packaged as *good*. If he can encourage expressions of "man's basic goodness" that are high-minded, altruistic, and spiritual, but *without Christ*, Satan is very pleased.

249

Satan's goal is to pervert the conscience to such an extent that his *lie* is embraced as God's *truth*. Far from desiring to destroy all religion, Satan seeks to be the leader of a *false religion* whose adherents unknowingly worship him. And of course that false religion, as we have seen, must be a perverted form of Christianity, inasmuch as the Antichrist pretends to be Christ.

While raw Satanism is exploding, most people are repelled by it. Satan is most seductive when he masquerades as *God*. Playing God has been his consuming passion ever since that rebellious outburst in ages past: *"I will be like the most High"* (Isaiah 14:14). It is in this mode that "the god of this world" (2 Corinthians 4:4) will manifest himself through his messiah, the Antichrist.

Just as the true Christ is God "manifest in the flesh" (1 Timothy 3:16), so the Antichrist will be Satan manifest in the flesh. Since Christ is God, Antichrist, who poses as Christ, must also pretend to be God: "He as God sitteth in the temple of God, showing himself that he is God" (2 Thessalonians 2:4). Satan knows the Bible—and has a craving to be worshiped. While he takes great pleasure in so corrupting men that they worship him as the personification of evil, he desires even more to be worshiped as *God*.

In Revelation 13:3 the apostle John is given a mysterious vision of the Antichrist as one of the beasts that Daniel saw, the same Beast with "seven heads and ten horns" upon which the "whore of Babylon" rides: "I saw one of his heads as it were wounded to death; and his deadly wound was healed, and all the world wondered after the beast." Based on that Scripture many prophecy writers believe that the Antichrist "will literally be raised from the dead"[1] to counterfeit Christ's resurrection. Some even suggest that the Antichrist is a man "who lived before . . . [having] ruled one of the previous seven great empires which directly impacted Israel."[2]

If that theory is true, it certainly cannot be derived from what John tells us. To recover from what seemed to John "as [though] it were" a mortal wound is a far cry from bringing back to life a totally decomposed, 2500-year-old corpse—to say nothing of bringing back soul and spirit from hell! On the contrary, the phrase *as it were* seems to indicate that he never actually died. It was a wound from which one would be expected to die, but Antichrist recovers. It is the closest thing to a resurrection that Satan can produce.

Others suggest that one of earth's previous tyrants, perhaps Hitler, will come back to life. It sounds like science fiction. Proponents try to make their back-from-the-dead theory more palatable by calling it a "counterfeit resurrection" because, unlike Christ, the Antichrist will die again.[3] But that would mean that the resurrections of Lazarus and the others whom Jesus raised were also "counterfeit resurrections," because they died again. No, a resurrection gives life to the dead, and Satan has no such power.

Only God can transcend His own laws and thereby do genuine miracles. Satan can no more transcend the universal laws that God has established than can man. Demonic intrusions from the spirit world into our physical universe are often mistakenly referred to as "supernatural" because they seem to transcend the laws of physical science as we understand them. Satan and his demons, however, are bound by the laws of the spiritual universe and only seem from our limited perspective to be doing miracles.

Satan's intrusion into and interference with the physical universe is limited to what God allows. When the time has come, God will remove *all* restraint and allow the Antichrist to exercise "the working of Satan with *all power* and signs and *lying* wonders, and with *all deceivableness* . . ." (2 Thessalonians 2:9,10, emphasis added). Trickery is apparently an integral part of the display of Satan's power upon earth in order to make this power appear to be greater than it actually is. That delusion will reach its zenith under the Antichrist.

The resurrection of Christ is the ultimate miracle—absolute proof that He is God the Savior—and cannot be duplicated by anyone. It isn't easy to pretend to come back from the dead, which is reason enough why the world's religions have not dared to make this claim for their leaders. Instead, their followers make shrines of their tombs. Furthermore, Hinduism, Buddhism, Islam, and other religions don't even recognize the *necessity* for the resurrection.

By contrast, the resurrection of Christ is the very heart of Christianity. As Paul said, if there were no resurrection, then the apostles were all liars for claiming to have seen the risen Christ. Christ would be proved a false prophet as well, for He declared that He would rise from the dead. The Bible would also be exposed as false, because it both foretold His resurrection and reported that it had occurred. The entire message of Scripture from beginning to end would be a lesson in futility, for it says that death is a result of God's judgment upon sin and promises that God would provide a Savior to conquer this enemy once and for all.

The death, burial, and resurrection of Christ as historic events upon planet Earth make any kind of ecumenical union with the world's religions both impossible and abominable. A dead Buddha or Muhammad has nothing in common with the resurrected Lord Jesus Christ. There is no point in discussing ethical and moral beliefs which many religions hold in common with Christianity. That fact is a result of God's law having been written in the consciences of all mankind—and that law cannot save, but only condemns. Christ alone paid the penalty demanded by the law, which He proved by His resurrection, and He alone can save. There are only two options: to accept Him or reject Him. "Dialogue" is rejection, an attempt to "climb up some other way," as Jesus put it, rather than coming to God through the One who alone could say in truth, "I am the door: by me if any man enter in, he shall be saved . . ." (John 10:9).

It will not do to say that Jesus was a good teacher if in fact He didn't rise from the dead, for then He would be a false prophet and His disciples liars, or that the Bible offers good morals and presents a sublime religious philosophy, if Jesus didn't rise again. One cannot "accept the teachings" of Jesus and reject

His resurrection, for victory over death was the essence of His message.

Mankind's great enemy, death, no longer has any power over those who receive Christ as Savior and Lord. The resurrection of Christ offers a hope that goes beyond this world and even beyond this universe to the new universe that God has promised to create in its place. For those who reject Christ, however, only eternal doom awaits, for which they cannot blame God but only themselves.

What does all of this have to do with the subject of this book? Everything! It is as the Conqueror of death in His resurrected and glorified body that Christ confronts and destroys Antichrist at His second coming. As we have seen, it is by the marks of His crucifixion that Israel, when He comes to rescue her, will realize that Jesus of Nazareth is both Jehovah and Messiah. Seven years earlier, when they meet Him in the air above this earth, Christians will recognize their risen Lord in the same way: by the nailprints in His hands and feet and the spear wound in His side. God will not allow those evidences of victory over sin and death and Satan to be counterfeited by Antichrist or anyone else.

The Antichrist won't even pretend to be Jesus crucified and *resurrected*. On what basis, then, will he claim to be Christ? Almost certainly he will claim to be the latest *reincarnation* of the "Christ Spirit" that was allegedly in Krishna, Rama, Buddha, Jesus, Muhammad, et al—a deception which God's Word anticipated and warned against: "It is appointed unto men *once* to die, but after this the judgment" (Hebrews 9:27). As Christ ascended into heaven two angels told the disciples that "this *same Jesus*" (not a reincarnation of the "Christ Spirit" or "Christ Consciousness") would return in the same way. John wrote that the spirit of Antichrist denies that Christ has come once-and-for-all in the flesh (1 John 4:3)—i.e. was resurrected and continues to live in the same body.

A belief in reincarnation enables the world to accept a "Christ" without the marks of crucifixion—a clever lie indeed! It can hardly be coincidence that just at this time, along with the many other last-days signs, the theory of reincarnation is gaining millions of followers in the West after being largely confined to the East for thousands of years. One more piece of the puzzle falls into place to signal the nearness of Antichrist's rise to power and the second coming which will follow as day after night.

Just as the ancient world rejected Christ, so the modern world will accept the Antichrist. This is not surprising. The Antichrist will represent all that a self-centered species wants to become on its own terms and independently of its Creator. As we have already noted, Jesus said to those who He knew would soon cry out for His death: "I am come in my Father's name, and ye receive me not; if another shall come in his own name, him ye will receive" (John 5:43).

In his own name is the key. Antichrist represents himself, not the God of heaven. Through him "Christianity" becomes the ultimate humanism. The satanic power manifest through Antichrist will be hailed as psychic powers of the mind and thus proof of man's innate Godlike potential. It will seem to be the ultimate triumph of self in fulfillment of the humanistic selfist psychology that permeates not only the secular world but now the church as well. And it will be the pledge that each of his followers, in the New Age that has dawned, can experience the same Godlike powers.

In contrast to the Antichrist's religion, which exalts self, Christ taught that we must *deny* self and take up the cross to follow Him. Jesus didn't have His disciples quickly sign up would-be followers as "church members" before they changed their minds. Nor did He suggest getting them involved in the choir or some committee in order to keep them active in the church. Instead He tested the quality of their commitment.

"If you really want to follow me," Christ would say, "then let me tell you where we're going. I'm heading for a hill outside Jerusalem called Calvary where they'll nail me to a cross. So if you would be faithful to me to the end, you might as well take up your cross right now, because that's where we're heading!" (see Luke 9:23-26). Such "negativism"! Yet if we are to avoid filling our churches with "Christians" who will worship the Antichrist, then we must take our example from our Lord in evangelizing the world.

Unfortunately, many of today's church leaders are far too sophisticated to present the gospel in the same "negative" terms used by Jesus and His apostles. They have taken success-oriented motivational seminars, studied psychology, and adopted Dale Carnegie techniques of "How to Win Friends and Influence People," which they consider to be ideal for "winning people to Christ." They persuade millions to "make a decision for Christ" who imagine that Christ's mission was to make them feel good about themselves by building up their self-esteem, answering their selfish prayers, and fulfilling their self-centered agendas. John points out:

> Now when he was in Jerusalem at the passover, in the feast day, many believed in his name when they saw the miracles which he did.
> But Jesus did not commit himself unto them, because he knew all men, and needed not that any should testify of man, for he knew what was in man (John 2:23-25).

Why did He "not commit Himself" to these people who believed that He was the Messiah? Because He knew that they misunderstood the Messiah's mission and were not willing to be corrected. They were only interested in experiencing His *miracles*, but would not take up the *cross* to follow Him. Yet they would be welcomed in most churches today, and many pastors would be careful not to challenge their false thinking for fear that they might leave and the church would lose their tithes. Jesus simply did not commit Himself to such persons.

In contrast to these people, the next chapter introduces us to Nicodemus, who was equally impressed by the miracles Christ did, but who also had a hunger to know the full truth. There we have the famous passage where Christ explains to Nicodemus that He had come to die for the sins of the world, and that in order to be saved one had to be "born again" through faith in Him.

In John 8 the same lesson is driven home again. In verse 30 we read, "As he spoke these words, many believed on him." In today's language many "went forward at the altar call." The Jews were believing on Christ in large numbers! What a revival! It is most instructive to see how Christ dealt with these "converts":

> Then said Jesus to those Jews which believed on him, If ye continue in my word, then are ye my disciples indeed, and ye shall know the truth, and the truth shall make you free (John 8:31,32).

It is difficult for us to grasp the shocking effect that this statement had upon His listeners. *"My disciples"?* Who was He claiming to be? In their excommunication of the man who had been blind from birth and to whom Christ had given sight, the rabbis declared contemptuously, "Thou art his [Jesus'] disciple, but we are Moses' disciples" (John 9:28). Clearly Jesus was claiming to be greater than Moses! And *"my word"*? The Jews prided themselves that they followed the Word of *God*. Was Jesus claiming to be God?

There was no doubt that He was claiming to be the Messiah, the Promised Deliverer, and they were willing to accept Him as such—provided He delivered them with the sword from their Roman oppressors. But this talk of setting them free through *truth* was both a disappointment and an insult. The Romans were militarily in control, but the Jews considered themselves to be intellectually free because they had the law of Moses and the temple. How dare anyone suggest that they did not have the *truth*!

When Christ tried to explain that He wanted to free them from sin and self, they argued heatedly. Denying the evil in their hearts, they insisted that they were the children of God: "We have one Father, even God" (John 8:41). Christ's response must have cut them like a knife: "Ye are of your father the devil, and the lusts of your father ye will do" (verse 44). Infuriated, they "took up stones to cast at him [to kill him]" (verse 59).

Jesus was not the kind of Messiah the Jews wanted, but Antichrist will be exactly what the whole world, including the Jews, desires. Christ offers to bring mankind into a right relationship with the true God who created the universe, and He is rejected. Antichrist will offer, as Satan promised Eve, to turn humans into gods, and he will be accepted. This profound difference between Christ and all antichrists is expressed eloquently by a popular Christmas card:

> History is crowded with men who would be gods [pictured are Alexander the Great, Julius Caesar, Maharishi Mahesh Yogi, Hitler, Lenin, Buddha, Mao Tse Tung, et al], but, only one God who would be man [followed by an artist's representation of Christ as the babe of Bethlehem].[4]

Again the question arises: What does all of the above have to do with the rise of Antichrist and Christ's second coming and the final conflict between them? Again we say: Everything! That face-to-face meeting at Armageddon is only to consummate what was already settled at Calvary and upon the basis of which Satan was defeated and each of us must make our own eternal choice.

The battle between Christ and Antichrist is fought to the finish in every human heart. We must know on whose side we are now. It will be too late to choose or change sides at the second coming. It is absolutely essential that we understand who Christ is and why He came and what He expects of us—or we could be deceived and in the end find ourselves on the wrong side of the cross for eternity.

It is solely on the basis of Christ's sacrifice upon the cross that He will destroy Antichrist at His second coming and Satan will be consigned to the lake of fire eternally. Though, like His disciples, we find it difficult to understand, the Bible makes it very clear that God became a man so that "*through death* he might destroy him that had the power of death, that is, the devil" (Hebrews 2:14). An old hymn puts it beautifully:

> By weakness and defeat
> He won the victor's crown,
> Trod all His foes beneath His feet
> By being trodden down.
>
> He Satan's power laid low;
> Made sin, He sin o'erthrew.
> Bowed to the grave, destroyed it so,
> And death by dying slew.

Behold in the cross, for the entire universe of all time and eternity to see, the awfulness, the horror, the contemptibleness and repulsiveness of sin laid bare. Be astonished, for in that hour that divides all mankind and all time and eternity, when the evil in the human heart was being vented against God, He joined sinful man in unleashing His fury against the same Victim upon the cross. Behold God's hatred of sin and His wrath poured out upon His own Son, as the sinless One: "For he [God] hath made him to be sin for us . . . that we might be made the righteousness of God in him" (2 Corinthians 5:21).

What her own prophets declared—that Israel would hate and slay her long-promised Messiah when He came—should have shocked and awakened an apostate and religiously proud Israel. Yet in spite of such clear warnings, that was exactly what happened. The very Son of God, the perfect Man, without a physical or moral blemish, presented Himself to Israel, healed the sick, cured the blind and lame, raised the dead, fed the hungry, brought love and joy—and was hated and reviled, given a mock trial, and publicly executed.

What an enigma! As one old classic hymn exclaims: "Thou the King of Glory wearing for our sake the crown of thorns!" How could it be possible? Charles Wesley wrote: "Amazing love, how can it be, that thou my God shouldst die for me!" After becoming a Christian, space scientist Werner von Braun declared in amazement:

> Evil had reached such proportions on this planet that the stage was set for a scenario unknown in the history of the cosmos: God would visit His creatures and they would nail Him to a cross!

Angels looking on in horror must have trembled with rage, anticipating at any moment the command to intervene and destroy those who abused, spat upon, scourged, and condemned to death the One who had created them. What an affront to see puny man mockingly put upon the Lord of Glory a crown of thorns, when the crown of the universe was His by right! And He let them do it, suffering each humiliation silently and patiently! Satan must have danced with glee, neither heeding nor comprehending the words that Jesus had spoken as He looked forward to the cross:

> Now is the judgment of this world; now shall the prince of this world [Satan] be cast out.
> And I, if I be lifted up from the earth [upon a cross], will draw all men unto me [either for salvation or judgment] (John 12:31,32).

Adam and Eve had hidden in guilt and disgrace when God had visited the Garden after their disobedience. When Jesus came, however, He was greeted by a brazen self-righteousness which even justified in its own eyes its rejection of Him. Adam and Eve had at least known God's voice, but now when He walked among His creatures the Creator was unrecognized. Hatred, guilt, fear, and defensive pride were the natural human reactions of those who came face-to-face with the God-man. Jesus was everything they knew they ought to be but were not, and they hated Him for it with a passion.

While demons rejoice and angels hide their faces, the religious and civil authorities join to slay the innocent. The mask of human goodness has slipped, exposing the truth about human depravity. These vile creatures vent their hatred upon the Perfect One who has done only good and who returns their revilings with love and forgiveness. Those despicable monsters circle the base of the cross like so many bloodthirsty hyenas! Worse than beasts, they take pleasure in His agony and savor what they foolishly imagine is their sweet revenge against this One whose perfect life condemned their hypocrisy and whose righteous words pierced their hearts.

They gloat as He winces in pain and His blood drains into the ground, yet it is being shed for their sins. Here once again we confront reality beyond our ability to grasp: "The very spear that pierced His side drew forth the blood that saves!" The blood that flowed for sin, however, only cleanses those who are willing to repent and to be reconciled to God. For those who reject the salvation that Christ has purchased, who spurn God's love and mercy—what just and awesome judgment awaits them!

The cross is the ultimate proof not only of God's love, but also of His righteousness and integrity. He could not compromise His holy standards. His justice must be satisfied. Grace could not be dispensed at the expense of truth. There could be no forgiveness of sin, no reconciliation of rebellious man to a holy God simply by a bookkeeping entry in heaven. The full price that justice demanded had to be paid. And God Himself was willing to pay it all.

What love! We respond with love toward those who love, attract, and please us—but He loves those who hate and torture and crucify Him. Stand back in amazement as He prays from the cross for those who have nailed Him there: "Father, forgive them, for they know not what they do" (Luke 23:34). Again Charles Wesley put it so eloquently:

> And can it be that I should gain
> An interest in the Savior's blood?
> Died He for me who caused His pain,
> For me who Him to death pursued?
> Amazing love, how can it be,
> That thou, my God, shouldst die for me!

The cross does not end in history past. It has not lost its power to save, to inspire both love and hate, and to divide mankind into two camps. That process continues today. Christ's disciples are to share in His rejection and sufferings at the hands of a world that would crucify Him again if it could. In His absence, it vents its hatred upon those who bear His name and are true to Him.

How dare anyone pervert the cross to make it appealing to the world that crucified the Lord of glory! At the cross we must die to life as we would have lived it in exchange for a new life—the resurrected Christ living in us. Paul wrote triumphantly:

> I am crucified with Christ; nevertheless I live—yet not I, but Christ liveth in me; and the life which I now live in the flesh I live by the faith of the Son of God, who loved me and gave himself for me (Galatians 2:20).

Christ's victory over Antichrist in a final confrontation at Armageddon would be empty if all of mankind went down to hell with that impostor. To God's eternal glory billions have been rescued by Christ from Satan's grasp. In spite of his satanic power Antichrist is defeated even before the second coming by those followers of Christ whom he martyrs in the great tribulation. Of them over whom Antichrist seemed victorious it is written in heaven:

> And they [the martyrs] overcame him [Antichrist] by the blood of the Lamb, and by the word of their testimony; and they loved not their lives unto death (Revelation 12:11).

20 | *Preparation for Delusion*

OUR CONCERN HAS BEEN with the rise of Antichrist and events preparing the world for that great delusion. It would take another volume to deal with what happens after he assumes power—the horrors of his rule and the great tribulation. Suffice it to say that after a brief period of Utopian unity and peace, the revived Roman Empire of "iron mixed with clay" that Daniel said "shall not cleave one to another" (2:43) will begin to fall apart. This earth will turn into a veritable hell when Satan, operating through the Antichrist, plays his last cards as his long-standing cosmic struggle with God reaches its climax.

In a furious battle in heaven itself between "Michael and his angels . . . and that old serpent, called the Devil, and Satan, which deceiveth the whole world," the latter will be "cast out into the earth, and his angels . . . with him" (Revelation 12:7-9). Planet Earth will be Satan's last bastion. In his fury to retain dominion, all pretense of being an angel of light will be stripped away. Those inhabiting this earth will begin to discover at last the horror of what it means to be the servants of sin and Satan. An angel from heaven will pronounce their doom:

> Woe to the inhabiters of the earth and of the sea! for the devil is come down unto you, having great wrath, because he knoweth that he hath but a short time (Revelation 12:12).

Seeking to retain his leadership, the Antichrist will find a scapegoat to blame for the increasing destruction as God pours out His wrath upon this earth. After breaking his pact with Israel, he will rally the world to accomplish what Hitler called "the final solution to the Jewish problem." The Bible calls it "the time of Jacob's trouble" (Jeremiah 30:7). The last act of togetherness on the part of the nations of the world will be an attempt to destroy Israel once and for all. Unwittingly, they will fulfill God's purpose: "I will gather all nations against Jerusalem to battle, and the city shall be taken . . ." (Zechariah 14:2).

Seeing Israel's defeat within their grasp, the world's armies will turn upon one another in a desperate contest for control of planet Earth. Armageddon will become a holocaust. Certainly Israel, which has a nuclear arsenal, will not allow itself to be annihilated without using its ultimate weapons. Christ's statement that He would have to intervene or all flesh would be destroyed (Matthew 24:22) suggests that a nuclear exchange of dreadful proportions will have begun when He comes in power and glory to rescue Israel. "Then shall the Lord go forth, and fight against those nations. . . . And his feet shall stand in that day upon the mount of Olives . . ." (Zechariah 14:3,4).

It will take no great struggle for Christ to liquidate the Antichrist and all the armies of this world. A mere word will suffice from the One who bears the marks of crucifixion, who "was dead" and is "alive for evermore" and has "the keys of hell and of death" (Revelation 1:18; 2:8; etc.). Satan will be locked away for 1000 years (Revelation 20:1-3) with his Antichrist and false prophet, while Christ rules the millennial kingdom from David's throne.

Science fiction? That the world in the last days will irrevocably turn its back upon truth and righteousness and opt for a false peace, and thus reap God's judgment and its destruction, is one of the clearest teachings in the Bible. Yet at the same time it is one of the most puzzling revelations of the stubborn perverseness of the human heart. Men and women everywhere long for peace, but the path that must be followed to reach it is repugnant to human pride. Mankind is like a terminally ill patient who desires the cure the doctor offers, yet finds the prescribed medicine ("repentance toward God, and faith toward our Lord Jesus Christ"—Acts 20:21) too distasteful to swallow—and takes a sugar-coated but deadly pill instead.

Even with all of the evidence we have given, it may still seem unbelievable that Antichrist could so thoroughly deceive mankind. Once again it will help to turn to a man whose rise to power continues to intrigue and mystify historians. Adolf Hitler emerged suddenly out of obscurity and rose to a power unequaled in modern times. He deceived not only Germany but nearly the entire world for a surprising length of time. There is no rational explanation.

Film footage of the public appearances of Hitler with their pageantry—solemn marchers carrying huge banners displaying the swastika, and fanatically repeated "Sieg heils" from hundreds of thousands of throats—reveal an unmistakable but mysterious *religious* element. Demonic? Without doubt. Hitler evoked a spontaneous mass hysteria that bordered on *worship*. William Shirer, author of *The Rise and Fall of the Third Reich*, who went to Germany in 1934 to report on what was taking place, wrote in his diary at the time:

> Today, as far as the vast majority of his fellow-countrymen are concerned, he [Hitler] has reached a pinnacle never before achieved by a German ruler.
>
> He has become—even before his death—a myth, a legend, almost a god. . . .[1]

There was a twisted genius in Hitler that accomplished some great things. Between 1933 and 1937, while the rest of the world was still wallowing deep in the Depression, Germany's unemployment dropped from 6 million to less than 1 million. National output doubled. The Volkswagen went into production and the world's first major highway system, Germany's famous autobahn, was begun. So much good camouflaged the evil. Simone Veil, who spent time in Auschwitz, where most of her family died, confessed: "We had great difficulty believing that people were actually being killed. Nobody imagined that there could be a plan for extermination."[2]

After a honeymoon of peace, love, and brotherhood, the terror of Antichrist's rule will make Hitler's rule seem benevolent. Those who refuse to worship him and submit to the new world order will be summarily executed—and the whole earth will know and approve. After all, mankind will have just experienced the incredible disappearance of millions of people. Fear of being snatched from earth will keep everyone in line—for awhile.

The most fascinating aspect of Hitler's deception was the heavy "Christian" element that was involved—an element that will be absolutely essential under Antichrist. Most of the church in Germany went happily along with the new order. Hitler promised "liberty for all religious denominations," much like the promises now being made in Eastern Europe.

In his March 23, 1933, speech, when he took over as dictator, Hitler praised the Christian faith and promised to respect liberty of conscience. A few excerpts from his wartime speeches reveal an incredible pretense of being on God's side:

> 1940: "We pray our Lord that He would continue to bless us in our battle for freedom. . . ."
>
> 1941: "We believe we shall earn the blessing of the Supreme Leader . . . the Lord God has given His approval to our battle. He will be with us in . . . the future."
>
> 1942: "And we will pray the Lord God for that, the salvation of the nation. . . ."
>
> 1943: "We will continue to give our whole strength to our nation this year. Only then can we . . . pray to our Lord God, that He will help us as He always has. . . ."[3]

Thousands of German pastors joined the newly organized "German Christians' Faith Movement," which supported the Nazi doctrines and promoted a "Reich Church" that would unite all Protestants under the state. A minority of pastors, led by Martin Niemoeller (who had originally welcomed Hitler to power), realized at last that Hitler's "Positive Christianity" was in fact anti-Christian, and so opposed the Nazification of the church.

The "Reich Church," formed under leaders picked by Hitler, was formally recognized by the Reichstag on July 14, 1933. On November 13 a massive rally was held in the Berlin Sportpalast by the "German Christians' Faith Movement." Leaders of the rally proposed abandonment of the Old Testament and revision of the New Testament to fit National Socialism. Resolutions called for "One People, One Reich, One Faith," an oath of allegiance to Hitler to be signed by all pastors, and the exclusion of Jewish Christians by all churches. The Gestapo's reign of terror against followers of Christ began with the arrest of 700 pastors in the fall of 1935.

Always the justification under Hitler, as under Constantine, was ecumenical "unity." We are hearing the same appealing slogan today—nor can the tide of ecumenism be stemmed. Those who oppose it are accused of being narrow-minded bigots. *Truth*, which we are not to sell at any price (Proverbs 23:23), is already being bartered for a humanistic and mythical *peace* and *unity*.

All the time that he was deliberately moving to destroy Christianity and replace it with his neopagan occultism, Hitler continued to pretend that he was the champion of *real* Christianity. The following excerpt from a speech by Dr. Hans Kerrl, Nazi Minister of Church Affairs, reveals how blatant the lie can become while still being eagerly embraced by "Christians":

> The Party stands [for] . . . Positive Christianity, and Positive Christianity *is* National Socialism. . . .
>
> National Socialism is the doing of God's will . . . God's will reveals itself in German blood. . . . That Christianity consists in faith in Christ as Son of God makes me laugh. . . .
>
> True Christianity is represented by the Party, and the German people are now called by the Party and especially by the Fuehrer to a *real* Christianity. . . .
>
> The Fuehrer is the herald of a *New Revelation*.[4]

We are reminded by the homage afforded to cult leaders that the world remains vulnerable to delusion. The Dalai Lama, for example, is highly honored worldwide by political and religious leaders and greatly admired by the masses. Yet his public claims are similar to those which will be made by the Antichrist: That he is the 14th *reincarnation* of the original Dalai Lama and that he is literally *"God."* He proposes to bring global peace through a heavily demonic Yoga visualization technique into which he is initiating tens of thousands of persons around the world. For this he was awarded the Nobel Peace Prize in 1989! This forerunner of the Antichrist continues to be feted by the Roman Catholic Church, which previously gave Hitler its blessing.

With all genuine Christians removed from earth and the Holy Spirit no longer convicting consciences, mass deception will be a thousand times easier for the Antichrist than for Hitler. Almost any "positive" belief will be acceptable that supports the delusion of infinite human potential, builds up self-esteem and self-worth, and concerns itself with social justice through humanistic efforts. It is already a crime punishable under the Genocide Treaty, which was recently signed by the United States, to suggest that any religion is wrong. To be ecumenical and "positive" is required by international law. It is but a small step to Antichrist's harsh rule.

Today's "Positive Christianity"—which, like Hitler's, dresses occultism in Christian language—has virtually taken over in America and is now being exported into Eastern Europe. Those who promote Positive Thinking, Possibility Thinking, and Positive Confession are among the most influential radio/television preachers and church leaders in America. Any correction is rejected as "negative." As for "new revelations," the Charismatic movement is spawning "prophets" whose pronouncements are being blindly followed by growing numbers of Christians even though the "prophecies" often contradict the Bible. Like the world, the church too is being set up for a great delusion.

Even for many evangelicals, "faith" no longer requires God as its object, but is touted as a "positive" power of the mind that creates what we firmly and sincerely *believe.* Thus what we "pray" for will come to pass, not if *God* wills it, but if *we* can only *believe it will happen.* "Your unconscious mind . . . [has a] power that turns wishes into realities when the wishes are strong enough,"[5] promises a "Christian" leader whose writings are read each month by 16 million persons. His protégé, one of the most popular promoters of this occultic delusion that "faith" is a force wielded by our minds, explains this seductive gospel enthusiastically:

> What is the magic ingredient that can insure success and eliminate failure from our lives? It is FAITH! Possibility Thinking is just another word for faith.[6]
>
> You don't know the power you have within you! . . . You make the world into anything you choose. Yes, you can make your world into whatever you want it to be.[7]

Enticed by such false teaching, Christians begin to view prayer as a religious technique for getting their own way. They set their sights upon what they want, then try to have "faith" to make it happen. Seminars in *How To Write Your Own Ticket With God*[8] by thinking certain thoughts, speaking certain words, or visualizing goals are eagerly attended by thousands.

Today's false gospel is spawning "Christians" who have been attracted to a "Christ" who has the attributes of Antichrist. This widely-presented false "Christ" no longer calls sinners to repentance before a holy God but excuses ungodly behavior as a psychological problem resulting from traumas suffered in childhood. Instead of requiring his disciples to "deny self and take up the cross," he teaches them to love and accept themselves and to recognize their inherent "self-worth." Nor does this "Christ" promise the "meek" that they will inherit the earth, but offers "self-assertion" training. Instead of blessing those that "mourn," he warns against "low self-esteem" and promotes a new "positive self-image." And rather than promising heaven to the "poor in spirit," this false "Christ" offers to the financially poor the enticing gospel of a hundredfold return for gifts to certain ministries.

Furthermore, the dynamic, motivating hope of Christ's imminent return is being denied by many who claim to belong to the Lord. That Christ will come back to earth visibly and in person is a view that is being increasingly rejected in favor of some kind of "spiritual" second coming. Popular author M. Scott Peck, though a New Ager, professes to be a Christian and is so accepted even by evangelicals. He speaks for a growing sector of the church:

> When I think of the enormity of the changes required [for global peace]...it sometimes seems that a virtual Second Coming is required. I am not talking about a bodily second coming. In fact, I am profoundly pessimistic about a church that would sit around passively waiting for its messiah to appear in the flesh.
>
> Rather, I am talking about the resurrection of Christ's spirit, which would occur in the church if Christians took him seriously.[9]

Here we have one of the most persuasive New Age lies that was ever inspired by Satan. Many Charismatic leaders are now promoting the idea that the second coming is not the return of our Lord *personally* in His resurrected individual body to earth, but the attainment by His *spiritual body*, the church, to a higher spiritual state evidenced by great signs and wonders. A leading New Ager presents this lie persuasively:

> So as we accept Christ in our hearts...not just a simple emotional conversion that the electronic evangelists call for, but a radical transformation of consciousness...we experience personally the coming of Christ, now....
>
> There is no Second Coming of Christ, that is a false concept....There is only, as the Bible puts it, the coming of Christ, through you and through me, as we ascend in consciousness....
>
> The final appearance of the Christ will not be a man in the air before whom all must kneel...[but] an evolutionary event....A new race, a new species will inhabit the Earth— people who collectively have the stature in consciousness that

Jesus had. And in that process the kingdom of God will truly be established on Earth under the rule of the Christ in the hearts and minds and souls of all people.[10]

How diabolically clever! The author does not argue as an *anti*-Christian but as a *true* Christian. He does not *reject* the Bible but claims to *correct a false interpretation* of the Bible. His thesis is very persuasive. To rise to the full stature of one's innate perfection seems far more ennobling than to repent of one's rebellion before a holy God. And this thesis fits perfectly with the Antichrist's probable claim that he is the reincarnation of the Christ Spirit that was in Jesus—a "higher state of consciousness" into which he promises to lead the world.

The Roman Catholic Church, by its dogmas, also denies the rapture. The best that most Catholics hope for after death is to awaken in purgatory, a place where they must suffer for their sins for an indeterminate length of time, depending upon how many indulgences they have earned and how many Rosaries and Masses and alms and good deeds others perform for them after their death. Thus the teaching that "the dead in Christ shall rise first, then we which are alive and remain shall be caught up together with them in the clouds to meet the Lord in the air" (1 Thessalonians 4:16,17) must be ignored or reinterpreted. After all, some good Catholics may have to spend several thousand years in purgatory, others only a few days or weeks. The Church has no clear guidelines to say how long anyone will be there. Therefore all Christians could not be resurrected at once and, together with the living believers, taken to heaven simultaneously, as the Bible teaches.

Moreover, the Pope has apparently received a most interesting "revelation" from Our Lady of Fatima: that a great disaster is coming which will transform human thinking and catapult him into a position where he will play a key role in bringing order out of chaos. It sounds very much like the mass disappearance of millions in the rapture. Malachi Martin, "former Jesuit and professor at the Vatican's Pontifical Biblical Institute," writes:

John Paul is waiting. God must first intervene, before John
Paul's major ministry to all men can start. . . .

He is waiting . . . for an event that will fission human
history, splitting the immediate past from the oncoming future. . . .

John Paul's waiting and watching time will then be over. His
ministry as the Servant of the Grand Design will then begin . . .
when the fissioning event occurs. . . .[11]

As we have seen, the rapture of the church will be a "fissioning event" indeed! Unity and peace will not come as "Our
Lady of Fatima" has revealed, but that will not matter. The
disappearance of multiplied millions will create the opportunity which both the Antichrist and the Pope await. Neither
will realize that Christ has taken His bride home to heaven, but
they will know that their time has come.

The great delusion will be furthered by the spurious "Holy
Spirit" which is so evidently operating within the Charismatic
movement—a movement that includes an estimated 10 million
American Roman Catholics. One of the first "prophecies"
that was spoken at the inception of the Catholic Charismatic
movement, which began in the mid-1960's, promoted the
delusion that "what Mary promised at Fatima is really going to
take place."[12] The "gift of tongues" was received spontaneously by many Catholics as they were engaged in unbiblical
prayers to Mary: "With Tom N. it was as he was finishing his
rosary . . . with Sister M., it came as she knelt in silent prayer
to the Blessed Virgin."[13] The general effect upon Catholics of
the "baptism in the Spirit" has been to increase their heretical
devotion to Mary and to make the many other abominable
dogmas of Romanism all the more acceptable and meaningful.[14] The "spirit" that endorses such delusion will also endorse Antichrist.

That spirit operating through Catholic leaders is already
deceiving Protestants. This was demonstrated again at "Indianapolis 1990," an ecumenical Charismatic conference on
"the Holy Spirit and World Evangelization" where Roman
Catholics had the largest representation among the 23,000 in

attendance. *Charisma* magazine reported enthusiastically that the "Roman Catholic [evangelism training] session...was centered on leading people to salvation in Christ, not on persuading them to join the Catholic Church as was feared by some people."[15] That session was, however, a dishonest misrepresentation. One wonders why those who claim miraculous gifts of the Spirit so often lack the discernment to know that they are being deceived.

Tom Forrest, a priest who directs Rome's "New Evangelization 2000" from the Vatican, used all the right evangelical terms when speaking before the joint Protestant-Catholic audience. He drew applause from Protestants when he called for "Christian unity" in "World Evangelization." But when he spoke to a Catholic-only workshop he let it be known, to repeated loud applause from fellow Catholics, what he really believed:

> Our job is to make people as richly and as fully Christian as we can make them by bringing them *into the Catholic Church*... our visible sacrament of salvation. I like saying those words... "Our visible sacrament of salvation." That's what the Church is, and... we have to be evangelizing *into the church*....
>
> No, you don't just invite someone to become a Christian, you invite them *to become Catholics*. Why would this be so important?... there are seven sacraments, and the Catholic Church has all seven.... we have the body of Christ, we drink the blood of Christ. Jesus is alive on our altars, as offering.... We become one with Christ in the Eucharist....
>
> As Catholics we have Mary... Queen of Paradise....
>
> As Catholics—now I love this one—we have purgatory. Thank God! I'm one of those people that would never get to the Beatific Vision without it. It's the only way to go.
>
> ...our job is to use this remaining decade evangelizing everyone we can *into the Catholic Church*... and into the third millennium of Catholic history.[16]

On top of her heresies, the Roman Catholic Church consorts with "seducing spirits" such as those that have appeared at Fatima in the form of "Mary" and the *child* "Jesus." These apparitions and their "doctrines of devils" (1 Timothy 4:1) have been embraced by every Pope in the past 60 years and thus by hundreds of millions of Catholics. Similar appearances have increased around the world, from Lipa City in the Philippines to Bayside, New York, to Medjugorje, Yugoslavia. Always there are "miracles" and "warnings" to the world of coming judgment, with the promise that through the rosary and "Our Lady's" intervention peace can come. One Roman Catholic expert on such appearances has written:

> ... we are solicited on all sides by extraordinary mystical phenomena: apparitions, visions, prophecies, ecstasies, stigmatisations, etc.... There is Fatima, of course ... [and daily appearances at] Medjugorje....
>
> There is also Dozule ... and Kibeho in Rwanda, with apparitions of a very new kind. We also hear of apparitions of Our Lady at Akita in Japan ... apparitions in Chile, in Australia and in Poland ... in Canada ... Garabandal, San Damiano, Cairo ... Amsterdam.[17]

In Spain's village of Garabandal alone, there were about 2000 apparitions accompanied by occultic phenomena and messages to the world. The "Virgin Mary" is now appearing all over the earth with increasing frequency. There is a mixture of fraud (as exposed at Medjugorje, for example) and genuine demonic power. The message that comes from the "Virgin" is consistent with other demonic revelations and is important for the Antichrist: that all religions are basically the same and must come together for peace. Offering a gospel that can be "accepted by Catholic, Protestant, Moslem or Jew,"[18] "Mary" declares: "Everyone worships God in his own way with peace in our [*sic*] hearts."[19]

Contact with demonic spirits is accelerating, making both the world and the church of our day far more vulnerable to satanic deception than was the case in Hitler's time. Involvement in the occult, Yoga, and other practices from Eastern mysticism and New Age philosophies is even greater today than in Hitler's Germany of the 1930's. The United Nations has a Meditation Room containing Babylonian occult symbolism, where followers of all religions, who visit by the hundreds of thousands each year, may awaken the "god within." The Pentagon has its own Meditation Club, which seeks to prevent war by creating a "psychic peace shield" around the earth with positive thoughts. The Soviets have a similar program. Dabbling in the occult in order to "develop human potential" has gained a large following among political leaders. As one syndicated columnist recently pointed out:

> ... a new day is dawning at the Central Intelligence Agency, the Pentagon and Congress: The New Age has arrived. ... highly placed officials are consulting psychics ... engaging in past-life regressions or consulting mediums. ...
>
> At any given time, about one-fourth of congressmen are engaged in exploring psychic phenomena, according to Rep. Charles Rose of North Carolina. "That would be healing, prophecy, remote viewing or physical manifestation of psychic powers such as bending spoons or erasing computer tapes," he said.[20]

Through his pursuit of the occult and New Age medicine, Prince Charles, the next King of England and thus the next head of the Church of England, has concluded that all religions are basically the same. He considers himself to be psychic and believes in guidance from the spirit realm. The Queen (also involved in spiritism) and the Prince both believe that he, Charles, "is the Chosen One—placed in line for the throne through a divine, preordained plan."[21]

Prince Charles is representative of many other prominent world figures who are also involved in the occult and anticipate the coming of a humanistic one-world religion. Scientists, too, are supporting the belief in psychic forces. *Foundations of Physics* recently published an article by Princeton University researcher Roger D. Nelson to the effect that scientific experiments demonstrate that the human mind can influence computers at a distance.[22] The increasing openness to paranormal events and alleged psychic forces is an important preparation for the coming Antichrist, who will manifest such powers to a degree never before known.

With the new freedom in Eastern Europe, occultists are going public and being enthusiastically received. The *Chicago Sun-Times* reported, "First newspaper horoscope leaves Soviets starry-eyed."[23] The *New York Times* headlined a major article on exploding occultism and spiritual renewal in the USSR: "An Unnamed 'Healing Force' Debuts on Soviet TV."[24] For 70 years there were about 40,000 lectures a day in factories, schools, and on radio and TV "proving" that God didn't exist and that "scientific materialism" was the only truth. Now the Soviets are resentful of having been deprived of other viewpoints and are ravenous for spiritual experiences.

Unfortunately, this new openness to the *spiritual* without the guidance of *the Bible and the Holy Spirit* opens the door to satanic deception. Again, the stage is set for the Antichrist. That this trend is gathering such great momentum at this time is another sign that we are nearing the return of Christ. The *Washington Post* reported:

> If there is a new "cult of personality" in the Soviet Union, it is centered not on Mikhail Gorbachev but rather on a Ukrainian psychologist who [by visualization] "applies anesthesia from a distance" and has an audience of up to 200 million people whenever he appears on "Good Evening Moscow."
> Kashpirovsky claimed to cure everything from sterility and arthritis to cancerous tumors, and there were plenty of the grateful to attest to his remarkable powers.[25]

Visualization is the most powerful occult technique known. Practitioners, from Siberian shamans (witch doctors) to success seminar leaders, know that it is the fastest way to make contact with "spirit guides." Carl Jung said of "Philemon," his spirit guide: "I went walking up and down the garden with him . . . he was what the Indians call a guru."[26] Jungian psychologist Hal Zina Bennett assures us, "I have never met a person who could not contact an inner guide . . . within thirty minutes of coaching."[27]

A typical seminar, "The Power of Imagination," has been taught to thousands of people across the country by two Catholic schools, Marquette and Loyola Marymount Universities. Participants learn to contact a visible "inner guide" that literally speaks to them, is never wrong, and will be with them for life. This practice has exploded in the areas of education, business, medicine, and psychology since the "First World Conference on Imagery" (sponsored by Marquette University and the Medical College of Wisconsin) was held in 1985.

One no longer need travel to a distant place where "Mary" has appeared. Visualization techniques are being taught, from kindergarten to top management seminars, which enable anyone to make contact with "Jesus" or the "Virgin Mary" or "extraterrestrials" or any person from the past or even the future. Through this ancient and powerful method of opening oneself to satanic delusion, demons posing as Jesus are being contacted for "inner healing" and "prayer" even among evangelicals.

Psychologists and medical doctors are among the foremost promoters of "visual imagery" for healing everything from a poor self-image to the most deadly diseases. Their endorsement gives a respectability to techniques that witch doctors have been using for thousands of years. Alfred S. Alschuler, former president of John F. Kennedy University and now the head of the Institute for Transpersonal Psychology, has "no explanation" for what he calls "inner teachers" but suggests that therapists should "help patients maintain a healthy relationship with their 'inner voices' " in order to benefit from the "wisdom they offer." He admits that these entities can be evil, but rejects a belief in demons, which is the only explanation for "spirit guides" that fits all the facts. Addressing a convention of psychologists, Alschuler confessed:

> Ten years ago I started hearing an inner voice. As a clinical psychologist I was worried that this might be the beginning of a breakdown. . . .

Dorothy Maclean, a co-founder of the Scottish Findhorn community, admitted that "the personal side of me resisted and did not want to listen—yet in the presence of my resplendent God-self (her name for her inner voice) I was transformed...."

When I asked for the name of my own voice, it said, "We are the Great White Brotherhood" [a group of "Ascended Masters" well-known in the occult].[28]

Dr. Martin L. Rossman, who uses visualization of spirit guides in his medical practice and teaches it to others, calls this technique "the essence of Shamanism [witchcraft]." "Working with imagery like we do," says Rossman, "is making Shamanism contemporary and relevant.... Some of my patients astrally project themselves and have a spirit guide on the astral plane."[29] This is *medicine*?

Dr. Rossman and others now utilizing this ancient witchcraft technique liken the inner guide to the Holy Spirit. And Christians are only too happy to accept this outrageous claim as "scientific support" of the pseudo-Christian occultic practices which they have picked up from psychology.[30] Thus the great delusion deepens!

Alschuler says, "Whether it is called God, Jesus, Daimon, Master, Adept, Guardian Angel, Mentor, ordinary earth names or exotic aliases, the role of the voice is to teach."[31] Indeed it is.

What these seducing spirits would teach in the last days, Paul warned, would be "doctrines of devils." Both the world and the church are being deceived for the epitomy of diabolical delusion, which is yet to come. It is not difficult to see the day when untold millions of such spirit guides will identify the Antichrist as the Christ and will be believed. What a setup!

21 | *The Christian's Hope*

THE CHRISTIAN LIFE SHOULD be one of great joy for many reasons. First of all, the knowledge that one has been forgiven by God of every sin, and that no appeasement need be made, gives a joyful release from the fear of coming judgment. Then there is the deep gratitude that Christ would suffer the eternal judgment we deserved in order to have us in His presence in heaven forever. There is also the joy of love awakened by the Holy Spirit in response to His great love—a love that is beyond anything earth can offer. This love gives the believer a consuming desire to please the One who said, "If ye love me, keep my commandments" (John 14:15).

Perhaps the greatest joy of all is the discovery that we can indeed please the One who loves us so—that our hearts have been changed so that we now hate sin and love righteousness. Words fail to express the joy that comes from knowing that Christ Himself is living within us and empowers us by His Holy Spirit to live a new life that honors and glorifies Him. Instead of fearing to meet God, we long to be in the presence of our heavenly Father when at last, as part of the church which is Christ's bride, we will see the Bridegroom and be united with Him forever.

To be caught up at the rapture to meet Christ in the air and to be taken to heaven without experiencing physical death is the great hope of the Christian. In comparison, any earthly ambition fades into insignificance. Paul reminded the Philippians, "Our conversation [citizenship] is in heaven, from whence also we look for the Savior, the Lord Jesus Christ" (3:20). To Titus he wrote: "Looking for that blessed hope, and the glorious appearing of the great God and our Savior Jesus Christ" (2:13). Hebrews 9:28 declares, "Unto them that look for him [Christ] shall he appear the second time without sin unto salvation."

One does not look for someone who cannot possibly appear for months, much less for years. If the rapture could not occur until after the Antichrist had first appeared, or until the end of the great tribulation, surely such language would not have been used. There can be no doubt that the imminent return of Christ to take them to His Father's house of many mansions was the daily hope and expectancy of the early Christians. And so it should be for us today. These words of our Lord should both encourage and warn us:

> Let your loins be girded about and your lights burning, and ye yourselves like men that wait for their lord. . . .
> Blessed are those servants whom the lord when he cometh shall find watching. . . .
> Be ye therefore ready also, for the Son of man cometh at an hour when ye think not (Luke 12:35-37,40).

"At an hour when ye think not"! That expression would suggest that the nearer the coming of the Lord, the fewer there will be who are really looking for Him. It seems odd that it should be so, yet the expectancy in the church of Christ's return has been steadily decreasing and is now at a very low ebb. It also suggests that the conditions in the world will be such when Christ returns that Christians will be so contented and at ease that they will not be longing to leave this earth for a better place. Paul's warning, which we have quoted several times, bears repeating yet again: "When they say 'Peace and safety' . . ." then the big surprise will come!

There are Christians today who complain that those who are looking for Christ to return at any moment are "so heavenly-minded that they're no earthly good." But that cliché has it backward. Jesus, who is our example, was the most heavenly-minded Person in history—yet at the same time He did the most earthly good. True heavenly-mindedness actually makes one more useful here upon earth.

Others suggest that those who are waiting for the rapture to take them to heaven are just sitting on their hands and doing nothing. Critics call this an "escapist mentality." Logically, however, the more we are convinced that Christ is coming very soon, the more diligent we will be to do God's will, live for Christ, and win others for Him because of the conviction that the time is short. This "blessed hope" of being with our Lord in heaven at any moment is in fact the greatest motivation of all for holy and victorious living. John said that everyone who has this hope "purifieth himself, even as he [Christ] is pure" (1 John 3:3).

In Colossians 3 Paul gives as complete a description as we can find anywhere in Scripture of the Christian life—what we should and what we should not be and do. The Christian is to mortify his bodily passions: "fornication, uncleanness, inordinate affection, evil concupiscence, and covetousness, which is idolatry . . . anger, wrath, malice, blasphemy, filthy communication . . ." and so forth. Having done that, he is to express in holiness and love "mercies, kindness, humbleness of mind, meekness, longsuffering. . . ." The list goes on, providing a complete pattern of godliness. In that one chapter the apostle Paul clearly presents the Christian life in unmistakable and practical terms.

Of course, most religions have moral standards and require a code of behavior for their adherents to follow. Buddha had his Four Noble Truths and his Eight-fold Path, Confucius his secular ethical philosophy. Other religions have their standards, which to some extent reflect God's moral laws written in everyone's conscience. It is axiomatic, however, that no ethical philosophy can provide the moral strength to live up to its standards. No law can save; it can only condemn. Christianity, which sets by far the highest standard of all, is alone in providing the power to live a holy life. Therein lies another element of the uniqueness which separates it from every religion the world has ever known.

Paul did not impose upon the Colossian believers, and upon us today, a strict moral code that we must struggle to live up to in our own strength. The key to living the Christian life is found in one word in verses 5 and 12: *therefore*. "Mortify *therefore*" the sins of the flesh. "Put on *therefore*" the holiness and graces of Christ. Whatever *therefore* refers to, it gives both the *reason* for obedience and the *power* to obey. To what, then, does it allude? The answer is found in the preceding verses:

> If [since] ye then be risen with Christ, seek those things which are above, where Christ sitteth on the right hand of God.
>
> Set your affection on things above, not on things on the earth.
>
> For ye are dead, and your life is hid with Christ in God.
>
> When Christ, who is our life, shall appear, then shall ye also appear with him in glory.
>
> Mortify *therefore*. . . .
>
> Put on *therefore*. . . .

The power to live the Christian life comes from confidence in and gratitude for the marvelous, historic fact that Christ died for our sins, rose from the dead, and is now in heaven at the Father's right hand. Yet there is another dynamic: the great hope of His soon appearing and of our appearing with Him as His bride at His side! This is no mere theoretical religious philosophy but a vital, real relationship with One who could come at any moment to take us to be forever in His presence in a new, eternal dimension of living! Once that hope has gripped us, we have the motivation and power to live as truly born again and as God's dear children, partakers of His divine nature.

Moreover, true Christians have a deep sense of the holiness of God and an awesome, respectful fear of the One to whom they must give account. They have a keen awareness of having broken His law, and they know the awful consequences of this.

That is why they are so grateful that their sins have been forgiven. Until a person has been brought to these convictions he is not ready to become a Christian on the terms that God offers in the Bible.

Yes, the Christian is crucified with Christ, dead to sin and to this world, and intimately identified with Christ in His cross. He has been raised with Him into new life—in fact, Christ *is* our life. But in addition to all of this, wonderful as it is, Paul exhorts us to live in this expectancy: "When Christ, who is our life, shall appear, then shall ye also appear with him in glory." The knowledge of that destiny delivers us from lusts and fears and causes this world to lose its attractiveness to us once and for all.

Christ could come at any moment to take us to His Father's house, where we will be united with Him eternally. Then, when He appears and "every eye shall see Him" and Israel will recognize Him, we will be at His side in glorified bodies to rule and reign with Him—"and so shall we ever be with the Lord!" That is the Christian's hope. Heaven is our real home and that is where our hearts are—with Him. The world has lost its appeal, sin has lost its power, and Satan must relinquish his claim upon those who belong to Christ. We have been set free!

Moreover, it is essential that the imminent rapture once again become not only the great expectancy and hope of the church, but that Christians testify to the world of this soon-coming event and of Christ's second coming to judge the world and to establish His millennial kingdom that will follow. If we believe in the Christ whose birth the angels proclaimed, then we must also embrace what the angels declared to be the purpose of His birth: that He would bring peace to this earth, as only He can, by personally reigning on the throne of His father David in Jerusalem. This is not stated as an ideal possibility with other options available; it is man's only hope.

Those who believe in Christ must necessarily oppose and condemn as false and deceitful every attempt to bring "peace on earth" that does not include Jesus Christ as world ruler. If that seems like an extreme statement, it is only because so few

284 ◆ *Dave Hunt*

Christians take seriously what the Bible says about global peace, the rapture, the rise of Antichrist, and the second coming.

There are only two persons who will rule over this world: The first is the Antichrist, and the other is the Lord Jesus Christ. Each individual must choose between these two antagonists and their opposing kingdoms. There is no neutral ground.

Those who set out to establish international peace through a world government over which the Lord Jesus Christ is not invited to reign are necessarily on the side of the Antichrist. They are preparing the world for his rule, whether they acknowledge that fact or not. Such is the danger that lies before the world at this moment when the prospect for international peace and unity resulting from mankind's own efforts seems so encouraging.

Those who suggest that we can retain the idea of Christ's return to reign over this earth as the symbol of some "spiritual truth" suitable for all religions deny the very foundation of the Christian faith. The significant distinction between Christianity and every other world religion is found in the central and essential *personal* role that Christ plays as compared with that of a Buddha, Muhammad, Krishna, or Confucius. In contrast to the others, Christ did not offer a mere religious philosophy to live by; He offered *Himself*.

Christ *personally* died for our sins upon the cross and He promises to *personally* come to live within the hearts of those who receive Him as Savior and Lord. Furthermore, He promised just as clearly to come *personally* to this earth to establish His kingdom in peace and righteousness. It is as much a denial of the Christian faith to refuse to take seriously Christ's offer to reign personally upon earth as it is to reject His offer to personally be one's Savior from sin and its penalty.

Christianity is based upon the claims that Christ made about *Himself* and the eyewitness accounts of His life, death, and resurrection as recorded in the New Testament and verified by Old Testament prophecies. The distinctions that make Christianity unique are irreconcilable with any other religious belief, and any attempt at ecumenical unity is a denial of biblical Christianity. Consistent with the distinctiveness of Christianity, the Bible also teaches that peace will not come to this world through the triumph of Christ's *teachings*, but only through His *personal return to reign from Jerusalem.* In fact, His teachings cannot be believed apart from Himself. That was the very challenge with which Jesus confronted the Jewish religious leaders:

> Search the Scriptures, for in them ye think ye have eternal life; and they are they which *testify of me.*
> And ye will not *come to me* that ye might have life (John 5:39,40).

How dare anyone think that a world ripening for judgment can be rescued by Christians working together in political/ social activism with the followers of all religions, and with humanists and atheists! Scripture says repeatedly that nothing but the personal and physical return of Christ to this earth can put an end to its wickedness and suffering. Paul declared that "the whole creation groaneth and travaileth in pain together" as it longs for a release that can only come through "the manifestation of the sons of God" (Romans 8:19-22). He makes it very clear what this means: that only when Christians have received their immortal bodies and are glorified with Christ (verses 23-25), ruling and reigning upon this earth with Him, will earth be delivered from its pain.

The last days before Christ's return are indeed prophesied as a period of growing evil, error, and spiritual delusion, manifested in both the world and the professing church. There are also, however, indications in Scripture that in the last days millions of people around the world will receive Christ as Savior and Lord, thus hastening His return. Many of them will be the most unlikely candidates for salvation—New Agers, drug addicts, prison inmates, Communists, Muslims, Catholics, the poor, and the outcasts of society—as Christ seemed to indicate in the parable of the great supper:

> Then the master of the house being angry [at those who accepted his invitation, then failed to come to the feast and tried to cover up their unwillingness with pitiful excuses] said to his servant, Go out quickly into the streets and lanes of the city, and bring in hither the poor, the maimed, the halt, and the blind.
>
> And the servant said, Lord, it is done as thou hast commanded, and yet there is room. And the lord said unto the servant, Go out into the highways and hedges, and compel them to come in, that my house may be filled (Luke 14:21-23).

At least 50 million people, and perhaps many more, turned to Christ in China during the brief period of increased freedom that followed the demise of Mao Tse Tung and his totalitarian regime. Concerned by this revival, Chinese authorities had already begun to imprison and even execute Christian leaders long before the student uprising and massacre at Tiananmen Square in early June 1989—peaceful demonstrations which was led to a large extent by Christians. Since that time, and particularly since the fall of Communist regimes in Europe, conditions in China have grown increasingly difficult. There is great fear on the part of the leaders that the army could rise up as it did in Romania, and measures are being taken to prevent popular demonstrations of any kind. It seems likely that a new wave of repression against religion will be launched.

The new breath of freedom in Eastern Europe could well bring a similar revival there. As this book goes to press there are indications that multitudes are coming to Christ. The following are brief excerpts from a very few representative letters among the many in the Soviet Union who are believing the gospel after hearing it for the first time:

> I was a member of the Communist Party for 25 years. How much harm I caused Christians! But God forgave me. I can't believe the depth of His love. (From Rovno.)
>
> Together with some friends, I decided to rob a church. . . . I came to the church to case the place and heard a sermon that was just for me. . . . I repented. My friends think I am crazy but

I am praying for them. I want to tell everyone about Jesus. (From Grodno.)

I was a hardened atheist. . . . But now by God's will I am proving that He does exist. (From Arkhangelsk.)

I am already 80 years old and I just received my first copy of the Bible. . . . I weep with great joy that God has sent me bread from heaven. (From Zaporozhe.)[1]

There are reports of many people who, upon hearing their first sermon or getting their first copy of the Bible, are being set free from sin and self for eternity. The following letter to the editor from a young man in Novosibirsk, Siberia, was published in the popular Soviet weekly *Ogonyok*. It eloquently tells the story of what is happening to thousands:

I just turned over the last page of a great book, and I am overcome by feelings of gratitude and happiness. But there are some bitter questions which remain unanswered: Why only now, why so late? Half of my life is gone! Oh, if it could only have been 10 years earlier! . . . At the age of 30 I was able to read the Gospel for the very first time.

It was entirely by chance that this small book fell into my hands . . . and I was gripped by what I read. . . . But gradually I began to boil with indignation: To think that such a treasure had been hidden from me! Who decided and on what grounds that this book was harmful to me? I realized that I have never been and never will be an atheist.

In our time of unrest and brokenness, when crystal palaces turn out to be cardboard shacks, when once majestic kings are now covered with shame, when under the granite edifices are unstable foundations of clay, then I know that there is a book to which I can always return, and it will help, comfort and support me in the darkest hour.

That "darkest hour" is probably nearer than most of us imagine. There is an old saying that the night seems the darkest just before the dawn. The Bible, on the other hand, cautions us that things will seem the brightest for mankind just before earth's darkest hour. Unperturbed by events, whatever they may bring, the Christian's hope remains firm:

For I reckon that the sufferings of this present time are not worthy to be compared with the glory which shall be revealed in us (Romans 8:18).

For our light affliction, which is but for a moment, worketh for us a far more exceeding and eternal weight of glory... (2 Corinthians 4:17).

If we suffer [for him], we shall also reign with him; if we deny him, he also will deny us (2 Timothy 2:12).

To "reign with Him"! That hope is not fueled by a selfish lust for power but by love and compassion for this suffering earth and its inhabitants. The King with whom we will reign over this world in resurrected, glorified bodies is the Creator and Lord of the universe. He is also the One who loved mankind so much that He became one of us in order to die for our sins. How different His benevolent rule of perfect righteousness will be, not only from the destructive rule of Antichrist but from the best that humanistic politicians could possibly offer!

The most heroic efforts of environmentalists can only fall short of rescuing earth's ecological system from the cumulative results of human carelessness, abuse, and exploitation. In contrast, Christ will restore this earth to its pollution-free, Edenic beauty and peacefulness. In the millennium there will no longer be any need for a Society for the Prevention of Cruelty to Animals. Nor will the creatures themselves bite and devour one another. The pitiful suffering of even a fly caught in a spider's web will be ended:

The wolf also shall dwell with the lamb, and the leopard shall lie down with the kid, and the calf and the young lion and the fatling together, and a child shall lead them.

And the cow and the bear shall feed; their young ones shall lie down together, and the lion shall eat straw like the ox.

The sucking child shall play on the hole of the asp, and the weaned child shall put his hand on the cockatrice's den (Isaiah 11:6-8).

Poverty and famine and the crippling diseases of old age will be gone forever. Robust good health and happiness will bless all mankind. With abundance for all, there will be little cause for greed, envy, anger, and hatred. Satan's confinement and Christ's perfect reign for 1000 years will make even the pettiest crimes rare. Earth will be a paradise of blessing and joy beyond present comprehension. The millennium will display the beauties of the colorful, flowering, fruitful environment that God originally planned—a world of love and peace and joy in human relationships as well.

Wonderful though it will be, however, the millennium is not the ultimate kingdom that the prophets foretold: "Of the increase of his government and peace there shall be no end . . ." (Isaiah 9:7). It ends after 1000 years—tragically and violently—in war. The millennium is, in fact, the final proof of mankind's incorrigibly sinful and selfish nature. The theories of psychologists and sociologists, which blame "society" and "environment" for mankind's ills, will be laid to rest. Just as Satan incited Eve to rebellion in the perfect Garden of Eden, so he will, when released after 1000 years, entice the nations to attack Christ:

> And when the thousand years are expired, Satan shall be loosed out of his prison, and shall go out to deceive the nations which are in the four quarters of the earth, Gog and Magog, to gather them together to battle, the number of whom is as the sand of the sea.
>
> And they went up on the breadth of the earth, and compassed the camp of the saints about and the beloved city; and fire came down from God out of heaven and devoured them (Revelation 20:7-9).

God's ultimate kingdom is far more wonderful than human imagination can even conceive: "Eye hath not seen, nor ear heard, neither hath it entered into the heart of man, the things which God hath prepared for them that love him" (1 Corinthians 2:9). The entire universe, so contaminated and debilitated by Satan's cosmic rebellion, will vanish in one huge nuclear explosion, to be replaced instantly by a "new heavens and a new earth, wherein dwelleth righteousness" (2 Peter 3:13).

The new universe will be inhabited by those who have repented and received God's remedy so that He could create them anew (Ephesians 2:8-10). In perfect bodies, no longer susceptible to temptation and sin, and filled with Christ's love, theirs will be eternal bliss in God's presence and the inconceivable adventure and joy of the wonders He has planned for all eternity.

At any moment it could be too late to respond, but as yet Christ's gracious offer of pardon and eternal joy is still open: "He that heareth my word and believeth on him that sent me hath everlasting life, and shall not come into condemnation, but is passed from death unto life" (John 5:24). "Therefore if any man be in Christ he is a new creature: Old things have passed away; behold, all things are become new!" (2 Corinthians 5:17).

Appendices
and
Notes

Appendix A

Was Peter the First Pope?

There is no evidence that Peter ever enjoyed the position of leadership in the early church which the Popes claim for themselves as his alleged successors. Christ's promise, "I will give unto thee the keys of the kingdom of heaven" (Matthew 16:19), could be interpreted as having been fulfilled when Peter opened the kingdom to the Jews on the Day of Pentecost (Acts 2:14-41) and to the Gentiles in the home of Cornelius the centurion (Acts 10:34-48). Christ's further promise to Peter that "whatsoever thou shalt bind on earth shall be bound in heaven, and whatsoever thou shalt loose on earth shall be loosed in heaven" was no more than His identical promise to all of the disciples (Matthew 18:18-20). Like wise the statement "whosoever sins ye remit, they are remitted unto them..." (John 20:23) was made to all of the disciples.

That the special authority which has been claimed by the Roman Catholic popes as Peter's alleged successors was never exercised by Peter as the head of the church (nor as the chief apostle) is clear. In his epistles Peter exhorts equals; he does not command subordinates: "The elders which are among you I exhort, who am also an elder" (1 Peter 5:1). He offers as the basis for his writing not any official and exalted ecclesiastical position or power, but the fact that he has been "a witness of the sufferings of Christ... [an eyewitness] of his majesty" (1 Peter 5:1; 2 Peter 1:16).

The first church council (Acts 15:4-29), which was held in Jerusalem around 45-50 A.D., was not convened on Peter's initiative but on Paul's. Furthermore, it was James and not Peter who seemed to take the leadership. While Peter made an important statement, it was not doctrinal. It was mainly a summation of his experience in first bringing the gospel to the Gentiles. James, however, drew upon the Scriptures and argued from a doctrinal point of view. Moreover, it was James who said, "Wherefore my sentence is..." and his declaration became the basis of the official letter sent back to Antioch.

Fear of James and his influence caused Peter to revert to Jewish traditional separation from Gentiles. As a result, Paul, who wrote far more of the New Testament than Peter and whose ministry was obviously much larger, publicly rebuked Peter for his error (Galatians 2:11-14). Thus the specious claim that Peter held a special leadership position and was given the chief place among the apostles, much less that he was the first Pope, is refuted by numerous passages in the New Testament.

Roman Catholicism bases its false claim solely upon Christ's statement "Thou art Peter, and upon this rock I will build my church" (Matthew 16:18). One need not argue from the Greek that Peter (*petros*) is not "this rock" (*petra*). The truth of the matter does not depend upon a disputable interpretation of this one verse; it depends upon the totality of Scripture. That Romanism's view is not valid is demonstrated fully not only by the passages in the New Testament to which we have already referred, but by the fact that the entire Bible, rather than supporting the Roman view, actually refutes it.

God Himself is clearly described as the only unfailing "Rock" of our salvation throughout the entire Old Testament.[1] As for the New Testament, it declares that Jesus Christ is the Rock upon which the church is built and that He, being God, is alone qualified for that position. The rock upon which the "wise man built his house" was not Peter, but Christ and His teachings (Matthew 7:24-29). Peter himself points out that Christ is the "chief cornerstone" upon which the church is built (1 Peter 2:6-8) and quotes an Old Testament passage to that effect which Christ fulfilled. Paul also calls Christ "the chief cornerstone" and declares that the church is "built upon the foundation of [all] the apostles and prophets" (Ephesians 2:20)—a statement which clearly denies to Peter any special position in the foundation thereof.

As for the testimony of history, it is not certain that Peter ever resided in Rome, much less that he was the first Bishop of Rome. Even if that were conceded on the basis of the insufficient evidence offered, we are certain that Peter was not the Pope. The evidence already given above proves that neither Peter nor anyone else was recognized as the Pope or head of the church. That concept was unknown until much later. History, too, bears this out.

While Catholics seek to show that the Bishop of Rome was recognized as the head of the church, there is no proof of this claim prior to Constantine. It was he, in fact, who decreed that the Bishop of Rome should be the head of the church. Constantine created the office of Pope for his own purposes, and the popes themselves for hundreds of years thereafter acknowledged this fact.

Even Catholic historians admit that during the Middle Ages the popes and hierarchy of the Roman Catholic Church circulated a fraudulent document to justify their position and power. It made no attempt to trace papal authority to Peter by apostolic succession, nor did it attempt to justify that office from the Bible. Instead, the document, known as *The Donation of Constantine*, justified the office of Pope and the authority which the popes were exercising as having been granted to them by imperial decree. Purportedly written by Constantine, the forged document declared:

> And we [the Roman Emperors] command and decree that he [the Bishop of Rome] should have primacy over the four principal Sees of

Antioch, Alexandria, Constantinople and Jerusalem, as well as over all the Churches of God throughout the whole world; and the Pontiff who occupies at any given moment the See of that same most holy Roman Church shall rank as the highest and chief among all the priests of the whole world and by his decision all things are to be arranged concerning the worship of God or the security of the faith of Christians.

The fact that the popes relied upon this fraud proves two things: 1) the dishonesty of the popes in claiming their office; and 2) that even in the Middle Ages the popes, rather than laying claim to an authority that was received by apostolic succession from Peter, acknowledged that their office had been created by Constantine, thus admitting that there had been no Pope prior to that time.

Clearly, if the tradition had already been established in the Middle Ages that Peter was the first Pope and that those occupying this office had received their position and power by apostolic succession traceable back to him, then there would have been no need for forging such a document as *The Donation of Constantine*. The fact that the popes found this necessary proves a further fraud: the claim of the Roman Catholic Church today that the popes can trace their authority back to Peter.

One of the Roman Catholic Church's proudest claims is that the alleged infallibility of its popes and its ability to trace them back to Peter has kept it unified since the beginning. In contrast, Protestants are criticized for the many denominational divisions among them. In fact, however, there are as many if not more divisions among Catholics as there are among Protestant denominations.

There are always numerous factions at theological odds with the Vatican. Pierre Teilhard de Chardin is one of many examples. His heresies were considered so great that Rome forbade him to publish his writings—yet he remained unrepentant and a priest within the church. Matthew Fox's beliefs are more in harmony with Starhawk, a witch who teaches at his Holy Names College in Oakland, California, than they are with Rome. Yet this popular priest, though recently silenced by the Vatican for a year, has renounced none of his heresies and remains in the church, one of thousands who reject Rome's attempts to bring them in line theologically.

Heretics of almost any stripe can remain within the church as priests, monks, bishops, cardinals so long as they acknowledge the headship of Rome while disobeying her. The "unity" within the Roman Catholic Church is thus more institutional than doctrinal in spite of the claims she makes of being able to trace her roots through apostolic succession back to Peter.

Appendix B

The Immaculate Heart

The popular Catholic dogma of the "Immaculate Heart," whether of Mary or of Jesus, has no basis in the Bible, but comes out of the realm of the occult. The "Immaculate Heart" is depicted as a visible object glowing within the bosom of Jesus or Mary, and often held in Mary's hand. A strange heart indeed! Here we have a magical source of power and protection, with an uncanny identity of its own. Devotion is directed to this mystical object in what becomes a subtle replacement of a personal relationship with Christ and devotion to Him.

The heart of Jesus Christ is, of course, immaculate, perfect, without sin. Though fully man, He is also God. No other person has ever been without sin: "There is no man that sinneth not" (1 Kings 8:46); "There is not a just man upon the earth, that doeth good and sinneth not" (Ecclesiastes 7:20). If it is argued that these Scriptures were written before Mary's birth, then the following were written after her death: "For *all* have sinned and come short of the glory of God" (Romans 3:23); "If we say that we have not sinned, we make him a liar, and his word is not in us" (1 John 1:10). These statements leave no room for any exception, which both Paul and John should have made had Mary been a special case.

To attribute an "Immaculate Heart" to Mary is to deny her sinful humanity. In fact, this is borne out by another related dogma: the Immaculate Conception. That heresy was first popularized through the efforts of British monk Eadmer in the twelfth century and was at last declared a dogma by Pope Pius IX in 1854. It teaches that Mary was "from the first moment of her conception, by a singular grace and privilege of Almighty God, in view of the merits of Christ Jesus the Savior of mankind, preserved free from all stain of original sin" and that she remained without sin during her life.

It is argued that unusual grace was extended to Mary to keep her sinless. That claim flies in the face of logic and the entire Bible. If it were possible to keep Mary sinless, then why didn't God do the same for Adam and Eve and thus prevent sin from entering the world in the first place? Adam and Eve were not immaculately *conceived* by sinful parents; they were *created* sinless by God and placed in a perfect, sinless environment—yet they sinned. Any being with the power of choice, except God Himself, would inevitably sin. If that were not the case, then God would never have allowed sin to occur.

The only way to prevent mankind from sinning would be by removing the power of choice. But that would turn man into a robot and thus make it impossible for humans to love God and one another, for the essential ingredient of love is free will. The problem of sin is overcome (without destroying the power of choice) *only* through the full plan of redemption: Christ's payment of the penalty of sin, the awakening of love in the hearts of the redeemed out of gratitude for what He has done for them, Christ's indwelling of the believer by faith, the creation of a new body without the sensual properties that contribute to sin, and the ushering of the redeemed into heaven itself to be forever with Christ and in the presence of God. This complete redemption, which is the entire message of Scripture, is superfluous if sinlessness can be realized simply by the extension of unusual grace, as it is claimed was done for Mary. That heresy undercuts the entire Bible.

In the end, the denial of Mary's place as a "sinner saved by grace" has the effect of deifying her. Though Catholics would deny that accusation, that is what it amounts to in practice. The "Immaculate Heart" of Mary demands not only equal but greater devotion than that given to Christ. Thus the apparitions at Fatima did not demand that in order to bring peace to earth "reparation" be made to the "Immaculate Heart" of *Jesus*, but of *Mary*.

Appendix C

The Mass and Transubstantiation

John the Baptist hailed Christ as "the Lamb of God, which taketh away the sin of the world" (John 1:29). Hebrews 9:26 declares of Christ: "But now *once* in the end of the world hath he appeared to put away sin *by the sacrifice of himself.*" The next chapter goes on to explain that the animal sacrifices in Old Testament times could never take away sins. Thus they had to be repeated daily by the Jewish priests. The writer then argues the efficacy of Christ's sacrifice, which the animal sacrifices prefigured, on the basis that it was *never to be repeated*: "But this man [Christ], after he had offered *one sacrifice for sins forever*, sat down on the right hand of God [in heaven] . . . for by *one offering* [of Himself for sins] he hath *perfected forever* them that are sanctified" (Hebrews 10:4, 10,12,14).

The Bible could not state more clearly that the redemption of mankind was obtained once and for all by the sacrificial death, burial, and resurrection of Christ: "For this he did *once* when he offered up himself"—Hebrews 7:27. Nor is anything further needed for the complete reconciliation of mankind to God: "He that believeth on the Son hath everlasting life . . . and shall not come into condemnation, but is [already] *passed from death unto life*" (John 3:36; 5:24).

Christ's *one sacrifice* has fully and eternally accomplished our redemption, salvation, forgiveness of sins, and deliverance from the penalty demanded by God's justice. His death has procured eternal life and a home in heaven as a free gift of God's grace for those who receive Christ as Savior and Lord. Just before He yielded His spirit into His Father's hands, Christ cried from the cross in triumph, "*It is finished!*" To attempt to make any further offering or to do anything else in order to be forgiven of sin and accepted by God is to deny the sufficiency of that which Christ Himself has already accomplished and which God has already accepted.

Indeed, any attempt to offer to God something in addition to Christ's once-for-all sacrifice constitutes a *rejection* of the salvation God offers. If the one sacrifice that Christ made of Himself upon the cross is not sufficient, then what is—and how do we know? How many more times must He be offered on Catholic altars? While Catholicism insists that the sacrifice of

298

Christ was not enough, it cannot and does not tell how many Masses must be offered, how many Rosaries must be said, how much alms must be given, or how much and how long one must suffer in purgatory in order for the debt owed to God's infinite justice to be paid and the soul to arrive in heaven at last. Consider the following Roman Catholic teaching:

> At the hour of death the holy Masses you have heard devoutly will be your greatest consolation.
> Every Mass will go with you to Judgment and will *plead* [How effectively?] for pardon [How much?] for you.
> By every Mass you can *diminish* [By how much?] the temporal punishment due to your sins, more or less [How vague!], according to your fervor [How is it measured?]. . . .
> Through the Holy Sacrifice, Our Lord Jesus Christ supplies for *many* [Which ones? Why not all?] of your negligences and omissions. . . .
> By piously hearing Holy Mass you afford the Souls in Purgatory the greatest possible relief. . . . You shorten [By how much?] your Purgatory by every Mass.[1]

Roman Catholic dogma is clear: Christ's death upon the cross, rather than being, as the Bible teaches, the once-for-all and complete sacrifice for sins, is instead merely the first installment. Even after Christ died for our sins and rose in triumph, a huge debt still remains to be paid off by numerous Masses—plus alms, good deeds, Rosaries, suffering here and in purgatory, etc. That this is *another gospel* than that which Paul preached and to which the entire Bible bears witness cannot be denied. It is thus appropriate to be reminded once again of Paul's warning:

> But though we or an angel from heaven preach *any other gospel* unto you than that which we have preached unto you, let him be accursed (Galatians 1:8).

In the place of the faith in Him who gives eternal life as a free gift of God's grace, Roman Catholic teaching concerning the Mass substitutes the physical act of eating bread and drinking wine (which has allegedly been magically turned into the literal body and blood of Christ). Salvation is effected, then, not through the once-for-all act of Christ giving Himself upon the cross for our sins, but by Roman Catholic priests reoffering His body and blood endlessly and the faithful repeatedly partaking of it. The Mass thus nullifies the sacrifice Christ fully accomplished when He "offered himself without spot to God" (Hebrews 9:14) and contradicts the biblical teaching that "by one sacrifice He has perfected forever them that are sanctified."

The Mass also nullifies Christ's resurrection. Through the Mass, His immortal resurrected body, which no longer contains blood (Luke 24:39) because that was poured out in death upon the cross, is turned back into the mortal, flesh-and-blood-sustained body which Christ had before the cross, thus undoing His perfect sacrifice. No wonder thousands died at the stake rather than confess to heresy through denying such Scriptures as the following:

> Nor yet that he [Christ] should offer himself often . . . for then must he often have suffered . . . but now *once* in the end of the world hath he appeared to put away sin by the sacrifice of himself.
>
> So Christ was *once* offered to bear the sins of many . . . we are sanctified through the offering of the body of Jesus Christ *once for all.*
>
> . . . after he had offered *one sacrifice for sins forever,* [Christ] sat down on the right hand of God. . . .
>
> For by *one offering* he hath perfected forever them that are sanctified. . . . This is the covenant . . . saith the Lord . . . their sins and iniquities will I remember *no more.*
>
> Now where remission of these is, there is *no more offering* for sin (Hebrews 9:24–10:18).

According to Roman Catholic dogma, the physical partaking of the Sacrament of the Mass (like the physical act of baptism) produces spiritual benefits. This teaching is derived from two statements that Christ made: 1) When to a group of unbelieving Jews He said, "Except ye eat the flesh of the Son of man, and drink his blood, ye have no life in you" (John 6:53); and 2) when at the Last Supper He took bread and wine and said to His disciples, "This is my body . . . this is my blood . . . eat ye all of it" (Matthew 26:26-28). A careful reading of these passages, however, confirms what common sense demands: that Christ was not advocating the cannibalistic eating and drinking of His literal flesh and blood. Nor did He ever teach that to do so would contribute to one's salvation.

In the first instance, in the same discourse Christ said that those who *believed* on Him would have eternal life. Thus He made it very clear that by "eateth" and "drinketh" He meant *believeth*—that it was necessary to *believe* that He, the Creator of the universe, had come to earth not as an apparition or in a "spirit body" but as a *real flesh-and-blood man* to die for our sins:

> I am the bread of life; he that cometh to me shall never hunger, and he that *believeth* on me shall never thirst.
>
> And this is the will of him [God] that sent me, that every one which seeth the Son, and *believeth* on him, may have everlasting life; and I will raise [resurrect] him up at the last day.

He that *believeth* on me hath everlasting life. I am that bread of life.

It is the spirit that quickeneth [gives life]; the *flesh profiteth nothing*: the words that I speak unto you, they are spirit and they are life (John 6:35,40,47,48,63).

In the second instance, He was sitting in the presence of His disciples in His physical body when He said of the bread which He held in His hands, "This is my body." None of the disciples there with Him could reasonably have thought that He meant that the bread had become His literal physical body, which was clearly visible to them in its normal form. Nor did He say that the bread would *later become* His body, but "This *is* my body." The only possible meaning was that the bread and wine were *symbols* of His body and blood.

Catholicism prides itself upon taking Christ *literally* in these passages.

Yet for centuries the Catholic Church allowed *only the priests* to drink the wine that had been allegedly turned into Christ's blood. Thus if, as Rome teaches, Christ's requirement to *eat* his flesh and *drink* his blood is not a command to *believe* in him, then she deliberately consigned billions of Catholics to eternal damnation by denying them the life-giving blood of Jesus.

The rule for discerning when to take Scripture literally and when to take it figuratively is always to take it literally unless it neither makes sense nor is necessary to do so. Surely it makes no sense to suggest that Christ, while present in His physical body, meant that the loaf of bread He held in His hands was also His literal body. Nor does it make sense that the body of Christ should be multiplied endlessly all over the world so that millions could eat of it again and again. Nor could that belief be called taking Christ literally, for such a "magical body" could not be His literal body.

It is no more necessary to take Christ literally when He says that He is "the *bread* of God come down from heaven" and "the bread that I will give is my *flesh*" than it is to believe that He is literally a *shepherd* and Christians are literally *sheep* (John 10:11), or that He is literally a *door* (verse 7), or literally a *light* (John 8:12). Furthermore, to interpret Christ's statements concerning eating and drinking His flesh and blood literally contradicts and undermines the very gospel which Christ is attempting to preach—that salvation is through *believing* in what He has done, not through some physical work we accomplish.

The effect of the heresy of transubstantiation is to make salvation dependent upon the physical and *repeated* act of eating and drinking the miraculously reconstituted, precrucifixion/preresurrection flesh and blood of Christ—with no indication of how often this must be done. Thus salvation is never complete, but the priest must again and again change more bread and wine into the alleged body and blood of Christ so that it can be repeatedly offered and partaken of in the Mass. This magical transformation of bread and wine into Christ's body and blood and the reoffering thereof can only be performed by a priest upon Roman Catholic altars. Thus for a Roman Catholic, salvation depends not upon one's personal faith in and relationship to the resurrected and glorified Christ who died for one's sins, but upon one's relationship to the Church and participation in those sacraments which she performs and decrees are essential to salvation.

Furthermore, the doctrine of transubstantiation denies that Christ has come *once for all in the flesh*, just as it denies that He has died and been sacrificed once for all. This is an Antichrist teaching, according to 1 John 4:3. Christ comes *again and again in the flesh* to thousands of Roman Catholic altars around the world as wafers are repeatedly turned into His body. Nor does He have one physical body as the Bible teaches, but His "body" is on display in thousands of places at once. As God, Christ is omnipresent in *Spirit*, but there is no such thing as an omnipresent *body*.

One of the explanatory sheets given out at L'Eglise de le Sacre Cour (the Church of the Sacred Heart), perched high above Paris in Montmartre, declares:

> Above the high altar a monstrance containing the bread which has become the body of Christ through the mass has been solemnly exposed since 1885 for the uninterrupted adoration during the night as during the day. Those who take part in this prayer of adoration are the link between Christ and the people of their social sphere, of their country and of the entire world which the far-reaching view [from] the avis enables them better to recall to mind.

Even after attributing to them heretical powers, Baptism and Mass are not enough. Catholicism's insistence that "the blood atonement of the cross" does not fully cleanse from sin or deliver from its penalty requires much more ritual and effort. A person's good works, prayers, penance, repetition of the Rosary, and suffering (and the list goes on and on, limited only by the ingenuity of those inventing new "means of grace" for the Church to minister) are also necessary in order to reach heaven at last. And no one, not even the Pope himself, can calculate when enough Masses have been said, enough sufferings endured, enough Rosaries recited. Catholicism never says when enough is enough. The Church remains strangely silent concerning that most important question.

Appendix D

Baptismal Regeneration

Baptismal regeneration" IS A vestige of heretical Catholicism from which Martin Luther and other Reformers were never able to free themselves and to which some Protestant groups still cling. The United Pentecostal Church, for example, declares: "Water baptism is an essential part of New Testament salvation. . . . Without proper baptism it is impossible to enter into the Kingdom of God." Far from teaching such a doctrine, however, the Bible pointedly tells us that Christ, the Savior of sinners, never baptized anyone (John 4:2) and that Paul baptized very few, which seems odd if baptism is essential to salvation.

The chief apostle wasn't certain whom he had baptized in Corinth. He remembered that he had baptized "Crispus and Gaius . . . and the household of Stephanas," but added, "I know not whether I baptized any other" (1 Corinthians 1:14-16). Clearly someone else baptized most of the Corinthian believers. Yet Paul calls himself their "father," and explains, "for in Christ Jesus I have begotten you through the gospel." Paul had been the means of their salvation—*without baptizing them*. If baptism were essential—in fact the means by which we are "born again"—then he could not have called himself the "father" through whom they were begotten (i.e. born again) in Christ Jesus.

Far from being saved through baptism, the Corinthians, as Paul reminded them, were saved *through believing the gospel*: "that Christ died for our sins according to the Scriptures, and that he was buried, and that he rose again the third day according to the Scriptures . . ." (1 Corinthians 15:1-4). Nowhere does Paul even suggest that baptism saves, but instead he consistently teaches that salvation comes *only through believing the gospel*. Paul declares this repeatedly. Note Romans 1:16: "For I am not ashamed of the gospel of Christ, for *it is the power of God unto salvation to everyone that believeth*. . . ." There is not a word here about baptism in Paul's declaration of the gospel. In fact, Paul goes so far as to state, "For Christ sent me *not to baptize*, but to preach the gospel" (1 Corinthians 1:17).

Then what about Mark 16:16, which says, "He that believeth and is baptized shall be saved"? Clearly it does not say that baptism saves, but that

304 ◆ Dave Hunt

it should accompany salvation. It is saved people who get baptized. The rest of the verse says, "but he that *believeth not* shall be damned." Nowhere does the Bible say that "he that is not baptized shall be damned." Nor does it warn us that believing is not enough, by stating, "If you only believe but don't get baptized you are lost."

There are scores of verses which say, "He that believeth is saved." There is only one verse which says, "He that believeth and is baptized is saved." Again, there are scores of verses declaring that if we don't believe the gospel or don't believe on Christ we are lost, but *not one* which says that if we don't get baptized we are lost. Surely the Bible would not leave out such a warning if indeed a failure to be baptized would damn the soul for eternity!

Baptism is a public declaration that one has believed in Christ and in so doing has accepted His death, burial, and resurrection as his very own. It is an act of obedience to the Lord's command, and as such should be the experience of every Christian—but it is not essential to salvation. The thief on the cross was never baptized. Suppose a person about to die, pinned in the wreckage of a car, cries out with his last strength, "What must I do to be saved?" Must one respond, "I'm sorry, there is no hope for you because you must be baptized to be saved, and that isn't possible for you"? Praise God that the Bible never requires that one must be baptized to be saved!

Then what did Jesus mean when He said, "Except a man be born of water and of the Spirit, he cannot enter into the kingdom of God" (John 3:5)? The evidence we have already considered refutes the idea that by "born of water" He meant baptism. Nicodemus knew that water in the Old Testament was used for cleansing. Of course water could not cleanse from sin, but was a symbol of the cleansing that comes through believing and heeding the Word of God. Thus Paul wrote of "the washing of water by the word [of God]" (Ephesians 5:26) and "the washing of regeneration" (Titus 3:5). Peter stated that we are "born again . . . by the word of God" (1 Peter 1:23).

The Catholic Church on the other hand believes that a child can be regenerated, that is, made Christian, through infant baptism. Such is the heresy of "sacramentalism," which attributes spiritual power to a physical act. The Roman Catholic Church administers seven such sacraments. Clearly it undermines the gospel, which the apostles preached, to teach that an infant, without exercising the requisite moral choice and faith in Christ, of which it is incapable, can nevertheless be "born again" through a priest's solemn pronouncements and a wet hand laid upon it.

The heresy, of course, is in believing that a physical act can contribute to one's salvation. Nor is this error confined to baptism. It extends to taking communion, wearing a scapular, saying the Rosary, and other acts prescribed by the Catholic Church as essential and/or contributing to salvation. Once faith is placed in anything else, one is no longer trusting totally in Christ for salvation. Sacramentalism is thus the enemy of the cross and of the gospel and has led untold millions astray.

Appendix E

The Gospel of the Kingdom

We have noted the confusion among those of Christ's day concerning when, how, by whom, and for whom the kingdom of God would be established. That confusion remains in the church today. There are those, for example, who try to find a distinction between the kingdom of heaven and the kingdom of God. In fact, there is no difference. The former is used exclusively by Matthew, but the other three Gospels say exactly the same thing about the kingdom of God that Matthew says about the kingdom of heaven.

Where is the kingdom? New Agers take Christ's statement "the kingdom of God is within you" (Luke 17:21) to mean that the kingdom is a mystical reality inside of every person, a reality which may be experienced in a "higher state of consciousness." The Greek preposition *entos* could also be translated "among you" or "in your midst," and should be in this case. Christ the King, and thus the kingdom, was in their midst, unrecognized. Of course, the kingdom of God does exist in every heart that has received Christ the King. On the other hand, it would be both unbiblical and unreasonable to suggest that the kingdom of God is within individuals who have never received Christ but who, in fact, reject Him—which was the case with those to whom Christ addressed these words.

When is the kingdom? It is present within the hearts where Christ has entered and reigns. It will be visibly present upon the earth during the thousand years that Christ will reign from David's throne. The millennium, however, is not the ultimate manifestation of the kingdom because it comes to an end, whereas the Bible clearly and repeatedly states, "Thy kingdom is an everlasting kingdom" (Psalm 145:13; Daniel 4:3,34; 2 Peter 1:11; etc.). Moreover, the millennium ends in a war, whereas the Bible declares that the kingdom involves peace that will never end (Isaiah 9:7; 32:17; etc.).

Further proof that the millennium is not the ultimate kingdom is found in Christ's statement that "except a man be born again he cannot see the kingdom of God" (John 3:3) nor can he enter into it (verse 5). Yet there will be an innumerable multitude upon the earth during the millennium who have not been born again and who will end up in the lake of fire, according to Revelation 20:7-15. Paul adds that "flesh and blood cannot inherit the kingdom of God" (1 Corinthians 15:50), yet there will be many "flesh-and-blood" people alive on earth during the millennium—so again it cannot be more than a temporary and earthly manifestation of the kingdom which is yet to come.

Ultimately the kingdom will be the entirely new universe that God will create to replace the present one when He destroys it (2 Peter 3:7-13). That fact is an integral part of the gospel we are to proclaim: that all of man's efforts to rescue planet Earth and to make it a beautiful, safe, and peaceful place in which to live are doomed. Man is called upon to be reconciled to God and to look to God to restore mankind to paradise. That is the "gospel of the kingdom" which Christ preached.

Are we to preach it today as well, or was it only for that time? The simple answer is found in the fact that Christ preached the gospel of the kingdom (Matthew 4:23; Mark 1:15; etc.), spoke of it after His resurrection (Acts 1:3), and commissioned His disciples to preach it (Matthew 28:19; Mark 16:15). That the apostles preached the gospel of the kingdom is stated repeatedly (Acts 8:12; 20:25; Romans 14:17; 1 Corinthians 4:20; Colossians 4:11; etc.) and this is the same gospel which we are required to preach today.

Appendix F

Purgatory

According to Catholic dogma, the sufferings of Christ upon the cross were not sufficient to pay the full penalty demanded by God's judgment for sin. To make up for that alleged deficiency, each person who believes in Christ must also suffer for his own sins either in this life or in purgatory—or, as is the general expectancy of Catholics from the Pope on down, in both places. Like so much else in Roman Catholicism, purgatory is an invented doctrine that cannot be found in or supported by the Bible, but contradicts its clear teaching. It was proposed by Pope Gregory I in 593 and dogmatized by the Council of Florence in 1439 as a required belief of every Catholic who hopes to get eventually to heaven. The Council of Trent anathematized (eternally damned) all who would not believe it.

Other people can also suffer for one's sins to make up for the deficiency in what Christ allegedly failed to accomplish. Catholics have been taught that various "saints," such as St. Catherine of Genoa, "Patroness of the holy souls in purgatory," have had a special commission from God to suffer in their own bodies in order to obtain the early release of those in purgatory. On November 10, 1910, having been a priest for only three months, the soon-to-become-famous Padre Pio "wrote to his Father Provincial":

> My dear Father, I want to ask your permission to do something. For some time past, I have felt the need to offer myself to the Lord as a victim for poor sinners and for the souls in Purgatory. . . .
> I have begged the Lord to pour out upon me the punishment prepared for these souls, so that they may be consoled and quickly admitted to Paradise. [1]

While Padre Pio's desire to be punished for sinners was an admirable sentiment, it was an insult to the One who claimed to have fully paid that debt and on that basis to be the *only* Savior of sinners. Padre Pio, over a period of 30 years, allegedly evidenced his suffering for the souls in purgatory through the stigmata, a mysterious bleeding in his palms in a presumed sharing of the sufferings of Christ.

Yet, as we have already noted, Christ's triumphant cry "It is finished!" announced that the penalty demanded by Infinite justice had been paid in full. His suffering had ended. He is now in a resurrected and glorified body in heaven that has no blood in its veins and is certainly no longer bleeding! For Roman Catholicism to claim that bleeding and suffering continues through others in order to help pay the debt that Christ has already paid in full is the rankest heresy. Yet that lie is inherent in the Mass and in the other sacraments of the Roman Catholic Church.

His deliberate rejection of the clear teaching of the Bible caused Padre Pio to come under heavy demonic delusion. Deeply devoted to Our Lady of Fatima, who allegedly cured him of an illness in 1959, he claimed that *millions* of souls of the dead attended his Masses and "stopped in his cell to thank him for his help on their way to Paradise." These spirits were not figures of his imagination. He claimed that he saw them with his physical eyes.[2] It is almost beyond comprehension that a man could be so certain that he was serving God and yet be consorting with demons. Pope John Paul II held Padre Pio, whom he had met personally, in high esteem and has performed the Mass at his tomb.

Purgatory stands between every Catholic, no matter how devout, and heaven. Church dogma requires that some must suffer there much longer than others, depending upon how many Rosaries they have said, how many Masses have been performed for them, and how many indulgences they have earned by various means. Some will be in purgatory no longer than a week, for Mary, who can accomplish what Christ could not, has promised a special deliverance to those who faithfully wear her "scapular."

The scapular consists of two pieces of brown cloth containing Mary's promise on one and her picture with "baby Jesus" on the other. One piece is worn in front and one in back, and they are connected over the shoulder by two strings. Mary allegedly appeared to St. Simon Stock on July 16, 1251, and gave him "The Great Promise" that has comforted millions ever since: "Whosoever dies wearing this Scapular shall not suffer eternal fire." In 1322 Pope John XXII received a further promise from "Mary" known as "The Sabbatine Privilege": "I, the Mother of Grace, shall descend on the Saturday after their death and whomsoever I shall find in Purgatory [who was wearing the Scapular when they died], I shall free." St. Simon Stock's famous prayer ends thus: "O Sweet Heart of Mary, be our *salvation!*"

Another obvious effect of the doctrine of purgatory is to eliminate the hope of a simultaneous resurrection of all who have died believing in Christ. This would be impossible unless every soul were required to wait until the last Catholic had been purged in purgatory or released by Mary. Nor could there be a rapture of living believers, who hadn't even gone to purgatory and thus were not yet sufficiently "purged" to enter heaven.

Thus Catholics are not expecting Christ to catch them up to meet Him in the air. They would have no reason to be surprised, however, if "Christ" should be identified by their Pope as the miracle-working figure who has suddenly taken the reins of the revived Roman Empire.

Appendix G

The Spirit of Antichrist

*And every spirit that confesseth not that Jesus Christ is come in the flesh is not of God: and this is that spirit of antichrist....*1 John 4:3a

It is often taught that Antichrist is not a man but a spirit. Though the above verse refers to the "*spirit* of antichrist," John earlier makes it clear that Antichrist is a *person*: "...as ye have heard that antichrist shall come, even now are there many antichrists..." (1 Jn 2:18). Many antichrists were already present, operating in the "spirit of antichrist." None of them, however, was *the* Antichrist who, John assures us, will eventually come.

Paul refers to Antichrist as "that man of sin...the son of perdition...that Wicked [one]...whom the Lord...shall destroy with the brightness of his coming: Even him whose coming is after the working of Satan with all power and signs and lying wonders..." (2 Thes 2:3-10). If this is not *the* Antichrist, who would this supremely evil man be, who will sit "in the temple of God [to be rebuilt in Jerusalem in these last days], shewing himself that he is God" (v 4)? Who else but Antichrist, Satan's world ruler, would have such authority? "And all that dwell upon earth shall worship him..." (Rv 13:3-4, 8).

Paul declares, "And now ye know what withholdeth [prevents] that he might be revealed *in his time*" (2 Thes 2:6). Yet many try to identify Antichrist *before* his time. This evil man, who is almost certainly alive right now, may not even know the eventual role for which Satan has been grooming him. Nor can Satan put him into power until God prepares the way.

Two events *must* precede Antichrist's revelation to the world. First must come the great apostasy, already underway in Paul's day and reaching its climax in ours:

> ...for that day [of Christ, or the Lord, see v 2] shall not come, except there come a falling away [apostasy] first, and that man of sin be revealed, the son of perdition.... (2 Thes 2:3)

This verse does not teach that Antichrist must appear before the day of the Lord and thus before the Rapture, which we believe initiates that day. Paul only states that the *apostasy* must come first. As for Antichrist, "that day shall not come, except...that man of sin be revealed...." Clearly the Antichrist will be revealed in "that day" and not before.

Paul reminds the Thessalonian believers of what must occur in order for Antichrist to be revealed: the *removal* of the One who prevents this revelation. At the time Paul wrote this epistle a *Person* was preventing Antichrist from being revealed; and Paul explains that this same Person will continue to do so until He is taken out of the way: "For...he who now letteth [prevents/hinders] will let [prevent], until he be taken out of the way. And then shall that Wicked be revealed..." (2 Thes 2:7-8).

That God himself is the One preventing Antichrist from being revealed is clear for two reasons: 1) This One has prevented Satan's takeover for more than 1,900 years; 2) Only God is more powerful than Satan. That God, therefore, who is omnipresent, will be "taken out of the way" is the key.

There is only one possible interpretation: that the Holy Spirit indwelling the believers is the One preventing Antichrist from being revealed. In the Old Testament the Holy Spirit came *upon* men, but did not indwell them, and could leave them. Thus David prayed, "...take not thy holy spirit from me" (Ps 51:11). We offer no such prayer today, for we are "sealed with that holy Spirit of promise" (Eph 1:13) whom Jesus declared would "abide with you for ever" (Jn 14:16). Christ told His disciples, "...he [the Holy Spirit] dwelleth *with* you; and shall be *in* you" (Jn 14:17). This special presence of God, unknown on earth until the day of Pentecost, can be "taken out of the way"—but *only* at the Rapture.

Christ assures us, "He that believeth on me,...out of his belly [innermost being] shall flow rivers of living water." John explains, "[T]his spake he of the Spirit, which they that believe on him should receive: for the Holy Ghost was not yet given [to indwell permanently]; because that Jesus was not yet glorified" (Jn 7:38-39). It is from heaven when He was glorified to the Father's right hand that Jesus, on the day of Pentecost, sent the Holy Spirit to indwell the believers permanently, exactly as He promised ("the Comforter...whom I will send unto you from the Father..." –Jn 15:26), and the church was born. Thus Peter at Pentecost declared, "Therefore, being by the right hand of God exalted, and having received of the Father the promise of the Holy Ghost, he [Christ] hath shed forth this..." (Acts 2:33).

It is only this special indwelling presence of God, which began at Pentecost, that can be taken away—and only through the Rapture removing Christians from earth. If Antichrist appears before the Rapture, then believers would logically look for *him* first; yet we are told to look for Christ (Lk 12:35-40; Phil 3:20; 1 Thes 1:10; Ti 2:13; Heb 9:28, etc.). Nor could any other event except the Rapture unite the world under Antichrist.

Some suggest that the chaos caused by computer failures on January 1, 2000, will be the catalyst to usher in Antichrist's world government. In our opinion, the Y2K warnings of disaster border on extremism and alarmism, which we will attempt to deal with in a future issue. God has something far more electrifying and unifying in mind: the Rapture. In our opinion, nothing else could unite Hindus, Muslims, Jews, Catholics, Protestants, Orthodox, atheists, communists, capitalists and everyone else—except the unspeakable terror caused by the sudden mass disappearance of millions of believers all over the world.

"Where did they go? Who took them? Will I be next?" That hysterical cry will be on everyone's lips—from cowering individuals to the bewildered United Nations meeting in emergency session. Most terrifying of all will be the question, "How can I escape when whoever took them comes back for more?" Almost no one will believe the biblical Rapture has occurred, because of a "strong delusion" from God (2 Thes 2:10-12).

The pretrib Rapture, uniting the world in a common terror and grief, will offer the perfect opportunity for Satan to put his man into power. With God's restraint lifted, all of Satan's power will be unleashed through Antichrist "in signs and lying wonders, and with all deceivableness of unrighteousness" (vv 9-10). Antichrist may claim to be negotiating with an intergalactic council for the return of the missing. Should he promise that those who take his mark in hand or forehead would not be snatched from earth, multitudes would welcome that guarantee.

We believe that the Rapture (not the appearance of Antichrist and tribulation necessitating survivalist tactics) is the next event on the prophetic calendar, and that it must occur very soon. In the meantime, the "spirit of antichrist" is preparing the world and a false church for his appearing. Consider carefully what John has to say: "...try [test] the spirits whether they are of God: because many false prophets are gone out into the world" (1 Jn 4:1). Many spirits are involved in a common anti-Christ agenda, speaking through many false prophets.

John alerts us to a foundational truth which Satan undermines in any way he can: "that Jesus Christ is come in the flesh" (1 Jn 4:2). The denial of this truth characterizes what John calls "the spirit of antichrist."

Tragically, this antichrist spirit pollutes the teaching of many seemingly Christian churches and leaders. Remember, the Greek prefix *anti* not only means "in opposition to" but also "in the place of." The antichrist spirit opposes Christ under the pretense of representing Him and leading His church.

To warn of a denial "that Jesus Christ is come in the flesh" seems, at first, unnecessary. Very few people deny that Jesus Christ really lived. The date on coins and documents around the world attests to that historic fact. John, therefore, must have meant much more than that, as careful thought reveals.

Clearly, the phrase "is come in the flesh" indicates that Jesus Christ existed prior to His incarnation as a babe in Bethlehem. He is God the Son, one of three Persons of the Godhead (Col 2:9), "the Almighty...the Alpha and Omega" (Rv 1:8, 11); the Creator of all (Jn 1:3); the eternal Word "made flesh" (Jn 1:14). "For unto us a child is born" refers to the baby Jesus. The very next phrase, "unto us a son is given" (Is 9:6), refers to the Father giving His eternal Son into the world: "For God so loved the world, that he gave his only begotten Son..." (Jn 3:16); "the Lord God, and his Spirit, hath sent me" (Is 48:16, etc).

This *given* Son is called "The mighty God, The everlasting Father" (Is 9:6). To deny that God has come in flesh expresses the very spirit of antichrist. That spirit is manifested in the Jehovah's Witnesses' denial that Jesus is God. Islam and its Koran, though honoring Jesus as a great prophet, also deny His deity. So do a substantial percentage of those who call themselves born-again Christians. These people are lost, no matter how lustily they sing, "O how I love Jesus," and how faithfully they attend church; for Jesus himself said, "Before Abraham was, I AM" [this is God's name, Jahweh/Jehovah, from Ex 3:14] (Jn 8:58).

The Mormon's denial is more devious: At the time Jesus came into the world He was a spirit being, half-brother of Lucifer and of all of us in a pre-earth state. Our "Father in heaven" was once a sinful man on another planet and was redeemed by that world's Jesus. The heart of Mormon doctrine is "As man is, God once was; as God is, man may become." The Mormon's God is an exalted man with numerous wives through whom he has millions of spirit children who must come to earth in order to become gods, as Jesus did. The body Jesus took in order to achieve godhood was produced when "Father God" came to earth and had intercourse with Mary. Behind such teaching, writes John, is "the spirit of antichrist."

The Roman Catholic claim that Mary is "the Mother of God" and the "spouse of the Holy Spirit" offers an even more subtle anti-Christ twist. In fact, Mary is not the mother of Jesus as God, the Eternal Son of God *given* by the Father to be the Savior of the world. She is the mother of Jesus as man, the mother of the body the Father prepared for His Son in her womb: "Wherefore when he [Christ] cometh into the world, he saith...a body hast thou prepared me" (Heb 10:5). Nor is she "the spouse of the Holy Spirit." The creation by the Holy Spirit in Mary's womb of the body which Jesus took when He became man had nothing to do with a relationship to her that could in any way imply that the Holy Spirit was Mary's *spouse*.

The Mary of Catholicism and Orthodoxy, inspired by the spirit of antichrist, has been elevated above Jesus, who is almost always pictured as a babe in her arms or a child at her side. Far more prayers are said to this false Mary than to Jesus and the Father combined. Many prayers ask *her* for the salvation which Christ, who is the Savior, promises all who believe in *Him*.

Reincarnation as taught by Hinduism (or New Age) is another denial that "Jesus Christ is come in the flesh." It requires that He come repeatedly in other bodies in successive lives. At His incarnation, Christ took up permanent residence in human flesh; the same body that was laid in the grave was raised from the dead, never to die again, leaving the grave empty. In that resurrected, glorified body, Christ now lives at the Father's right hand. Yet as surely as that fact is denied by the teaching of reincarnation, so surely is it also denied by Roman Catholicism's dogma that Christ comes in the flesh over and over to die continually on its altars as a wafer turned into His literal physical body.

Such teaching comes through the spirit of antichrist. The *sacrifice* of the Mass denies the clear teaching of the Bible: "So Christ was *once* offered to bear the sins of many...we are sanctified through the offering of the body of Jesus Christ *once*...after he had offered *one* sacrifice for sins for ever...there is no more offering for sin" (Heb 9:25-10:18). Defying such Scriptures, Catholicism declares, "Hence the Mass...[is] a sacrifice in which the sacrifice of the cross is perpetuated...in the sacrifice of the Mass our Lord is immolated...the eucharistic sacrifice is the source and the summit of...the Christian life.... In the sacrifice of the Mass in fact, Christ offers himself for the salvation of the entire world" (*Vatican II, Eucharisticum Mysterium*, 3.,18.).

Through this false teaching, the spirit of antichrist has Catholics literally worshiping the wafer as God ("all the faithful ought to show to this most holy sacrament the worship which is due to the true God"- Ibid., 3.f.). They think that salvation comes gradually by repeatedly ingesting Christ's physical body and blood—this wafer.

The errors of both reincarnation and the Sacrifice of the Eucharist are refuted by Scripture. "And as it is appointed unto men once to die, but after this the judgment" (Heb 9:27) refutes reincarnation. "Christ was once offered to bear the sins of many...there is no more offering for sin" (Heb 9:28; 10:18) refutes the alleged sacrifice of the Mass.

Christ's entrance into flesh to become a man took place only once—and is *permanent in that same body*. He was not "raised" a spirit being as His disciples imagined: "Handle me, and see;" Jesus told them, "for a spirit hath not flesh and bones, as ye see me have" (Lk 24:39). One must believe in the *bodily* resurrection of Christ in order to be saved: "That if thou shalt ...believe in thine heart that God hath raised him from the dead, thou shalt be saved" (Rom 10:9); "Moreover, brethren, I declare unto you the gospel...

By which also ye are saved,...how that Christ died for our sins...was buried, and...rose again the third day" (1 Cor 15:1-4). No other gospel will save the soul. Let us proclaim it without compromise and thus counter the lies perpetuated by the spirit of antichrist.

—Dave Hunt, *The Berean Call*, September 1998

Appendix H

Does It Matter?

"And, behold, I come quickly; and my reward is with me, to give every man according as his work shall be.... Surely I come quickly" (Rv 22:12, 20). These, Christ's last recorded words, confirm His earlier promise: "I will come again, and receive you unto myself; that where I am, there ye may be also" (Jn 14:2-3). Paul refers to the fulfillment of this promise: "For the Lord himself shall descend from heaven with a shout,...and the dead in Christ shall rise first: then we which are alive...shall be caught up together with them...to meet the Lord in the air: and so shall we ever be with the Lord" (1 Thes 4:16-17).

In response to these promises from Christ, "the Spirit and the bride say, Come" (Rv 22:17), to which John adds his glad "Amen. Even so, come, Lord Jesus."

Who is this Bride? After declaring that husband and wife are "one flesh," Paul explains: "This is a great mystery: but I speak concerning Christ and the church" (Eph 5:22-32).

Neither the words of Christ and John nor those of the Spirit and the Bride would make any sense if this coming to catch away the believers to Himself had to await the appearance of Antichrist (prewrath view) or the consummation of the Great Tribulation (post-trib view). A post-anything coming of Christ for His bride simply doesn't fit these words of Scripture. If the Great Tribulation must occur first, for the Spirit and the Bride to cry "Come, Lord Jesus!" would be like demanding payment on a debt that wasn't due for seven years!

A post-anything rapture flies in the face of many scriptures which clearly demand a coming of Christ that could occur at any moment. Christ himself said, "Let your loins be girded about, and your lights burning; and ye yourselves like unto men that wait for their lord..." (Lk 12:35). Such a command would mock us if Christ could not come until after seven years of tribulation.

That the coming which Christ's bride longs for will bring the resurrection of the dead and the transformation of the living into new bodies is clear not only from 1 Thessalonians 4, but from other passages such as "... from whence [heaven] also we look for the Saviour, the Lord Jesus Christ:

who shall change our vile body, that it may be fashioned like unto his glorious body" (Phil 3:20-21). Many other passages also call upon believers to watch and wait expectantly. Such exhortations make sense only if Christ could catch His bride to heaven at any moment:

> ...waiting for the coming of our Lord Jesus Christ (1 Cor 1:7);...ye turned to God from idols to serve the living and true God; and to wait for his Son from heaven...(1 Thes 1:9-10); Looking for that blessed hope, and the glorious appearing of...our Saviour Jesus Christ (Ti 2:13);...unto them that look for him shall he appear the second time... (Heb 9:28); Be patient therefore, brethren, unto the coming of the Lord (Jas 5:7); etc.

Opinions about the Rapture do not affect salvation—but we should seek to understand what the Bible says. The early church was clearly expecting Christ at any moment. To be watching and waiting for Christ if Antichrist must appear first would be like expecting Christmas before Thanksgiving. Yet Christ exhorted, "Watch therefore, for ye know neither the day nor the hour wherein the Son of man cometh.... Lest coming suddenly he find you sleeping. And what I say unto you I say unto all, Watch" (Mt 25:13; Mk 13:36-37).

Nor does the following from Christ fit a post-trib coming: "Therefore be ye also ready: for *in such an hour as ye think not* the Son of man cometh" (Mt 24:44). It is absurd to imagine that anyone who had survived the Great Tribulation and had seen the prophesied events (the plagues and judgment poured out upon earth; Antichrist's image in the temple; the mark imposed to buy and sell; all killed who would not worship Antichrist's image; the three witnesses in Jerusalem killed, then resurrected and caught up to heaven; Jerusalem surrounded by the world's armies, etc.), and who had counted the foretold 1,260 days, could possibly imagine at that hour that Christ was not about to return! There is simply no way to reconcile a post-trib coming of Christ with His warning that He would come when He would *not be expected.*

That statement alone distinguishes the Rapture (catching the church up from earth to heaven) from the Second Coming (to rescue Israel at Armageddon), for the latter will surprise almost no one. In contrast to His warning that even many in the church will not be expecting Him, numerous scriptures foretell another coming of Christ when all the signs have been fulfilled and everyone knows that He is coming. To unbelieving Israel, Christ declared, "when ye shall see all these things, know that it [My coming] is near, even at the doors" (Mt 24:33). Even Antichrist will know: "And I saw the beast, and the kings of the earth, and their armies, gathered together to make war against him that sat on the horse, and against his army" (Rv 19:19).

Either Christ is contradicting himself (impossible!) or *He is speaking of two events.* Christ says He will come at a time of peace and prosperity when even His bride will not expect Him: "Be ye therefore ready also: for the Son of man cometh at an hour when ye think not" (Lk 12:40). Not only the foolish, but even the wise, will be asleep: "While the bridegroom tarried, they *all* slumbered and slept" (Mt 25:5)!

Yet Scripture says that the Messiah comes when the world is almost destroyed by war, famine and God's judgment and Israel is about to go down in defeat. Then, Jahweh declares, "they shall look upon me whom they have pierced" (Zec 12:10) and all Jews alive on earth will recognize their returning messiah as the "mighty God, the everlasting Father" (Is 9:6) who, exactly as their prophets foretold, came as a man, died for their sins, and has come again, this time to rescue Israel. Of this climactic moment, Christ declares, "But he that shall endure unto the end, the same shall be saved" (Mt 24:13). Paul adds, "And so all Israel [still living] shall be saved..." (Rom 11:26).

It is inescapable that two comings are yet future: one that could catch even His bride by surprise, and another that will hardly be a surprise to anyone. These cannot be the same event. But where does the New Testament say that two comings remain? Every Christian believes in two comings: Christ came once to earth, died for our sins, rose from the dead, returned to heaven and is coming again. Yet nowhere did the Old Testament say there would be two distinct comings.

That fact caused confusion for the rabbis, for Christ's disciples,and even for John the Baptist. "Filled with the Holy Ghost, even from his mother's womb" (Lk 1:15, 41, 44), John had testified that Jesus was "the Lamb of God, which taketh away the sin of the world" (Jn 1:29). Yet this last of the Old Testament prophets, of whom there was none greater "born of women" (Lk 7:28), began to doubt: "Art thou he that should come? or look we for another?" (Lk 7:19).

Only one coming of the Messiah was anticipated. He would deliver Israel and establish His kingdom upon David's throne in Jerusalem. Thus the rabbis, soldiers and jeering onlookers mocked Him on the cross (Mt 27:40-44; Mk 15:18-20, 29-32; Lk 23:35-37)! In spite of all the miracles He had done, the disciples likewise took His crucifixion to be conclusive proof that He could not have been the Messiah. The two on the road to Emmaus said, "...we trusted that it had been he which should have redeemed Israel" (Lk 24:19-21)—but now He was dead.

Christ rebuked them for failing "to believe *all* that the prophets have spoken" (Lk 24:25). That was the common problem—failure to consider *all* prophecies. Israel had a one-sided view of the Messiah's coming (and still does today) which allows her to see only His triumphant reign and blinds her to His sacrifice for sin. Even many Christians are so obsessed with thoughts of "conquering" and "dominion" that they imagine it is the church's responsibility to take over the world and to establish the Kingdom so that the King can then return to earth to reign. They forget His promise to His bride to take her to heaven, from whence she shall return with Him to help rule the world.

How could Christ come from heaven to execute judgment upon earth "with ten thousands of his saints [i.e., multitudes]" (Jude 14) if He had not first taken them to heaven? Here we have another reason for a pretrib rapture. Amazingly, Michael Horton, in *Putting Amazing Back into Grace* (p. 198), imagines that 1 Thessalonians 4:14 refers to Christ's Second Coming "*with* the saints" ("so we believe that God will bring with Jesus those who have fallen asleep in him"). On the contrary, it is the disembodied souls and spirits of physically dead believers which Christ brings at the Rapture to be reunited with their bodies at the resurrection and takes them and the transformed living to heaven. At the Second Coming it is *living* saints who have already been resurrected and previously taken to heaven whom He brings with Him back to earth.

Prior to Christ's return with His saints there has been a wedding in heaven of the Lamb to His bride (Rv 19:7). Having undergone the judgment seat of Christ (1 Cor 3:12-15; 2 Cor 5:10, etc.), the saints are "arrayed in fine linen, clean and white" (Rv 19:8). Surely they must also be the army "clothed in fine linen, white and clean" (19:14) that comes with Christ to destroy Antichrist. When were they taken to heaven? Certainly not at the Second Coming, for that would leave time neither for the judgment seat of Christ nor for the wedding. The Rapture *must* be a prior event.

Those who are looking forward to meeting a "Christ" with their feet planted on this earth have forgotten that the true Christ will catch us up to meet Him in the air and take us to His Father's house. They have forgotten, too, that Antichrist will establish an earthly kingdom before the true King returns to reign. Sadly, those who are working to establish a kingdom on this earth are preparing the world for the counterfeit reign of "that man of sin."

How could anyone in Old Testament times have known that there would be two comings of the Messiah? By implication only. Either the prophets contradicted themselves when they foretold that the Messiah would be rejected and crucified and yet that He would be hailed as King and reign upon David's throne forever—or they were speaking of two comings.

There was no way to put into one event what the prophets said. There simply *had* to be two comings of the Messiah: first as the Lamb of God to die for our sins, then as the Lion of the tribe of Judah (Hos 5:14-15;

Rev 5:5) in power and glory to rescue Israel in the midst of Armageddon. And so it is in the New Testament. Notice the many contradictions unless these are two events: 1) He comes *for* His saints and at a time when no one expects Him; but He comes *with* His saints and at a time when everyone knows He is coming; 2) He doesn't come to earth but catches the saints up to meet Him in the air (1 Thes 4:17); but He comes to this earth, His "feet shall stand in that day upon the mount of Olives" (Zec 14:4) and the saints come to earth with Him; 3) He takes the saints *to* heaven to His Father's house of many mansions to be with Him (Jn 14:3); but He brings the saints *from* heaven (Zec 14:5; Jude 14); 4) He comes for His bride at a time of peace and prospering, business and pleasure (Lk 17:26-30); but He comes to rescue His people Israel when the world has practically been destroyed and in the midst of earth's worst war, Armageddon.

Christ declared: "And as it was in the days of Noe...they did eat, they drank, they married wives;...also as it was in the days of Lot;...they bought, they sold, they planted,...they builded; but the same day that Lot went out of Sodom it rained fire and brimstone from heaven.... Even thus shall it be in the day when the Son of man is revealed [to His own]" (Lk 17:26-30). These world conditions at the Rapture could only be before the tribulation period; they certainly could not be at its conclusion!

Rapture? Critics claim that the word "rapture" isn't even in the Bible! In fact, it is—and has been—since Jerome's fifth-century Latin Vulgate translated the Greek *harpazo* (to snatch suddenly) as *raeptius*, from which "rapture" comes. The KJV renders *harpazo* "caught up." That is what Christ promised in John 14—to catch us up to heaven.

Other critics parrot Dave MacPherson's myth that a pretrib Rapture came from Darby early in the nineteenth century, who learned it from a Margaret MacDonald, who got it from Edward Irving, who learned it from the writings of the Jesuit Emmanuel Lacunza. That is simply not true (see *The Berean Call*, June 1995). A number of much earlier writers expressed this belief. One is Ephraem of Nisibis (306-73), well-known in Syrian church history. He stated, "All the saints and elect of God are gathered together before the tribulation, which is to come, and are taken to the Lord...." That sermon was popularly circulated in several languages.

Yes, there *is* a post-trib coming: "Immediately after the tribulation of those days...they shall see the Son of man coming in the clouds of heaven with power and great glory" (Mt 24:29-30). For His angels to "gather together his elect from the four winds" (vv. 29-31) is certainly not Christ himself rapturing His church to heaven, but the gathering of scattered Israel back to her land at the Second Coming.

Christ associated evil with the thought that His coming would be delayed: "But and if that evil servant shall say in his heart, My lord delayeth his coming" (Mt 24:48; Lk 12:45). Again, that statement is senseless if the Rapture is post-trib.

There is no greater motive for holy living and diligent evangelism than knowing that Christ could take us to heaven at any moment. May the Bride awaken from her sleep, fall in love again with the Bridegroom, and from her heart and by her daily life call out continually, "Come, Lord Jesus, come!"

—Dave Hunt, *The Berean Call*, September 2001

Notes

Chapter 2—When They Say "Peace and Safety"
1. Romans 15:33; 16:20; Philippians 4:9; 1 Thessalonians 5:23; Hebrews 13:20.
2. *USA Today*, December 26, 1989.
3. *Los Angeles Times*, February 1, 1990, pp. A19-20.
4. Dave Hunt, *Peace, Prosperity and the Coming Holocaust* (Harvest House, 1983), p. 18.
5. Paul Johnson, "Entering the 'Age of Deals,' " *World Press Review*, March 1990, p. 24, cited from the London *Spectator*.
6. William Manchester, *The Last Lion: Biography of Winston Churchill, 1932-40* (Little, Brown and Company, 1988), pp. 82-83.
7. *The Orange County Register*, August 9, 1990, p. A7.

Chapter 3—Fulfillment in Our Day?
1. Robert Dick Wilson, "What Is an Expert?" *Bible League Quarterly*, 1955, cited in David Otis Fuller, ed., *Which Bible?* (Grand Rapids International Publications, 1975), pp. 42-44.
2. Ibid., pp. 44-46.
3. George Will, "Hussein worse than Mussolini in viciousness, military might," syndicated column, Washington D.C.
4. Johnson, "Age of Deals," pp. 24-25.

Chapter 4—The Last of the "Last Days"?
1. *Satanism In America*, p. 34, published by Kerusso Company, Inc., P.O. Box 1168, Crockett, TX 75835, endorsed by The National Criminal Justice Task Force on Occult Related Ritualistic Crimes.
2. John Wauck, "Paganism, American Style," *National Review*, March 19, 1990, p. 43.
3. "The Meaning of Life," *Life* magazine, December 1988, p. 78.
4. Brochure of Peace on Earth, Baltimore, Maryland.
5. Bruce Narramore, *You're Someone Special* (Zondervan, 1978), p. 22.
6. *The Orange County Register*, August 17, 1990, p. A5.
7. Wayne W. Dyer, "A Letter to the Next Generation," *Time*, October 17, 1988, part of a five-page Volkswagen ad which folded out from the front cover and explained: "In 'Open Forum' sponsored by VOLKSWAGEN prominent figures in American culture pass on their ideas and views to those who'll inherit the earth . . . 100 years from now."
8. For a full discussion of this belief and those who teach it, see Dave Hunt and T.A. McMahon, *The Seduction of Christianity* (Harvest House, 1985).
9. Zig Ziglar, "How To Get What You Want," tape No. 1105 in W. Clement Stone's "Collections of Cassette Tapes" offered by PMA, Chicago, IL and advertised in Robert Schuller's *Possibilities* magazine.
10. By Kenneth Hagin.
11. A.W. Tozer, *Keys to the Deeper Life*, rev. expanded ed. (Zondervan, 1988), p. 18.

Chapter 5—A United Europe: Stepping-stone to Global Peace?
1. *Los Angeles Times*, December 2, 1989, p. A2.
2. *Los Angeles Times*, December 6, 1989, pp. A1, A8-10.
3. William Rusher, "Teaching the East Bloc how freedom works," *The Washington Times*, January 5, 1990, p. F3.
4. Donald S. McAlvany, *The McAlvany Intelligence Advisor*, December 1989.
5. *The Detroit News*, February 1, 1990.
6. *Time*, December 11, 1989, p. 37.
7. *Los Angeles Times*, December 1, 1989, p. A42.

Chapter 6—Daniel's Remarkable Prophecy
1. Available from Kregel Publications, Grand Rapids, MI 49501 as part of the Sir Robert Anderson Library Series.

Chapter 7—Two Great Mysteries
1. *Los Angeles Times*, November 8, 1989, pp. B1, B12.
2. *The News Democrat*, July 28, 1989, p. 7A.
3. *Los Angeles Times*, December 8, 1989, p. B11.
4. Richard Wurmbrand, *Was Karl Marx A Satanist?* (Diane Books, 1976), available at most Christian bookstores, or P.O. Box 11, Glendale, CA 91209.

5. Karl Marx, "Invocation of One in Despair," cited in David Tame, *Critique: A Journal of Conspiracies & Metaphysics*, No. 27, "Secret Societies in the Life of Karl Marx," Part 2, pp. 31-36.
6. Ibid.

Chapter 8—The Revived Roman Empire

1. Vaclav Havel, "The Chance That Will Not Return," *U.S. News & World Report*, Feb. 26, 1990, p. 30.
2. Mikhail Gorbachev, *Perestroika: New Thinking for Our Country and the World* (Harper & Row, 1987), p. 197.
3. *New York Times*, February 24, 1990.
4. Havel, "Chance," p. 30.
5. *Los Angeles Times*, May 14, 1990.
6. Johnson, "Age of Deals," p. 25.
7. From the Summary Report of the National Education Association Bicentennial Program.
8. Allan Bloom, *The Closing of the American Mind* (Simon and Schuster, 1987), p. 36.
9. Lynda Falkenstein, *Global Education: State of the Art Research Summary Report* (Northwest Regional Educational Lab., 1983), p. 14, distributed by the U.S. Dept. of Education, NIE, Education Resources Information Center, Washington, D.C. 20208. As cited by Eric Buehrer, *The New Age Masquerade: The Hidden Agenda in Your Child's Classroom* (Wolgemuth & Hyatt, 1990), p. 42.
10. Cited by Eric Buehrer, *New Age Masquerade: The Hidden Agenda in Your Child's Classroom* (Wolgemuth & Hyatt, 1990), p. 43.
11. *Focus on the Family Citizen*, January 1990, p. 10.
12. *Orange County Register*, June 6, 1990, article begins on p. 1.

Chapter 9—Emperors and Popes

1. Joseph Sobran, "God and Man in Rome," *The Washington Times*, December 8, 1989.
2. *Los Angeles Times*, December 2, 1989, p. A4.
3. *San Gabriel Valley Tribune* (San Gabriel, CA), May 1, 1988.
4. Gorbachev, *Perestroika*, p. 191.
5. *Newsweek* magazine, September 21, 1987, p. 26
6. *Los Angeles Times*, December 2, 1989, pp. A1, A4.
7. *Time*, December 4, 1989, p. 75.
8. "Soviet Economists Seek Ways To Pull Nation Out Of Crisis," *Investor's Daily*, November 14, 1989.
9. Johnson, "Age of Deals," p. 25.
10. *The Toronto Star*, May 5, 1987, p. A3.
11. *Focus on the Family Citizen*, January 1990, p. 10.
12. *Seattle Times*, May 8, 1990.
13. W.H.C. Frend, *The Rise of Christianity* (Fortress Press, 1984), p. 458.
14. Will Durant, *The Story of Civilization: Vol. 3, Caesar and Christ* (Simon and Schuster, 1944), p. 656.
15. Augustine, *de cat. rud.*, XXV, 48.
16. Durant, *Civilization: Vol. 3, Caesar and Christ*, p. 657.
17. *USA Today*, August 6, 1990.
18. *World Goodwill Newsletter*, 1989, No. 4, pp. 1, 3.

Chapter 10—The "Whore of Babylon"

1. *Houston Chronicle*, November 29, 1989, p. 22A.
2. Ibid., p. 22A.
3. Durant, *Civilization: Vol. 3, Caesar and Christ*, pp. 671-72.
4. R.W. Southern, *Western Society and the Church in the Middle Ages* (Penguin Books, Vol. 2 of Pelican History of the Church Series, 1970), p. 144.
5. Colman J. Barry, O.S.B., ed., *Readings in Church History*, Vol. 1, "From Pentecost to the Protestant Revolt," (The Newman Press, 1960), p. 233.
6. Cardinal Alphonsus de Liguori, *The Glories of Mary* (Tan Books, 1977), pp. 94, 136, 137, 141, 143, 180-81.
7. *Devotions in Honor of Our Mother of Perpetual Help*, Official Edition (Liguori Publications, One Liguori Drive, Liguori, Missouri 63057), Imprimi Potest: John F. Dowd, C.SS.R., Provincial, St. Louis Province; Imprimatur: John N. Wurm, S.T.D., Vicar General, Archdiocese of St. Louis, pp. 46-47.

8. *Catholic Twin Circle*, Sunday, August 26, 1990, p. 20.
9. *Lucia Speaks: The Message of Fatima According to the Exact Words of Sister Lucia, Published by the Most Reverend Bishop of Fatima* (Ave Maria Institute, 1968), p. 46.
10. *Lucia Speaks on the Message of Fatima* (Ave Maria Institute, Washington, NJ 07882), pp. 26, 30-31, 47.
11. *The Fatima Crusader*, November/December 1986, p. 9.
12. *St. Louis Review*, November 4, 1988, cited in *Christian News*, November 14, 1988, pp. 10-11.
13. Malachi Martin, *The Keys of This Blood: The Struggle for World Dominion Between Pope John Paul II, Mikhail Gorbachev and the Capitalist West* (Simon and Schuster, 1990), pp. 626-627; see also interview with Malachi Martin, *Washington Times*, Sept. 28, 1990, p. B6.
14. *The Fatima Crusader*, November/December 1986, p. 9.
15. *Our Lady of Fatima's Peace Plan From Heaven* (Tan Books and Publishers, 1983), inside back cover.
16. Ibid., back cover.
17. *The Fatima Crusader*, November/December 1986, p. 1 of letter of appeal inserted in middle of the magazine, which starts, "Dear Fellow Catholic. . . ."
18. Quoted at the beginning of each "Heaven's Peace Plan," a daily Catholic radio program produced by the International Fatima Rosary Crusade, hosted by Fr. Nicholas Gruner, who publishes *The Fatima Crusader* magazine with a readership of an estimated 1 million. The radio program claims to reach millions of people in the United States and Canada each week "with our Lady of Fatima's urgent message." The claim is also made at the beginning of each program: "It is only by obedience to our Lady of Fatima's message that we here in North America shall avoid being enslaved by Communist Russia. It is only by prompt obedience to our Lady of Fatima's message that the world will have peace. . . ."
19. *Soul Magazine*, January/February 1985, pp. 5-7.
20. Martin, *Keys of This Blood*, pp. 626-657.
21. *Lucia Speaks on the Message*, pp. 26, 29, 30-31, 47.
22. *Chicago Sun Times*, December 24, 1989.
23. *The Pope Speaks*, March/April 1990, pp. 130-31.
24. *Our Sunday Visitor*, November 13, 1988.
25. *Courier-Journal*, May 11, 1984, p. A7.
26. *The Voice*, Diocese of Newark, January 1989.
27. *Los Angeles Times*, January 7, 1989, Part II, p. 7.

Chapter 11—Communism, Catholicism, and World Destiny
1. "Soviets find religious TV good for the proletariat" (an interview with Robert Schuller), *The Washington Times*, June 1, 1990.
2. *Los Angeles Times*, September 7, 1990, p. A39.
3. The current deafening silence concerning criticism of the Catholic Church may have less to do with one's courage than with the practical concern that to oppose Rome severely limits one's audience.
4. *Los Angeles Times*, June 27, 1990, pp. A1, A16.
5. Rev. Peter Geiermann, C.SS.R., *The Convert's Catechism of Catholic Doctrine* (Tan Books and Publishers, Inc., 1977), pp. 36, VI.
6. Karl Keating, *Catholicism and Fundamentalism: The Attack on "Romanism" by "Bible Christians"* (Ignatius Press, 1988), p. 127.
7. Austin Flannery, O.P., ed., *Vatican Council II* (Costello Publishing Co., 1984), Vol. I, p. 755.
8. Ibid., Vol. II, 1982, p. 430.
9. Ibid., Vol. II, 1982, p. 392.
10. Geiermann, *Catechism*, pp. 26-27.
11. Ibid.
12. Flannery, *Vatican Council II*, Vol. I, p. 379.
13. D. Martyn Lloyd-Jones, *Roman Catholicism* (Evangelical Press, P.O. Box 2453, Grand Rapids, MI 49501), one in a series of "Pastoral Booklets," pp. 1-4.
14. J.J. Schroeder, O.P., trans., *The Canons and Decrees of the Council of Trent* (Tan Books, 1978), p. 46.
15. Ibid., p. 214.
16. Lloyd-Jones, *Roman Catholicism*, pp. 1-4, 16.
17. "Praise The Lord," Trinity Broadcasting Network, October 17, 1989, hosted by Paul and Jan Crouch.

Chapter 12—Ecumenism and the Coming New World Order

1. Eusebius Pamphilus, *Life of Constantine* (London, 1650), ii, pp. 63, 70, cited in Will Durant, *The Story of Civilization: Vol. 3, Caesar and Christ* (Simon and Schuster, 1944), p. 659.
2. Durant, *Civilization: Vol. 3, Caesar and Christ*, pp. 659-661.
3. *The Fresno Bee*, June 13, 1984, p. C12.
4. Desmond Doig, *Mother Teresa: Her People and Her Work* (Harper & Row, 1976), p. 156.
5. Abbot Thomas Keating, OCSO, M. Basil Pennington, OCSO, and Thomas E. Clarke, SJ, *Finding Grace At The Center* (St. Bede Publications, 1978), pp. 5-6.
6. "World Briefs," *The Boston Globe*, December 15, 1989.
7. *Valley Daily News* (Auburn, WA), December 15, 1989, from an Associated Press dispatch from Vatican City by Stephen R. Wilson.
8. "Spiritual Vision of Man," *L'Observatore Romano*, February 10, 1986, p. 5.
9. *The Tidings*, October 13, 1989.
10. *Time*, September 17, 1979, p. 96.
11. *Newsweek*, September 17, 1979, p. 115.
12. John Cotter, *A Study in Syncretism* (Canadian Intelligence Publications, 1983), pp. 90-91.
13. David DuPlessis, as told to Bob Slosser, *A Man Called Mr. Pentecost* (Logos, 1977), pp. 207-213; Stanley M. Burgess, Gary B. McGee, and Patrick H. Alexander, *Dictionary of Pentecostal and Charismatic Movements* (Zondervan, 1988), p. 253.
14. Stanley M. Burgess, Gary B. McGee, and Patrick H. Alexander, *Dictionary of Pentecostal and Charismatic Movements* (Zondervan, 1988), p. 125; *New Covenant*, February 1973, pp. 14-17.
15. Alan Geyer, "Religious Isolationism: Gone Forever?" *The Christian Century*, October 23, 1974, pp. 980-81.
16. *Catholic Register* (Toronto, Canada), September 21, 1974.
17. *The Orange County Register*, August 17, 1990, p. A5.
18. *The Orange County Register*, April 15, 1990, p. G4.
19. Carol M. Ostrom, "Trust is key, interfaith group agrees," *Seattle Times* (Seattle, WA), March 11, 1987.
20. *Our Sunday Visitor*, November 13, 1988.
21. *Catholic World*, May/June 1989, p. 140.
22. "60 Religious Leaders Join Pontiff, Streets of Assisi Ring with Prayers for Peace," *The Los Angeles Times*, October 28, 1986, Part I, p. 7, continued from front page.
23. *Shared Vision: Global Forum of Spiritual and Parliamentary Leaders on Human Survival*, Autumn 1987, p. 5.
24. From an official brochure of Global Forum of Spiritual and Parliamentary Leaders on Human Survival, 304 East 45th St., 12th Floor, New York, NY 10017, (212) 953-7947, Fax: (212) 557-2061.
25. "For Global Survival: The Final Statement of the Conference," *Shared Vision* (newsletter of Global Forum), Summer 1988, p. 12.
26. Ibid.
27. *USA Today*, March 23, 1989.
28. Numerous authors, *Little Masonic Library* (Macoy Publishing and Masonic Supply, 1977), Vol. 4, p. 32.
29. Albert Pike, *Morals and Dogma of the Ancient and Accepted Scottish Rite of Freemasonry* (Charleston, SC, The Supreme Council of the 33rd Degree for the Southern Jurisdiction of the United States, 1906), p. 226.
30. J. Blanchard, *Scottish Rite Masonry Illustrated* (Charles T. Powner, Co., 1979), Vol. 2, p. 320.
31. James Dobson, *Focus on the Family*, January 1987, p. 7.
32. John Hick and Paul F. Knitter, eds., *The Myth of Christian Uniqueness: Toward a Pluralistic Theology of Religions* (Orbis Books, 1988), Preface, pp. x-xi.
33. *Orange County Register*, September 8, p. A10.
34. *Time*, September 17, 1990, p. 23.
35. Ibid.
36. *Newsweek*, September 17, 1990, p. 27.
37. *The Bulletin* (Bend, OR), September 11, 1990, front page.
38. *Orange County Register*, September 8, 1990, p. A10.
39. Mikhail Gorbachev, "U.S.S.R. Arms Reduction: Rivalry into Sensible Competition," *Vital Speeches of the Day*, February 1, 1989 (City News Publishing Co., Mount Pleasant, SC), p. 230, delivered before the United Nations, New York City, New York.

Chapter 13—Ecological Concern and Global Peace
1. From a transcript of his talk as cited in *NRI Trumpet*, Cynthia B. Lindstedt, "Prince Philip Promotes 'Ecological Pragmatism' of Pagan Worship, Religious Syncretism," p. 4.
2. Ibid.
3. From Religious News Service syndicated to newspapers, cited in *Christian News*, February 5, 1990.
4. From the official program *Global Forum on Environment and Development*, Moscow, USSR, January 15-19, 1990; and from official transcript of "Address by Mikhail Gorbachev to Participants in the Global Forum on Environment and Development for Survival, Palace of Congresses, The Kremlin, 19 January 1990."
5. Carl Sagan, *Cosmos* (Random House, 1980), p. 243.
6. Mary Long, "Visions of a New Faith," *Science Digest*, November 1981, p. 39.
7. *Sequoia*, October/November 1988.
8. *Our Sunday Visitor*, February 4, 1990, p. 5.
9. *Religious Workers for Lasting Peace, Disarmament and Just Relations Among Nations* (Department of External Church Relations of the Moscow Patriarchate, 1978), pp. 11, 16.

Chapter 16—A Tale of Two Comings
1. John Randolph Price, *Practical Spirituality* (Quartus, 1986), pp. 17-19.
2. The gold record attached to the Voyager spacecraft contained a message to extraterrestrial intelligences it was hoped would encounter and decipher it. Conceived by Carl Sagan and signed by then President Jimmy Carter, the communication was to the effect that we earthlings were rapidly becoming one global family with the aspiration of eventually joining an intergalactic community.

Chapter 17—The Arab-Islamic-Israeli Question
1. Will Durant, *The Story of Civilization: Vol. 4, The Age of Faith* (Simon and Schuster, 1950), p. 588.
2. *Watertown Daily Times*, January 21, 1990, p. A5.
3. Gorbachev, "U.S.S.R. Arms Reduction," p. 233.
4. *Washington Post*, September 10, 1990, p. A22.

Chapter 18—That Mysterious Trinity
1. Brooks Alexander, "One-to-One Correspondence," *SCP Newsletter*, Vol. 13:2, 1988, p. 13.
2. This is stated in various ways all through the Old Testament and confirmed in the New Testament in such verses as: Isaiah 43:3,11; 45:21; 49:26; 60:16; Hosea 13:4; 1 Timothy 1:1; 2:3; Titus 1:3; 2:10; 3:4; Jude 1:25; etc.

Chapter 19—Christ and Antichrist in Final Conflict
1. Marvin Rosenthal, *The Pre-Wrath Rapture of the Church* (Thomas Nelson Publishers, 1990), p. 208.
2. Ibid.
3. Ibid., p. 209.
4. The card is available to donors of InterVarsity Christian Fellowship, 6400 Schroeder Road, Madison, WI 53707-7895.

Chapter 20—Preparation for Delusion
1. William Shirer, *Berlin Diary*, as quoted by Gerald Suster in *Hitler: The Occult Messiah* (New York: St. Martin, 1981), pp. 140-141.
2. *Time*, August 28, 1989, p. 43.
3. Taken from a German condensation of Hitler's key speeches that has not been translated into English as yet.
4. Dave Hunt, *A Study Guide for The Cult Explosion* (Eugene, OR: Harvest House, 1981), p. 121.
5. Norman Vincent Peale, *Positive Imaging* (Fawcett Crest, 1982), p. 77.
6. Robert Schuller, "Faith, The Force That Sets You Free!" *Possibilities*, September/October 1988, p. 22.
7. Robert Schuller, "Possibility Thinking: Goals," Amway Corporation tape.
8. The title of a booklet authored by Kenneth Hagin.
9. M. Scott Peck, *New Age Journal* May/June 1987, p. 51.
10. John White, "The New Age and the Second Coming of Christ," *Body, Mind and Spirit*, November/December, 1988, pp. 48-53.

11. Martin, *The Keys of This Blood*, pp. 639-56.
12. Edward D. O'Connor, C.S.S., *The Pentecostal Movement in the Catholic Church* (Ave Maria Press, 1971), p. 58.
13. Ibid., p. 128.
14. Ibid., pp. 166-67, etc.
15. "Ready to Evangelize the World: 23,000 charistmatics gather for Indianapolis '90," *Charisma and Christian Life*, October 1990, p. 25.
16. "Roman Catholic Double-Talk at Indianapolis '90," *Foundation*, pp. 14-16, excerpts from talk by Fr. Tom Forrest to the Roman Catholic Saturday morning training session.
17. Brother Michael of the Holy Trinity at the Sorbonne, "Messages from Heaven to Earth: Fatima, Medjugorje, Kebeho and Charismatic Renewal," *The Catholic Counter-Reformation in the XXth Century*, November-December 1985, p. 1.
18. Wayne Weible, *Miracle at Medjugorje*, April 1988, p. 8.
19. *Christian News*, January 2, 1989, p. 4, quoting an interview in the *St. Louis Dispatch*, December 25, 1988, with "Seer Vicka Ivankovic."
20. *The Arizona Republic*, August 13, 1989, p. C5.
21. John Dale, *The Prince and the Paranormal: The Psychic Bloodline of the Royal Family* (W.H. Allen & Co. Plc., 1986), pp. 14-18; *US*, January 14, 1985, pp. 18-19, etc.
22. "ESP exists, scientist reports," *The Orange County Register*, April 1, 1990, p. A10.
23. *Chicago Sun-Times* January 11, 1989.
24. *New York Times International*, November 26, 1989.
25. New Age beliefs and practices are literally exploding in the Soviet Union even among top politicians. Boris Yeltsin, new head of Russia, the largest Soviet Republic, while calling for spiritual/moral leadership from the Russian Orthodox Church, maintains close ties with Esalen, a New Age center south of San Francisco. Werner Erhard's Forum (formerly EST) is expanding its influence in the USSR, while the Association for Humanistic Psychology is spreading its occult teaching via training sessions. The direction of future events seems clear.
26. C.G. Jung, *Memories, Dreams, Reflections* (Pantheon Books, 1963), p. 183.
27. Hal Zina Bennett, Ph.D., "The Inner Guides," *Magical Blend*, Issue 16, p. 40.
28. Alfred S. Alschuler, "Recognizing Inner Teachers: Inner Voices Throughout History," *Gnosis Magazine*, Fall 1987, pp. 8-12.
29. David Bressler and Martin Rossman, "The Inner Advisor in Clinical Practice," Workshop #2, tape #1, from IAHB Conference titled "Guided Imagery: An Intensive Training Program For Clinicians" with continuing education credit.
30. See, for example, John & Paula Sandford, *Healing the Wounded Spirit*, (Bridge Publishing, Inc., 1985), pp. 439-40, where they equate the Holy Spirit with the "inner guides" conjured up through occult techniques.
31. Alschuler, "Recognizing Inner Teachers," p. 12.

Chapter 21—The Christian's Hope
1. These are from among thousands of letters being received in response to broadcasts into the USSR by Russian Christian Radio, P.O. Box 1667, Estes Park, CO 80517.

Appendix A—Was Peter the First Pope?
1. See, for example, Deuteronomy 32:3,4; 2 Samuel 22:47; 23:3; Psalm 62:1,2; and many similar verses.

Appendix C—Mass and Transubustantiation
1. *The Fatima Crusader*, The Official Publication of The International Fatima Rosary Crusade, November/December 1986, "The Tremendous Value of Holy Mass," p. 21.

Appendix F—Purgatory
1. *Newsletter: The Padre Pio Foundation of America and the Mass Association*, August 1988, p. 2.
2. Ibid., p. 3.

Index

G

Genocide Treaty 268
German Christians' Faith Move-
    ment 266-267
Gestapo 267
glasnost 20, 56, 59, 91
global (see also world) 6, 36, 37, 95-96,
    162, 203, 205-206, 223
    brotherhood 96
    citizens 94, 157
    community 93
    council 166
    destruction 93
    ecological crisis 164
    education 93-94
    holocaust 33
    kingdom 82
    peace 9-10, 13-15, 18, 55, 63, 125,
        147, 154-156, 163-164, 175, 181,
        217, 268, 270, 284
    regions 70
    religious unity 153
    survival 157
    systems 95
    unification, unity 63, 93, 165
Global Civil Order 95
Global Forum (of Spiritual and Parliamen-
    tary Leaders on Human
    Survival) 156-157, 166, 169-170, 173
God-self 278
Godhead 171, 235, 237-238, 242-243
godliness 84-86, 281
Golan Heights 226
Golitsyn, Anatoly 60
Gorbachev, Mikhail 10, 20, 23, 49, 56,
    58-62, 82, 87-88, 90-92, 95, 100-106,
    110-111, 115, 117, 119, 131, 133, 136,
    151, 155-156, 161-162, 169-170, 172,
    203, 227, 249
    Raisa 100
Gore, U.S. Senator Al 166
gospel 16, 46, 53, 80, 86, 105, 123, 125,
    133-135, 141-146, 149, 154, 158, 171,
    188, 204, 210-212, 224, 229, 255, 269,
    274, 286, 294, 302, 304, 307-309, 311
grace 37, 121, 123-126, 129, 137, 139,
    142-143, 190, 224, 226, 246, 298,
    301-302, 306
Graham, Billy 77
great tribulation 14, 31, 72, 201, 203-204,
    211-212, 215-216, 261, 263, 280
Great White Brotherhood 278
Greek Orthodox Church 130
Gulf Crisis (Persian Gulf Crisis) 161, 227
guru(s) 47, 174, 276

H

Haiti 128
Hammer, Armand 135

hate 81, 82, 131, 258, 260, 279
Havel, Vaclav 89, 90, 104
heaven 14, 16, 25, 28, 41, 65-67, 69,
    79-81, 86, 92, 106, 113, 116, 118-119,
    121-123, 131, 140, 142-143, 145, 151,
    160, 170, 176, 188-190, 193, 196, 198,
    200-201, 203, 211-212, 214-216,
    229-230, 234, 253-254, 260-261, 263,
    269, 271-272, 279, 281-283, 287, 289,
    293, 298, 300-302, 304, 306, 310,
    312-314
hell 79, 81, 84, 86, 116, 120-121, 123,
    125-126, 135, 139, 170, 176, 190, 211,
    217, 251, 261, 263-264
Helsinki 161, 227
Herod, King 180, 183, 195, 242
"higher self" 47
Hindu(s) 29, 105, 129-130, 149-151, 154,
    155, 159, 173-174, 204, 206, 219, 223
Hinduism 29, 115, 128, 151, 169, 252
Hitler, Adolf 21-22, 25-26, 35, 225-226,
    229, 251, 257, 264-268, 274
holiness 281-282
holocaust 13, 20, 33, 164, 203, 208, 225,
    264
Holy See 104
Holy War 10, 147, 161, 221, 222, 227-229
homosexuality 52, 80, 172, 221
human potential 268, 275
humanism, humanistic 14, 16, 48, 52, 78,
    135, 172, 210, 254, 267-268, 275, 288
Hungary 17, 77, 88, 90
Hussein, Saddam 72, 120, 161-162, 226,
    227, 228

I

idolatrous, idolatry 50, 66, 120-121, 129,
    151, 281
imagination 8, 32, 33, 60, 65, 66, 81, 205,
    289, 313
Immaculate Heart 123, 124, 125, 127, 175,
    297-299
immorality 52, 172, 221
India 88, 129, 147, 150-151
Indianapolis 1990 272
infallibility, infallible 28, 137-141, 149,
    187
iniquity 77, 83-84
"inner guides" 45
"inner healing" 46, 277
inner potential 15, 233
"inner teachers" 277
"inner voices" 277
Institute for Transpersonal Psychology 277
inter-faith, Interfaith, Interfaith Coun-
    cils 130-131, 155, 166
inter-religious 155
Inter-Religious Federation for World
    Peace 154

Other Books by Dave Hunt

THE GOD MAKERS
—*Ed Decker & Dave Hunt*

ISBN: 978-1-565077-17-1

DEATH OF A GURU:
A REMARKABLE TRUE STORY OF ONE
MAN'S SEARCH FOR TRUTH
—*Rabi R. Maharaj with Dave Hunt*

ISBN: 978-0-890814-34-5

THE SEDUCTION OF CHRISTIANITY:
SPIRITUAL DISCERNMENT IN
THE LAST DAYS
—*Dave Hunt & T. A. McMahon*

ISBN: 978-0-890814-41-3

IN DEFENSE OF THE FAITH VOLUME 1:
BIBLICAL ANSWERS TO CHALLENGING
QUESTIONS —*Dave Hunt*

ISBN: 978-1-928660-66-8

THE NONNEGOTIABLE
GOSPEL —*Dave Hunt*

ISBN: 978-1-928660-43-9

DEBATING CALVINISM:
FIVE POINTS, TWO VIEWS
—*Dave Hunt & James White*

ISBN: 978-1-590522-73-8

COUNTDOWN TO THE SECOND COMING:
A CHRONOLOGY OF PROPHETIC EARTH
EVENTS HAPPENING NOW —*Dave Hunt*

ISBN: 978-1-928660-19-4

A WOMAN RIDES THE BEAST: THE
ROMAN CATHOLIC CHURCH AND
THE LAST DAYS —*Dave Hunt*

ISBN: 978-1-565071-99-5

OCCULT INVASION:
THE SUBTLE SEDUCTION OF THE
WORLD AND CHURCH —*Dave Hunt*

ISBN: 978-1-928660-60-6

WHAT LOVE IS THIS?
CALVINISM'S MISREPRESENTATION
OF GOD —*Dave Hunt*

ISBN: 978-1-928660-12-5

SEEKING & FINDING GOD: IN SEARCH
OF THE TRUE FAITH —*Dave Hunt*

ISBN: 978-1-928660-23-1

A CALVINIST'S HONEST DOUBTS:
RESOLVED BY REASON AND GOD'S
AMAZING GRACE —*Dave Hunt*

ISBN: 978-1-928660-34-7

THE MIND INVADERS: A NOVEL
[THE ARCHON CONSPIRACY]
—*Dave Hunt*

ISBN: 978-1-928660-35-4

AN URGENT CALL TO A SERIOUS
FAITH: A PROPHETIC ALARM FOR THE
BRIDE OF CHRIST —*Dave Hunt*

ISBN: 978-1-928660-33-0

PSYCHOLOGY & THE CHURCH: CRUCIAL
QUESTIONS, CRITICAL ANSWERS
—*Dave Hunt & T. A. McMahon*

ISBN: 978-1-928660-61-3

YOGA AND THE BODY OF CHRIST:
WHAT POSITION SHOULD CHRISTIANS
HOLD? —*Dave Hunt*

ISBN: 978-1-928660-48-4

PEACE, PROSPERITY, AND THE COMING
HOLOCAUST: (REPRINT) —*Dave Hunt*

ISBN: 978-1-928660-65-1

JUDGMENT DAY! ISLAM, ISRAEL,
AND THE NATIONS —*Dave Hunt*

ISBN: 978-1-928660-32-3

COSMOS, CREATOR, AND HUMAN
DESTINY: ANSWERING DARWIN, DAWKINS,
AND THE NEW ATHEISTS —*Dave Hunt*

ISBN: 978-1-928660-64-4

ABOUT THE BEREAN CALL

*The Berean Call (TBC) is a non-denominational,
tax-exempt organization which exists to:*

ALERT believers in Christ to unbiblical teachings and practices
impacting the church

EXHORT believers to give greater heed to biblical discernment and
truth regarding teachings and practices being currently promoted
in the church

SUPPLY believers with teaching, information, and materials
which will encourage the love of God's truth, and assist in the
development of biblical discernment

MOBILIZE believers in Christ to action in obedience to the
scriptural command to "earnestly contend for the faith" (Jude 3)

IMPACT the church of Jesus Christ with the necessity for trusting
the Scriptures as the only rule for faith, practice, and a life
pleasing to God

*A free monthly newsletter, THE BEREAN CALL, may be received
by sending a request to: PO Box 7019, Bend, OR 97708; or by calling*

1-800-937-6638

*To register for free email updates, to access our digital archives, and to
order a variety of additional resource materials online, visit us at:*

www.thebereancall.org

BEND • OREGON